Inscriptions of Roman Britain

Sixth Edition

LACTOR Sourcebooks in Ancient History

For more than half a century, *LACTOR Sourcebooks in Ancient History* have been providing for the needs of students at schools and universities who are studying ancient history in English translation. Each volume focuses on a particular period or topic and offers a generous and judicious selection of primary texts in new translations. The texts selected include not only extracts from important literary sources but also numerous inscriptions, coin legends and extracts from legal and other texts, which are not otherwise easy for students to access. Many volumes include annotation as well as a glossary, maps and other relevant illustrations, and sometimes a short Introduction. The volumes are written and reviewed by experienced teachers of ancient history at both schools and universities. The series is now being published in print and digital form by Cambridge University Press, with plans for both new editions and completely new volumes.

Osborne	*The Athenian Empire*
Osborne	*The Old Oligarch*
Cooley	*Cicero's Consulship Campaign*
Grocock	*Inscriptions of Roman Britain*
Osborne	*Athenian Democracy*
Santangelo	*Late Republican Rome, 88-31 BC*
Warmington/Miller	*Inscriptions of the Roman Empire, AD 14-117*
Treggiari	*Cicero's Cilician Letters*
Rathbone/Rathbone	*Literary Sources for Roman Britain*
Sabben-Clare/Warman	*The Culture of Athens*
Stockton	*From the Gracchi to Sulla*
Edmondson	*Dio: the Julio-Claudians*
Brosius	*The Persian Empire from Cyrus II to Artaxerxes I*
Cooley/Wilson	*The Age of Augustus*
Levick	*The High Tide of Empire*
Cooley	*Tiberius to Nero*
Cooley	*The Flavians*
Cooley	*Sparta*

Inscriptions of Roman Britain

Sixth Edition

Edited by
C. W. GROCOCK
Bedales School

Shaftesbury Road, Cambridge CB2 8EA, United Kingdom

One Liberty Plaza, 20th Floor, New York, NY 10006, USA

477 Williamstown Road, Port Melbourne, VIC 3207, Australia

314–321, 3rd Floor, Plot 3, Splendor Forum, Jasola District Centre, New Delhi – 110025, India

103 Penang Road, #05–06/07, Visioncrest Commercial, Singapore 238467

Cambridge University Press is part of Cambridge University Press & Assessment, a department of the University of Cambridge.

We share the University's mission to contribute to society through the pursuit of education, learning and research at the highest international levels of excellence.

www.cambridge.org
Information on this title: www.cambridge.org/9781009383455
DOI: 10.1017/9781009383424

First published 2023

A catalogue record for this publication is available from the British Library.

A Cataloging-in-Publication data record for this book is available from the Library of Congress.

ISBN 978-1-009-38345-5 Paperback

TABLE OF CONTENTS

A map showing find spots of inscriptions is available online at www.cambridge.org/9781009383455

ILLUSTRATIONS

Coins

All coins are illustrated with photographs from the British Museum non-commercial images service, which remain copyright of The Trustees of the British Museum.

Line drawings of inscriptions

Photographs

As with the coins, the following photographs from the British Museum non-commercial images service remain copyright of The Trustees of the British Museum.

NOTES

Each entry in the collection consists of:

Title line: entry number; description of entry; date (usually the date of dedication or issue).

The text: coin legends are transcribed as well as translated. For other texts originally in Latin, the original text can be found either on *RIB* online, https://romaninscriptionsofbritain.org/ or in the Epigraphic Database Clauss / Slaby (EDCS) http://db.edcs.eu/epigr/epi.php?s. In translation, a few terms, which do not translate easily, are left in the Latin and defined in the text notes or Glossary.

Publication details: publication reference; findspot, with Latin name where known; nature of the inscription, when and where found; present (or intended) location.

Notes: brief comments on the significance of the inscription, drawing attention to recent work and, where appropriate, to alternative readings and interpretations. Full details of the publications to which reference is made appear in the Bibliography.

Illustrations: line drawings have been provided of a representative sample of the texts, designed to show a building inscription, a tombstone, an altar, an example of ligatured letters etc. *RIB* (book) volumes I to III contain line-drawings of all entries and photos of many; *RIB* online includes line-drawings of most inscriptions recorded in volume I. EDCS includes many illustrations, indicated here by an asterisk after the EDCS number.

Other sources of illustrations: pictures of most the objects from the British Museum can be found at http://www.britishmuseum.org/research/collection_online/search.aspx. Most other museums have websites with illustrations of their collections. The Vindolanda Tablets can be viewed on line on the website maintained by the Centre for the Study of Ancient Documents at Oxford University: http://www.vindolanda.csad.ox.ac.uk/.

ABBREVIATIONS

AE	*Année Épigraphique.*
Bloomberg *WT*	R. S. O. Tomlin, *Roman London's First Voices: Writing tablets from the Bloomberg Excavations, 2010–14* (2016). London.
BM	British Museum, London
BMC	*Coins of the Roman Empire in the British Museum*, ed. H. Mattingly (1923–62). London.
CIL	*Corpus Inscriptionum Latinarum,* eds T. Mommsen *et al.* (1866 cont.). Berlin.
CSIR	*Corpus Signorum Imperii Roman. Vol I, Britain.* Oxford.
EDCS	*Epigrafik-Datenbank Clauss-Slaby* http://db.edcs.eu/epigr/edcs_id.php
Hobbs	R. Hobbs, *British Iron Age Coins in the British Museum* (British Museum Press London, 1996)
ILS	H. Dessau (ed.), *Inscriptiones Latinae Selectae* (1892–1916). Berlin.
JRS	*The Journal of Roman Studies.*
LACTOR 11	Yvette Rathbone and D.W. Rathbone, *Literary Sources for Roman Britain. LACTOR 11.* (4th edition, 2012).
RIB	*The Roman Inscriptions of Britain.* *Vol. I: Inscriptions on Stone*, eds R.G. Collingwood and R.P.Wright (1965). Oxford. *RIB (number) add.* refers to the new edition (1995) with Addenda and Corrigenda by R.S.O. Tomlin. *Vol. II: Instrumentum Domesticum, fascs 1–8*, eds S.S. Frere and R.S.O. Tomlin (1990–1995). *Vol III: Inscriptions on stone found or notified between 1 January 1955 and 31 December 2006,* eds R.S.O. Tomlin, R.P. Wright and M.C.W. Hassall (2009).
RIC	*Roman Imperial Coinage*, eds H. Mattingly, E.A. Sydenham *et al.* (1923 cont.). London.
RMD III	M.M. Roxan, *Roman Military Diplomas 1985–1993.* Institute of Archaeology Occasional Publication No. 14 (1994). London. (Nos 136–201).
RMD IV	M.M. Roxan and P. Holder, *Roman Military Diplomas 1994–2002.* Bulletin of the Institute of Classical Studies Supplement no. 82 (2003). London. (Nos 202–322).
SHA	*Scriptores Historiae Augustae.*
Tab. Vindol. I	A.K.Bowman and J.D. Thomas, *Vindolanda: the Latin Writing Tablets.* Britannia Monograph No. 4 (1983). London. (Nos 1–117).
Tab. Vindol. II	A.K. Bowman and J.D. Thomas, *The Vindolanda Writing Tablets* (Tabulae Vindolandenses) *II* (1994). London. (Nos 118–573).
Tab. Vindol. III	A.K. Bowman and J.D. Thomas, *The Vindolanda Writing Tablets* (Tabulae Vindolandenses) *III* (2003). London. (Nos 574–853).

Tab. Vindol. IV	A.K. Bowman and J.D. Thomas, *The Vindolanda Writing Tablets* (Tabulae Vindolandenses) IV, part 1 (2010). *Britannia* 41 (2010), 187–224. Cambridge University Press. (Nos 854–869). (Tabulae Vindolandenses) IV, part 2 (2011). *Britannia* 42 (2011), 113–144. Cambridge University Press. (Nos 870–889).

PREFACE AND ACKNOWLEDGEMENTS

This, the fifth edition of LACTOR 4, *Inscriptions of Roman Britain*, is the latest in a long line of volumes which date back to 1969 under the title *Some Inscriptions of Roman Britain.* It is in large part based on the third and fourth editions produced in 1995 and 2005 by Valerie Maxfield and Brian Dobson, but incorporates nearly a hundred new entries, particularly benefiting from the rich finds excavated in London at the Bloomberg site, which, to quote Charlotte Higgins about another Roman site, 'is perhaps Britain's most recent example of the capacity of the sleeping earth to throw up anomalies, puzzles that disrupt the sense of what should be found.'[1]

The production of this edition has allowed for the proper incorporation of material from Vindolanda which appeared before in a separate section, 'Writing Tablets', and in an 'Addendum'. In addition, the decision was taken at the start of the editorial process to dispense with the Latin texts in this volume, partly for reasons of space and partly to bring it into line with other volumes in the LACTOR series, but also because any reader wishing to access the original inscriptional material now has ready access to it via the internet. Thus this fifth edition retains the traditional printed format, but makes full use of electronic resources which are freely available, of which these have been referred to most frequently:

- The British Museum website https://www.britishmuseum.org/research/collection_online/search.aspx;
- *Roman Inscriptions of Britain* online, at https://romaninscriptionsofbritain.org/ (this covers volume one of *RIB* and inscriptions published in *Britannia* since 1995)
- The *Epigraphik-Datenbank Clauss-Slaby*, at http://manfredclauss.de/gb/index.html.
- The Vindolanda tablets can be viewed at http://vindolanda.csad.ox.ac.uk/. .

This collection of inscriptions has profited, during the production of its five editions, from the advice and expertise of a large number of people, to all of whom we are most grateful. The list of their names reads like a litany of Romano-British scholarship.

The first edition of 1969 owed an enormous debt to Professors S.S. Frere, A.L.F. Rivet, and Michael Crawford, who has kindly revised his note on Roman Coinage for the fifth edition and steered its editor towards sources of additional help. Mr A.R. Burn provided kindly assistance in the assembly of the original collection prepared by members of the JACT Bureau in conjunction with the LACT Ancient History group; J.A. Bolton; R.W.J. Clayton; Miss P.M. Davies; K.R. Hughes; S.J. Miller; J.D. Moore; Miss E. Powell; J.A. Smith; M.A. Thorpe and the Editor, M.C. Greenstock. The second edition (1972) was corrected and improved by suggestions

[1] Charlotte Higgins, *Under Another Sky* (Vintage, London, 2014), pp. 17–18.

from correspondents, and Professor J.C. Mann contributed the *Note on Religion* which prefaces section J on 'Religion' in the present edition. For the third edition of 1995, Professor Colin Haselgrove provided a piece on British coinage (which has been revised for the fifth edition) and Mr P.J. Casey added a piece on Roman coinage. The map and line-drawings included in the third edition were done by Sue Rouillard, from the Archaeology Drawing Office, Exeter University, updated for the fourth edition by Mike Rouillard and by Melvin Cooley for the fifth edition. Thanks are due also to Dr Roger Tomlin for permitting reproduction of the drawings which appear as Fig. 3 and Fig. 4. The fourth edition was the production of Valerie Maxfield and Brian Dobson, whose work in the entries they included stands almost entirely unchanged. They quite properly acknowledged the kind help of Professor David Breeze, Dr Roger Tomlin and Mr Robin Birley, and of Professors Haselgrove and Crawford for their updated material on coinage. As editor of this fifth edition, I re-echo that debt and must add my thanks to Brian Dobson and Valerie Maxfield for providing such a superb piece of work which it has been my pleasure to use for many years as a teacher and writer of exams, and in whose footsteps it is an honour and privilege to have trodden in producing the present volume. As editors of this fourth edition they were also pleased to express their gratitude to series editor, Melvin Cooley, for assistance at numerous points; I re-echo that expression of thanks too, and must also now include Terry Edwards; both (and particularly the latter) have done meticulous editorial work on the text.

Christopher Grocock
Grayshott, Hindhead, Surrey, October 2016

LACTOR committee gratefully records the substantial financial help given to the original edition by the Cambridge Faculty of Classics and by the JACT Council. Line drawings from *The Roman Inscriptions of Britain* Vol. I, by R. G. Collingwood and R. P. Wright (with Addenda and Corrigenda by R. S. O. Tomlin), and Vol. II edited by S. S. Frere and R. S. O. Tomlin are reproduced by kind permission of the Adminstrators of the Haverfield Bequest. I would like to thank Christopher Grocock for his excellent work on this new edition. As a result of his serious illness at a very late stage of the project, I did some final editing. I therefore take overall responsibility and apologise for mistakes that have been missed, and in particular I beg Christopher's pardon for errors of my own that I have doubtless introduced inadvertently into his work.

M.G.L. Cooley
LACTOR Chairman and General Editor, March 2017

THE SOURCE-VALUE OF INSCRIPTIONS

According to Tacitus, in *Agricola* 21, the values which the Romans believed they were bringing to the peoples they made subject were summed up in the Latin word *humanitas* – even if in that chapter, Tacitus says that the unsuspecting Britons did not realize that it was actually 'a part of their slavery.' According to Pliny the Elder, *HN* 3.39; Italy was

> chosen by the power of the gods, so that it might make heaven itself more famous, so that it might unite what had been scattered, soften discipline and customs, and by the exchange of speech for conversation draw together the discordant wild languages of so many peoples and give humanity [*humanitas*] to mankind; in short so that it might become the one fatherland of all peoples in the whole world.[2]

Cooley calls it 'an expression of the role of language in Italy's imperialist mission to unite the world'[3] but notes the dangers of seeing it as ever realized in Italy, let alone over the Empire as a whole.

Jonathan Prag, referring to Ramsay MacMullen and the phrase 'the epigraphic habit': 'whatever the underlying explanations might be, Latin epigraphy reflects social *mores* rather than brute facts.'[4] This is a subtle but necessary qualification of the comments which Sheppard Frere made about inscriptions, and which began this section up to the last edition:

> In a Roman province such as Britain, which received only sporadic and often brief mention in the works of contemporary historians, the inscriptions erected by the inhabitants or by the garrison offer an invaluable independent source of information to the modern student. They are contemporary factual records, uncoloured by the conscious or unconscious bias of the ancient writer of history, and they provide a wide variety of information not found in other written sources and unlikely to be obtainable by purely archaeological investigation.[5]

We may welcome the idea that an inscription represents 'an invaluable independent source of information', though we might wonder at how 'independent' the writer or commissioner was; we may have little trouble with inscriptions being 'contemporary factual records' and accept that 'they provide a wide variety of information not found in other written sources'; what is far harder to accept with the development of differing approaches to evaluating the evidence which inscriptions provide is that they are 'uncoloured by the conscious or unconscious bias of the ancient writer of history.' This statement needs to be qualified carefully, because whenever we critically evaluate

---

2 Cited by Alison Cooley, in the Introduction to (ed. A. E. Cooley) *Becoming Roman, Writing Latin? Literacy and Epigraphy in the Roman West*, (JRA Supp. Series 48, Portsmouth, RI, 2002), p. 10.

3 ibid.

4 J. R. W. Prag, 'Epigraphy by numbers: Latin and the epigraphic culture in Sicily', in A. E. Cooley, ed., *Becoming Roman, Writing Latin? Literacy and Epigraphy in the Roman West*, (JRA Supp. Series 48, Portsmouth, RI, 2002), 15 – 31, at p. 15.

5 LACTOR 4, 4th edition, p. 8.

an inscription from Roman Britain we need to bear in mind that there are two sets of values in play.

First, there is the desire of the creator or commissioner of the inscription to communicate his or her message. This is obviously value-laden. I would avoid using the word 'bias' because students not yet in the tertiary level of education have a habit of using the word itself without qualification; but it is fairly obvious that all the inscriptions come from an fairly identifiable social standpoint, and may therefore be taken as indicating an acceptance of, or alignment with, that standpoint. The inscriptions were put up to communicate values, whether welcomed by a subject people (including auxiliary soldiers) or forced onto them, overtly or subconsciously.

The second set of values involved in interpreting an inscription is the set that we ourselves bring to the interpretation process. These values will largely depend on attitudes to imperialism – was the Roman invasion, put crudely, a 'good thing' or a 'bad thing'? Historically, classicists have quite naturally tended to side with the views expressed by Tacitus in *Agricola* 21, and regarded the invasion as bringing many benefits, along the lines of the 'What have the Romans ever done for us?' argument; these benefits are taken to include the 'epigraphic habit'. In the past half-century, a more left-wing approach with Marxist foundations has regarded imperialism of all types as a negative concept and its effects as equally negative; so in the past decade and more, 'Romanization' has become a matter of debate in universities and in the media generally; and in some circles the idea that the native population might actually *like* some aspects of 'occupation by a foreign power' is not to be countenanced: for example, it was recently put to me that

> the extent to which the local population, especially in the north, benefited from the presence of the army is highly debatable. It was an occupying force, after all. Asking (a question about how Britons might have benefited from the presence of the Roman army) without also bringing up the question of the negative effects of domination and imperialism, is, I think, deeply problematic.[6]

On the other hand, what often seems to be left out of the discussion is 'the extent to which, in different parts of the country, the Roman takeover was, if not actually welcomed, then greeted with alliance-making and acceptance rather than military resistance.'[7] Interested readers – and I think that this is a topic in which readers of this volume *should* be interested – might wish to compare the varied approaches taken, to give just two examples, by David Mattingly and Greg Woolf in two readily-available books.[8] Woolf's perceptive discussion of the differences between ancient imperialism

---

6 Anonymous academic reviewer of my contribution about the Roman Britain module to Bloomsbury's GCSE Ancient History set text, forthcoming 2017.

7 Higgins, *Under Another Sky*, p. 16.

8 David Mattingly, *An Imperial Possession: Britain in the Roman Empire* (Penguin Books, London, 2006, esp. pp. xii and 14–17, where Prof. Mattingly explains his view that Romanization is a 'defective paradigm'; Greg Woolf, *Becoming Roman: the Origins of Provincial Civilization in Gaul* (Cambridge University Press, 1998), especially chapter 1, 'On Romanization', and chapter 2 section 1, 'Imperialisms, modern and ancient.'

and more recent expressions of it is very valuable and is supported by Anthony Spawforth's comment about Roman influence in Greece in the imperial period that

> Roman imperial ideology in general did not arise from relations of class dominance and subjection in an anachronistically modern Marxist sense, but was constructed through 'inter-subjective relations' between the participating groups on a basis of shared core values.[9]

If the native Britons did find ways of coming to an accommodation with the new Roman regime to which they were subjected, then inscriptions may well have been one way of showing this. Writing was a part of the 'Roman way', and was obviously a part of army life, since the army was the 'official presence' of Rome in Britain. Military inscriptions may therefore pose less of a problem. What is harder to discern is the level to which some inscriptions – especially the ones in Section H, 'Civilian Life and Economic Activity' – may be taken to indicate the extent to which the *Britons* had assimilated this *humanitas*, as Tacitus puts it, by the medium of writing; it is hard enough to tell whether any were written by Britons, or incomers; rarely is any indication given that the commissioner or writer is a native (an obvious example is **H9**, Lossio Veda the Caledonian). In addition we have to say *commissioner or writer* because even the existence of an inscription such as this one is questioned by some as evidence for literacy: it could have been requested by a wealthy native with no knowledge of the language but a desire to play a part in a society where epigraphy *meant* something; the text could have been discussed in a language other than Latin before being agreed and then set out by a sculptor, leaving the patron to trust that what it said was what it was supposed to say! Such a radical view is harder to maintain when the examples of curse-tablets are examined, but it illustrates the ways in which attitudes about 'Romanization' have developed in the past half-century, varying from views of Roman Britain having only a veneer of *humanitas* and maintaining a sullen hostility to the Roman presence on the one hand, to welcoming the Romans with open arms and seeing opportunities for trade and social development. No doubt attitudes varied through time, from region to region, tribe to tribe, and would also depend on individual circumstances and the place an individual occupied in society. What must always be borne in mind is the fact that it was not only the people who had the inscriptions made, or made them themselves in the case of graffiti, who brought sets of values to the process; we bring our own values to them as well, and (equally subconsciously) may shape our interpretations thereby. J. Edmondson, discussing evidence from Lusitania (an area where Latin eventually took root and mutated into a Romance language – unlike Britain), makes this useful comment:

> The mere presence of formal written texts in Latin does not necessarily prove that Latin was the *spoken* language of all the inhabitants of the community in which the inscriptions appeared. But setting up a dedication to a god (whether Roman or native) or an epitaph for a deceased member was a distinctly *Roman* cultural act, and it betokens at least some acceptance

[9] A. J. S. Spawforth, *Greece and the Augustan Cultural Revolution* (Cambridge University Press, 2012), p 5, referring to C.Ando, *Imperial Ideology and Provincial Loyalty in the Roman Empire* (University of California Press, Berkley, 2000) esp. pp. 222–3.

> of the culture of the conquering power, and an acknowledgement that Latin was now the 'prestige language' in which to leave behind a public memorial of one's private act of devotion.[10]
>
> Tracing the errors in the Latin inscribed does not necessarily prove anything about the quality of the Latin that was spoken by the inhabitants of a given region, although it might say something about that of the *lapidarii*. However, one might expect that a *literate* customer would have refused to accept a text that was botched, so these errors may indeed suggest a less-than-perfect control of Latin among the stonecutters and an even lower grade of Latin among the customers. In short, monumental inscriptions remain problematic evidence for the nature of the language spoken in the given region in which they were set up. However, they *do* provide evidence for the desire on the part of the person or persons responsible for their erection to identify with a cultural practice that was quintessentially Roman.[11]

Different value may also be ascribed to the different surviving types of inscriptions, as Professor Frere noted in earlier editions:

Official building records often date more or less closely the erection or repair of the buildings to which they relate, thus filling in the outline chronology, e.g. of frontier history, which is obtainable from historical sources. By careful isolation of contemporary material found in excavation of such structures a firm chronology can be extended to remains such as pottery, which thus acquire validity as independent means of dating. Such inscriptions, too, often give the names of governors, officers or officials whose careers so attested are of interest to the student of government, and of military units whose distribution and movements throw light on the history and organisation of the Roman army. In addition they sometimes give clues to the status of towns or to the organisation of local affairs in Britain.

Their formulaic nature may also have been a limiting factor, as noted by Ralph Häussler:

> The perception that Latin epigraphy served as an appropriate form of status display and self-representation under a monarchical system is partly responsible for the 'stereotypical' forms of Latin inscriptions. This raises the question of the extent to which local epigraphic habits could use the standardized repertoire of Roman epigraphy in order to construct a sense of local identity. [12]

---

10 Jonathan Edmondson, 'Writing Latin in the province of Lusitania' in A. E. Cooley, ed. *Becoming Roman, Writing Latin? Literacy and Epigraphy in the Roman West*, (JRA Supp. Series 48, Portsmouth, RI, 2002), 41 – 60, at p. 43.

11 Edmondson, art. cit., p. 47.

12 R. Häussler, 'Writing Latin – from resistance to assimilation: language, culture and society in N. Italy and S. Gaul', in A. E. Cooley, ed., *Becoming Roman, Writing Latin? Literacy and Epigraphy in the Roman West*, (JRA Supp. Series 48, Portsmouth, RI, 2002), 61– 76, at p. 61.

Tombstones are often of use for the same ends, besides providing a wealth of information about the composition, thoughts or expectation of life of the ancient population. Dedications illustrate the workings of polytheism, the balance between official cults and those of major or minor Celtic deities, or the spread of novel religions from the oriental parts of the Empire.

Even **graffiti**, cut for instance on tiles or pottery vessels, can yield useful information on the names of manufacturers, the status of owners and the types and frequency of personal names used in Roman Britain, as well as on such subjects as the units of weight and capacity in common use (see Section H, 'Civilian Life and Economic Activity'). Scratching one's name on a pot or a prized possession showed at least that the letter-shapes indicated an individual – and presumably not only to the owner but also to anyone who might feel tempted to purloin it! Literacy seems to have been the norm among Roman soldiers, and was widespread among lower ranks in the army. Derks and Roymans, discussing a very specific type of evidence for literacy in the Rhine delta (seal-boxes), comment that

> The fact that letters were kept in native farmhouses does not necessarily imply that those receiving them were able to read them themselves or to write letters in return. Nevertheless, we should not under-estimate the degree of Latin literacy among the rural population in the Batavian area. Veterans returning to their homeland after their service undoubtedly played a key role here. Their presence is revealed not only in the occurrence of Roman *militaria* in almost every native settlement, but also in the finds of several military *diplomata.*[13]

The soldiers in question, moreover, were from regiments based for some time at Vindolanda, now crucial as a British locus of understanding the role of writing in Roman military activity.

Evidence both from writing-tablets, graffiti, and other evidence for writing – notably styli – has been used convincingly by Hanson and Conolly to demonstrate that 'access to writing materials and, presumably, both knowledge and use of literacy was not confined to the élite or more urbanized elements of Romano-British society.'[14] That a literate, fully-developed civilian society which conducted itself on Roman lines existed almost from the outset of the Roman occupation after AD 43 has now been shown by the finds from the Bloomberg site in London;[15] that literacy permeated to rural areas is also shown by the evidence of curse-tablets from Bath and especially from Lydney, some of which are to be found in Section J (d).

---

13 T. Derks and N. Roymans, 'Seal-boxes and the spread of Latin literacy in the Rhine delta', in A. E. Cooley, ed., *Becoming Roman, Writing Latin? Literacy and Epigraphy in the Roman West*, (JRA Supp. Series 48, Portsmouth, RI, 2002), 87–134, at p. 100.

14 W. S. Hanson and R. Conolly, 'Language and literacy in Roman Britain: some archaeological conclusions', in A. E. Cooley, ed., *Becoming Roman, Writing Latin? Literacy and Epigraphy in the Roman West*, (JRA Supp. Series 48, Portsmouth, RI, 2002), 151–64, at p. 156.

15 Roger S. O. Tomlin, *Roman London's First Voices: Writing tablets from the Bloomberg Excavations, 2010–14* (Museum of London Archaeology Monograph 72; London, 2016).

In all these ways epigraphy, the study of inscriptions, broadens our knowledge of Roman Britain and its place in the Roman Empire, and provides depth of focus to our study of the remains revealed by excavation.

Many inscriptions are broken, battered or fragmentary when found. A study of the selection offered in this book, mainly of the better-preserved pieces, will show that certain word-orders and formulae tend to recur, and that a number of widely-used abbreviations can be recognised. Experience shows that a knowledge of these, together with a consideration of the space available for missing letters, will often enable a reasonably certain restoration to be made. The ways in which this process has been applied are outlined in the pages which follow.

New discoveries of inscribed material are potentially important, however fragmentary, and should be communicated to Dr R. S. O. Tomlin, Wolfson College, Oxford OX2 6UD (roger.tomlin@wolfson.ac.uk) as soon as the inscribed material is ready for reporting, so that they can be included in the reports on discoveries published annually in *Britannia* by the Society for the Promotion of Roman Studies.

C. W. Grocock, with grateful thanks to the late Professor S. S. Frere.
Grayshott 2016

SOME NOTES ON ROMAN EPIGRAPHY

1. Types of Inscription and Formulae

(a) Religious dedications, usually of altars but sometimes of statues or whole temples (**F16** with fig. 6). These normally begin with the name of the deity or deities (in the dative), followed by the name and status of the dedicator (in the nominative) and a verb or formula, usually abbreviated (e.g. P = *posuit* ('put up'), REST = *restituit* ('restored'), or, most common of all, V.S.L.M. = *votum solvit libens merito* ('willingly and deservedly fulfilled his/her vow')) though this may be omitted (**G44**). The reason for the dedication is sometimes stated (**C21, C45**).

(b) Honorific inscriptions, often cut on the base of a statue (**C16**). These give the name and rank, and often the career, of the man who is being honoured (in the dative), followed by a statement of the dedicator, usually corporate (in the nominative), with or without a verb (**F27**).

(c) Commemorative plaques recording perhaps a victory or a vow of allegiance (**D14, D23**, **F17**).

(d) Building inscriptions recording the erection or repair of buildings. These vary from lengthy accounts to a bald statement of the man or body responsible (**F26**, **G43**).

The longer examples may include:

(i) The name and titles of the reigning Emperor – in the nominative if he is the builder, in the dative if it is in his honour, in the ablative if it is intended merely to record the date; this is expressed in terms of his consulship and tribunician power (see below).

(ii) The name and status of the builder, if other than (i); this may be either an individual or a military unit, with or without the name of its commander (**C38**).

(iii) The nature of the building – PORTAM ('Gateway'), PRINCIPIA ('Headquarters') etc (**D5**).

(iv) If it is a reconstruction, its previous condition may be noticed – VETVSTATE DILAPSIS ('collapsed through age' – **D10** and compare **F37**). If it is a complete reconstruction or a new building, it may be described in a form such as A SOLO RESTITVIT etc ('rebuilt from ground level' – **D10**).

(v) The name of the man in charge of the work, who may be the provincial governor (**C38**) or the commander of the unit (**D11**). A very important class of building inscriptions are the stones from Hadrian's Wall and the Antonine Wall which record the lengths constructed by different units (**C28–C30**).

(e) Milestones were set up when a road was first constructed or when it was repaired. They consisted of stone pillars bearing an inscription which gave, first, the name and titles of the reigning Emperor (in the nominative or ablative), secondly, his consulate and tribunician power, and finally the mileage from a stated town (the Roman mile, of 1,000 *passus*, measured 1618 yards = 1480 metres). Later, in the third and fourth centuries, new stones seem to have been erected purely for propaganda purposes and only the Emperor's name and titles are inscribed, but it is possible that the mileage figure was added in paint. (See **F48** with photograph, **F25**, **F28**, **F30**, **F31**, **F49** and **F50** for examples of milestones).

(f) Tombstones are very numerous and the appearance and form of words vary a great deal – see photographs of **B18, B22** and **F21**. The commonest beginning is DM or DIS MANIBVS ('To the spirits of the departed') followed by the name in the dative or nominative (or genitive, **B18**). But we also have MEMORIAE ('to the memory of ...') followed by the genitive, or the name may come first, either in the nominative or (with 'the tomb of' implied) in the genitive. The name may be given in full, with that of the deceased's father, his voting-tribe (if he is a Roman citizen) and his place of origin. The careers of soldiers and prominent men are often recorded; soldiers' tombs give the length of their service, and a statement of age is normal. The heir, relative or friend who erects the stone is commonly added (**F12**, **G30**). Common last lines are HSE (*hic situs est* – lies here) and STTL (*sit tibi terra levis* – may the earth lie lightly on you). But many other phrases occur, sometimes poignantly personal (**G29**, **J8**). The pagan formula DM curiously persists even on some Christian tombstones, but here the age is often given as, e.g. PLVS MINVS LX ('more or less sixty'), possibly to express unconcern over length of life in this world (**J80**).

(g) Military diplomas were the certificates issued to auxiliary soldiers on completion of 25 years' service or on discharge, confirming the grant of Roman citizenship on themselves and their children and legitimising their children. Each diploma consisted of two linked bronze plates, to be folded together and sealed, and was a copy of an edict posted up in Rome. Hence it included the name and titles of the Emperor, the units to which the edict referred, the province in which they were serving and the name of its governor, followed by the date, the name of the individual soldier, and the names of seven witnesses to the accuracy of the copy (**C5**). All of the military diplomas from Roman Britain, known up to 1989, have been republished together in *RIB* II.1, 2401, with general introductory comments by M.M. Roxan. A further four (or possibly five) diplomas relating to Britain appear in *RMD* III, three in *RMD* IV.

(h) Writing tablets were used for purposes for which today pen and paper (or electronic media) would be used. They are made of wood and are of two basic forms. In one, the 'stilus-tablet' (see **F4** with photograph), a rectangle of wood is hollowed out and the recess filled with wax. The message is scratched into the wax using an iron or bronze stilus, a 'pen' with a pointed end (for writing) and a flat end (for erasing). The wax itself rarely survives, but often the writing had penetrated through it into the surface of the wood below. It is these traces which can sometimes still be detected, see figure 3, page 25 for drawing and transcription of **H35** and also **F4, H23, H34, H37–H40.** Because this type of tablet can be reused (by smoothing down the used surface or

refilling with fresh wax) the traces of writing in the wood below may relate to more than one letter. Some 405 of the 407 writing-tablets recovered from the Bloomberg site in London belong to this category[16] (**B25–B27, F7, G1, G2, G31, H1, H15–H20, H33, H41–H47, H49**). The second type of tablet is the ink-tablet, formed of thin slices of wood which are written on using a pen and ink. The Vindolanda Tablets (**G4–G10**) were the largest and best-known collection of these tablets in Britain, but other examples are also known from London, Wroxeter and Carlisle (**F11, G1–G3, G34**). Both of these types of tablet may be linked together to form longer documents.

(i) Curse tablets (see fig. 4) are sheets of lead on which were incised messages invoking a deity to intervene in human affairs; in the case of the British examples, this is typically by assisting in retrieving stolen property and punishing the thief (**J57–J70**). Substantial collections of these curses were retrieved from the sacred spring at Bath (Tomlin 1988) and the temple of Mercury at Uley, Gloucestershire (Tomlin 1993a). Others are from London, Caerleon, Leicester, and Red Hill, on the banks of the Trent in Nottinghamshire.

(j) Other inscriptions include the stamps on tiles and ingots of metal (**B17** with photograph, **B21**), seals (**H2**), potters' and metalworkers' stamps (**H13, H21**), votive plaques (often bronze as illustrated in **H9**, sometimes silver or gold – illustration with **J22**), oculists' stamps (for impressing on ointment – **H31** with photograph). In several of these cases, the lettering may have had to be created in reverse on a die or stamp, so as to appear properly on the product (see **H31**). Generally less elaborate are graffiti – words and sentences scratched on various objects (**H3, H7, H14, H32, H51–H61**). The latter particularly may reflect spoken Latin, though this is evidenced also in more formal inscriptions (as for example nos **B5** and **F41**).

2. The Dating of Inscriptions

Under the Empire official Roman dating continued to be by reference to the consuls who took office at the beginning of the year. From the vast number of Roman inscriptions in existence, scholars have been able to work out who the consuls were in most years. Many inscriptions give the year in which military buildings or religious dedications were made, e.g. **C37, F23**. Some public (**D28, D39**) and private inscriptions (**F44, J2**) even specify the exact date and year when dedications took place: such exact dating was obviously important on documents concerning legal or financial matters, (**C5, G31, H15, H33, H37, H38, H42, H46**). Inscriptions can often be dated by reference to the titles of emperor. In some cases they may officially have been consul for the year anyway (e.g. **B17, B21, B24**). If not, their number of previous consulships and other honours which effectively form part of the imperial title often provide a range of dates: for example Trajan who reigned 98 to 117, was consul in 91, cos II in 98, III in 100, IV in 101, V in 103, VI in 112; he was PATER PATRIAE (P.P.) from autumn AD 98; he was saluted as IMPERATOR ('victorious commander') thirteen times in all, some of which are datable, and took titles for foreign conquests as follows, GERMANICUS in Nov. 97; DACICUS at the end of 102; PARTHICUS in Feb 116.

16 Roger S. O.Tomlin, *Roman London's First Voices: Writing tablets from the Boomberg excavations, 2010–14* (Museum of London Archaeology Monograph 72, London, 2016), p. xiii.

More straightforward, if available, is dating by another title of the emperor, his *tribunicia potestas* or 'Tribunician Power' invariably abbreviated to 'TRIB POT'. Down to the end of the third century, every Emperor assumed this power at or soon after his accession, and from Nerva onwards the normal pattern is that while his TRIB POT I may begin at any date, his TRIB POT II begins on 10 December. Hadrian, for example, who succeeded Trajan in August AD 117, dates his TRIB POT I from 11 August 117, his TRIB POT II from 10 December 117, his TRIB POT III from 10 December 118, and so on. See, for example, nos **C2**, **F17**, **F26**, **F31** and n, **F48**.

Sometimes a governor of the province may be mentioned, rather than the emperor. This can sometimes give us an exact or approximate date, where a particular governor is well known from other epigraphic or literary sources, e.g. **C7–C9**. Roman tombstones, though they given the age of the deceased, often with months and days, do not give any absolute dates, so can only be dated by other factors (see for example, **B22, D18, F21**). Because of local differences in style and variations in the skill of the engravers, it is extremely difficult to date inscriptions, even approximately, by the form of the letters; this can be attempted only by a very experienced epigraphist.

Note

A full list of Roman consuls and of the Emperors from Augustus to Justinian I, with the dates of their tribunician power, consulships, imperator numbers and titles can be found in A.E. Cooley, *The Cambridge Manual of Latin Epigraphy* (Cambridge 2012), Appendix 1, 449–487 (consuls) and Appendix 2, 488–509 (emperors). A.R. Birley, *The Roman Government of Britain* (Oxford 2005) includes all that we know about every Roman official to have served in Roman Britain.

3. Techniques

(a) Materials. The normal material for monumental inscriptions is stone, but wood and bronze were also used, and sometimes bronze letters were fixed to wood or stone. Military diplomas (see 3(g) above) are engraved on bronze. Letters may also be formed on metal by means of a series of punched dots (see illustrations of **H9** and **J22**). Pottery and tiles carry impressions of stamps, and the stamps themselves might be of clay, wood or metal (see **H31**). Metal ingots are cast in moulds with embossed letters, but may have additions incised (**B17**). Cursive graffiti (**H14**, **H51–H58**, **H60**, **J57**, **J59**, **J62–J65**, **J67–J69**) may be scratched on metal, clay or plaster, or written in ink on wood. Paint was also used.

(b) Lettering is always in capitals (except in informal texts such as letters and curses), but may be 'monumental', which is deliberately formal, or 'cursive', which is produced by the rapid use of a stylus or brush. The latter increasingly influenced the former, especially when the mason was working from letters chalked for him on stone. In good monumental work the strokes of the letters are cut with a chisel to a V-section, but in rough work a punch or mason's pick might be used; the guide-lines used by the mason to keep the lettering straight can occasionally be seen. In monumental inscriptions the letters were usually picked out with cinnabar; traces of it are occasionally found (**C1**, **G35**, **G47**), and some museums restore inscriptions to their original appearance by painting the lettering red (**B5**, **C23**, **G18**). Words are commonly abbreviated by docking their ends, and plurals are expressed by doubling,

trebling or even quadrupling the last letter (thus AVGG = two Augusti, AVGGG three Augusti, etc.). Ligatures, or combined letters, become increasingly common after the first century AD (see, e.g. **D30**, fig. 5). Greek letters are less uniformly capital (**F2**, **J47**). In letters, V is the normal form of U, and K often supplants C (e.g. KANOVIO, **F48**). In numerals, note that the forms IIII and VIIII may be used instead of IV and IX. Words are usually divided by stops, which may be simple or decorative and which are placed opposite the middle of the letter (i.e. not at its foot like a full stop). Words may be broken at any point to fit the lines; and stops are occasionally introduced in mid-word (**F22**, **G18**).

(c) Erasures were sometimes made deliberately as the result of a *damnatio memoriae* passed by the Senate on a deceased Emperor. Over 30 Emperors were condemned after death in this way, including Geta (e.g. **D8**) and Gordian I (see on **D25**).

A.L.F. Rivet
Keele University 1969 with revisions added by the editors, 1994, 2005 and 2016.

FROM INSCRIPTION TO TRANSLATION – SOME EXAMPLES

In this section a number of examples are given to illustrate how some of the items in this volume have been deciphered and written down as a 'diplomatic' transcription, expanded into a 'full' Latin text, and then rendered in English.

Note that in printing the Latin of inscriptions, the following conventions are in general use:

[...] Square brackets enclose letters which are thought to have been originally written but which have been lost through the breaking, defacement, or weathering. It is conventional to use three dots to indicate missing matter; no attempt is generally made to show the estimated length of the omission.

(...) Round brackets enclose letters which have been added by the epigraphist to complete an abbreviated word, or, less commonly, which have been substituted by her or him to correct a blunder.

< > Angular brackets enclose letters which the epigraphist believes were included in error.
A vertical bar indicates the beginning of a fresh line on the stone.

Ǣ ǣ Ligatures are indicated by a bar, straight or curved, over the letters which are joined. There are several examples in, e.g. Fig. 5, but they are not indicated in the text of this volume.

Ạ A dot placed under a letter indicates that it is not fully legible (through decay or erasure). This convention is not used in this volume where letters that can be confidently restored are included as though fully legible.

Various other conventions are sometimes employed and in using a work it is always worthwhile to look for a 'list of critical signs'.

1. B12, Tombstone of M. Favonius Facilis (legio XX), AD 43–49

Drawing of the original inscription (Fig. 1).

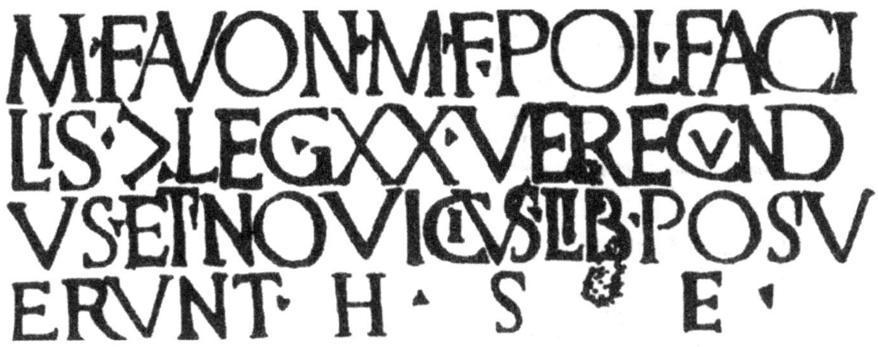

Diplomatic transcription:
M·FAVONI· M·F· POL· FACI
LIS· ›. LEG·XX·VERECVND
VS·ET· NOVICIVS·LIB·POSV
ERVNT · H · S · E ·

Latin text, expanded:
M(arcus) Favoni(us) M(arci) f(ilius) Pol(lia) Faci|lis c(enturio) leg(ionis) XX Verecund|us et Novicius lib(erti) posu|erunt h(ic) s(itus) e(st).

English translation:
"Marcus Favonius Facilis, son of Marcus, of the voting tribe Pollia, centurion of the Twentieth Legion; Verecundus and N›ovicius his freedmen set this up; here he lies."

Notes: the 'I' at the end of 'FAVONI' is the extended right-hand upright of the N. The symbol '›' represents centurion.

2. J56: dedication to Mithras 3rd century AD. *RIB* 1545.

Drawing of the original inscription (Fig. 2).

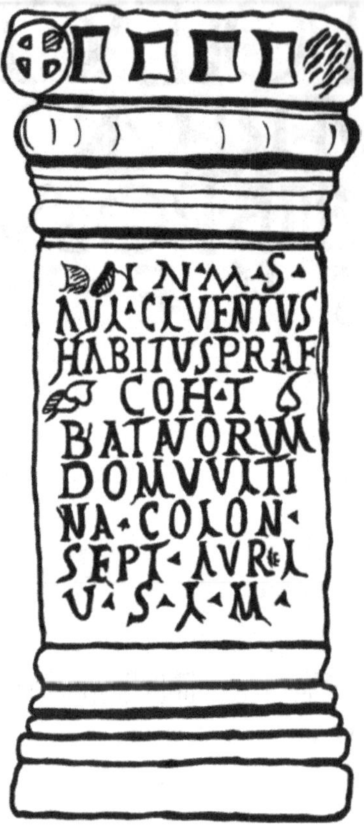

Diplomatic transcription:

D · IN · M · S ·
AVL·CLVENTIVS
HABITVS PRAF
COH · Ī
BATAVORVM
DOMV VLTI
NA · COLON ·
SEPT · AVR · L
V·S·L·M·

Latin text, expanded:
D(eo) In(victo) M(ithrae) s(acrum) | Aul(us) Cluen(t)ius | Habitus pra(e)f(ectus) | coh(ortis) I | Batavorum | domu Ulti|n(i)a (tribu) Colon(ia) | Sept(imia) Aur(elia) L(arino) | v(otum) s(olvit) l(ibens) m(erito).

English translation:
"Sacred to the Invincible god Mithras; Aulus Cluentius Habitus, prefect of the First Cohort of Batavians, of the Ultinian voting-tribe, from Colonia Septimia Aurelia Larinum, willingly and deservedly fulfilled his vow."

Notes: lettering influenced by 'cursive' style (see Fig. 3, page 25). There are some certain or possible mistakes: the T on CLVENTIVS' name may be there as a ligature with the N, but other letters and interpuncts seem to have been omitted, and other letters are badly carved (Ms and Ls).

3. H35: a writing-tablet from London Late 1st or early 2nd century AD

Dr Roger Tomlin's drawing of the cursive script on the tablet (Fig. 3)

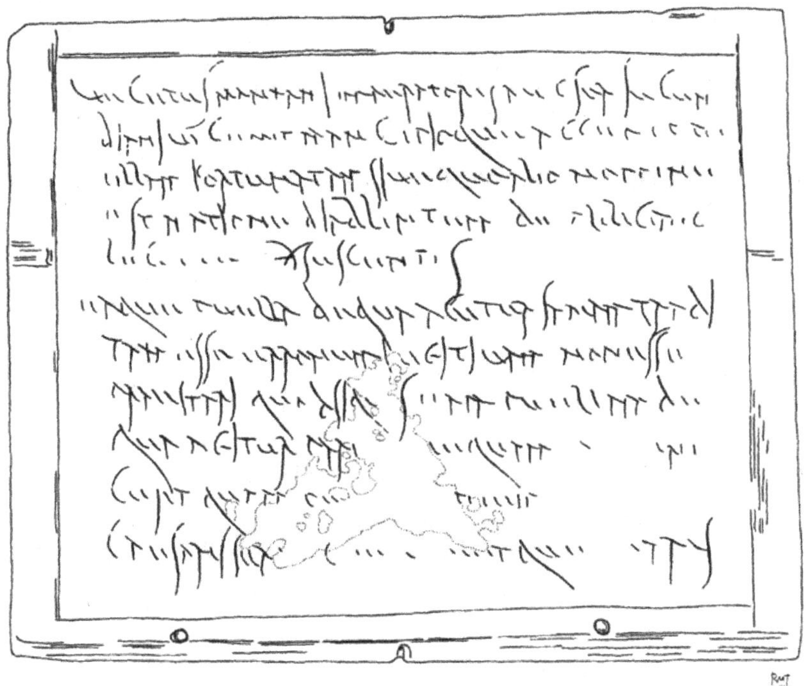

Diplomatic transcription:

VEG̣ETVS MONTANI IMPERATORIS AVG̣ SER SECVN
DIANI VIC EMIT MANCIPIOQVE ACCEPIT PṾ
ELLAM FORTVNATAM SIVE QVO ALIO NOMINE
EST NATIONE DIABLINTEM DE ẠḶBICIANỌ
ḶẸG̣3–4 X̶SESCENTIS *vacat*
EAQVE PVELLA DE QVA AGITVR SANAM TRADI
TAM ESSE ERRONEM F̣VGITIVAM NON ESSE
PRAESTARI QVOD SI QV[.]S EAM PVELLAM DE
QVA AGITVR PAR.[2–3]ṾẸ QVAM *traces*
CERA QVAM P̣Ẹ [...] ṾM [...]
CAESARIS SC̣R.[...]ṾỊṬQVE [2–3]ẠRIS

English translation:
Vegetus, assistant slave of Montanus the slave of the August Emperor and sometime assistant slave of Jucundus, has bought and received by *mancipium* the girl Fortunata, or by whatever name she is known, by nationality a Diablintian, from Albicianus […] for six hundred denarii. And that the girl in question is transferred in good health, that she is warranted not to be liable to wander or run away, but that if anyone lays claim to the girl in question or to any share in her, […] in the wax tablet which he has written and sworn by the *genius* of the Emperor Caesar […].

Notes: for an illustration of the letter forms used in handwritten 'old Roman cursive' script as found on tablets from Vindolanda, see http://vindolanda.csad.ox.ac.uk/exhibition/paleo-2.shtml from the Vindolanda website (together with a joke from a Roman comedy about how such writing might look like the scratchings of a chicken).

4. J57: a curse-tablet from Bath (4th century AD).

Dr Roger Tomlin's drawing of the curse-tablet (Fig. 4)

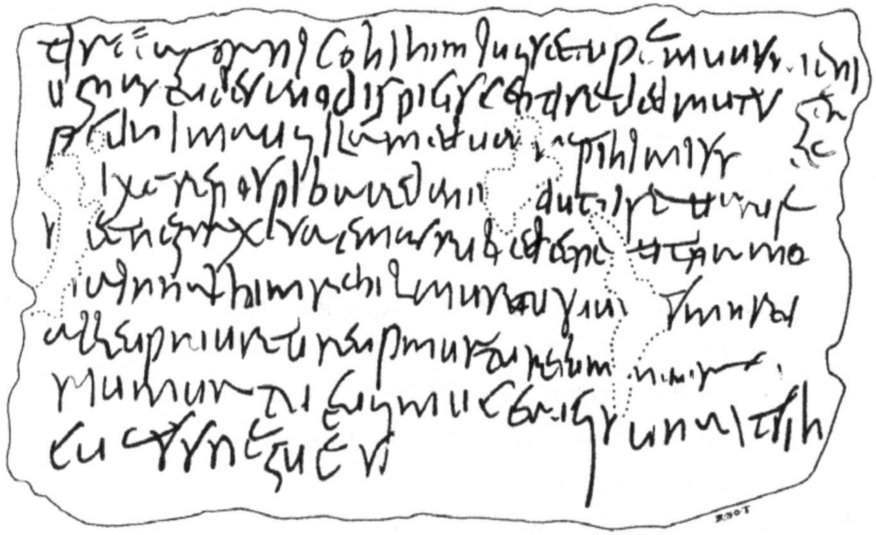

Dr Tomlin's expanded transcription of the cursive text (after restoring normal letter order)

sen gen(tili)s sen C|
h(r)istianus quaecumque utrum vir|
[u]trum mulier utrum puer utrum puella |
utrum s[er]vus utrum liber mihi Annian|o
ma<n>tutene de bursa mea s(e)x argente[o]s |
furaverit tu d[o]mina dea ab ipso perexi[g]|
e[.eo]s si mihi per [f]raudem aliquam in DEP |
REG[.]STVM dederit nec sic ipsi dona sed ut sangu|
inem suum EPVTES qui mihi hoc inrogaverit.

English translation:
"Whether pagan or Christian, whosoever, whether man or woman, whether boy or girl, whether slave or free, has stolen from me, Annianus, in the morning (?), six silver coins from my purse, you, lady Goddess, are to exact [them] from him. If through some deceit he has given me ..., and do not give thus to him, but [...] his blood who has invoked this upon me."

Notes: Written in cursive letters from left to right, but with the sequence of letters reversed from beginning to end of the side illustrated! See comments on **J57**.

Christopher Grocock.
Grayshott, Hindhead, Surrey, October 2016.

A NOTE ON ROMAN COINAGE

The legends and types on ancient coins can do two things: indicate the authority responsible for the coins, and convey a message put out by that authority. The first of these is essential for a coin to be a coin at all; the second is an optional extra. The Greeks, who took over the Lydian invention of coinage and spread it through the Greek world, on the whole only concerned themselves with the first possibility. The important coinages of Classical Greece, those of Athens, Corinth and Aegina, bore a more or less constant type which was the badge of the city. Thus the silver tetradrachms of Athens bore the head of Athena on one side and the owl of Athena (the mark also used to brand prisoners in the Samian War) on the other. With the advent of the Hellenistic monarchs the same approach to coin types was given a new twist – the coins bore their own portraits, as their badge and the symbol of their sovereignty, together with their titles, e.g. "PTOLEMAIOU BASILEOS" ("Of King Ptolemy") etc. The coinage of pre-Roman Britain is a distant barbarian derivation from the coinage of the Hellenistic world.

When the Roman Republic took over the notion of coinage in the late fourth century BC it entrusted production to a junior magistracy, holders of which were regularly chosen from the ranks of the aristocracy. These men naturally enough came to place their own distinguishing marks on the coins they produced, e.g. an allusion to a famous ancestor or to his great deeds. With the beginning of the Civil Wars, the heads of Caesar, Antony, Brutus etc. appeared on the coinage, in imitation of the coins of the Hellenistic monarchs. Augustus, the victor in the Civil Wars, made the coinage the property of himself and his family: the Emperor's head became the normal obverse type and an allusion to various aspects of his position or a commemoration of important events the normal reverse type. Neither evidence nor probability suggests that coin types were a matter of Imperial policy. We should rather envisage the artists in the Mint, whose patron was the Emperor, mingling on the coinage standard items (such as the Emperor's head and his principal virtues) with their own portrayals of the more striking events in the Imperial calendar. The precise significance of S(ENATVS) C(ONSVLTO) on the bronze coinage is disputed (its apparent absence on no. **D20** is probably due to the poor preservation of all recorded specimens). It is not now believed that the Senate had any effective control over the bronze coinage.

The standard equivalents and dimensions are as follows:

1 *aureus* (gold, 18mm diameter)	= 25 *denarii*	= 100 sesterces
1 *denarius* (silver, 18mm)	= 16 *asses*	= 4 sesterces
1 *sestertius* (brass, 35mm)	= 4 *asses*	= 1 sesterce
1 *dupondius* (brass, 28mm)	= 2 *asses*	= ½ sesterce
1 *as* (copper, 28mm)	= 1 *as*	= ¼ sesterce

The coinage of the Roman Empire, after the chaos of the late third century, was reformed by Diocletian, whose gold unit, slightly modified, became the *solidus* of Constantine and his successors. This was about the same size as the *aureus*, but weighed 4.5g compared to the original Augustan *aureus* which weighed 8g (but was gradually devalued).

Michael Crawford
Christ's College, Cambridge, 1969
Department of History, University College, London, 1994, 2005

GLOSSARY

ala: the basic word means "wing", but it is used to designate an auxiliary cavalry regiment, which usually fought on the wings.

ansate: with a triangular projection with base outwards at either end of the panel (see illustration of **H9**).

beneficarius: senior soldier serving on the staff of an officer commanding a unit, or, in the case of a legion, serving on the staffs of other officers down to a tribune.

beneficarius consularis: a personal assistant to the governor, performing administrative duties both civilian and military.

catafractata: adjective indicating that a cavalry regiment was heavily armoured.

civitas: a formal term of Roman administrative law referring to the smallest grade of urban community with its own local government, councillors and magistrates. In Britain, *civitates* were usually formed around pre-existing tribal centres.

cognomen: see *tria nomina*

cohors: an auxiliary infantry regiment, or a subdivision of a legion.

cohors equitata: a unit of infantry with a cavalry element attached to it.

damnatio memoriae: a phrase (= "condemnation of memory") used to refer to the destruction of statues and the erasure from inscriptions of the name of a person deemed to have been an enemy of the state. See further in Notes on Roman Epigraphy, 2c.

imperator ("victorious commander"): a Roman general was originally acclaimed as 'imperator' after a decisive military victory. While it becomes part of an emperor's name and title as early as Augustus, later emperors also use the title in its original sense to record the number of their military victories.

legatus Augusti pro praetor: the official title of the governor of an imperial province, as he is simply delegated that particular responsibility by the emperor. He himself may be an ex-praetor or ex-consul, depending on the importance of the province: the title is the same in either case.

milliaria: this, meaning literally a thousand strong, is applied to *alae* and *cohortes* which are of a larger size than the standard-size units, which are *quingenaria.*

nomen: see *tria nomina*

numerus: this means basically a unit which is neither an *ala, cohors* nor a legion.

pater patriae: *pater patriae,* literally father of the fatherland, was a title taken by most emperors from Augustus onwards, from different points in their reign.

patera: a small, flat dish used in religious offerings and often depicted on the side of tombstones.

pontifex maximus: Latin = "chief priest". Another role and title claimed initially by Augustus, and used by all subsequent emperors.

praenomen: see *tria nomina*

praeses: an informal name for governor which becomes the formal title in the later empire.

procurator: in a province like Britain, the chief financial officer, appointed by the emperor.

tria nomina: Latin = "three names". A Roman citizen would usually have three names. His *praenomen* or first name was chosen from only a dozen in common use. His *nomen,* the second of the three, was his family name. His *cognomen,* which might originally have been a nickname, often served to distinguish branches of extended families. In fact, not all Roman citizens did have three names: until the mid first century AD, a significant minority lacked a *cognomen*. Many members of the upper classes have four, five or more names. By the third century, the *praenomen* is often not recorded. A newly created citizen would take the *praenomen* and *nomen* of the person who enfranchised him, keeping his own name as a *cognomen* (so Togidubnus on being made a citizen by Claudius became Tiberius Claudius Togidubnus).

tribunician power: a tribune was traditionally a politician elected to represent the lower classes at Rome for a year. Augustus and all subsequent emperors adopt this as one of their range of powers and titles. See Notes on Roman Epigraphy, no.4 for how this title can date inscriptions.

quingenaria: this, meaning literally five hundred strong, is used to distinguish the smaller size of auxiliary cohorts and *alae*.

vexillum/vexillatio: a *vexillum* was a small flag of a unit or detachment. *Vexillatio* referred to any detachment. In the late Roman army it became the title of an army unit.

vicus/vicani: a formal term of Roman administrative law referring to a settlement of lesser importance and status than a *civitas*. A *vicus* was often subordinate to a bigger nearby town or military settlement. *Vicani* were the inhabitants of a *vicus*.

vigiles: the term used for the night watchmen, especially at Rome.

SECTION A

FROM CAESAR TO CLAUDIUS (55 BC–AD 43)

COINAGE IN PRE-ROMAN IRON AGE BRITAIN

Before the Roman invasion proper in AD 43, evidence of literacy is confined to coinage. Coins had come into gradual use over the preceding centuries, starting in the south-east, probably through diplomatic and trading links which provided channels for continental influence to penetrate the island of Britain. Only in the late first century BC did coins produced in Britain begin to show the names of kings in abbreviated form. As Jonathan Williams has noted, they are inscribed

> in both Gallo-Latin (a modified Latin alphabet developed in Gaul for writing local languages) and, to a greater degree, more orthodox Roman letters. In brief, after a period of uninscribed coin production in SE Britain beginning probably in the late 2nd century BC, both these scripts begin to appear on British coins more or less at the same time after the Roman conquest of Gaul, perhaps *c.* 25 BC. . . The appearance of inscriptions on coins in Britain also just precedes the rise of a new style of coin-design that broke with the local tradition, the roots of which lay in continental Iron Age Europe and ultimately in the coinage of Philip II of Macedon (4th century BC). Instead, coin types began to draw upon a range of contemporary Greco-Roman motifs, some but by no means all of which can be paralleled on Roman coins.[1]

The frequency of coins in pre-Roman Britain can easily be seen by searching on the British Museum's Online Collection for 'British gold staters'. Many of these are uninscribed, but names begin to appear during the period when the influence of Rome was beginning to have an impact on the tribes in the south of Britain following Caesar's invasions in 55 and 54 BC, as Roman sources such as the *Res Gestae Divi Augusti* make clear (LACTOR 11 B4. 1 and 2). The first coins to be produced in Britain were in gold or a cast bronze known as potin; coins in silver and bronze struck in a die, rather than cast, did not come into widespread usage until the middle of the first century BC.

Coins provide a valuable if not unique resource about developments among the tribes in Britain in the 96-year gap between the invasions of Caesar and Claudius, though their interpretation is obviously not unequivocal. For a start, they show an increasing interest in and adoption of continental customs and of burgeoning trade links, shown also by the importation of goods from the Roman world to archaeological sites such as Hengistbury Head in Dorset or Stanway in Essex. Apart from the writing on them, the symbolic horses, ears of wheat and vine-leaves may be indications of the key relationship between the coins themselves and the source of the agricultural wealth which permitted their minting, and the imported goods to which they in turn gave access. In addition the very material from which they are made – gold and silver in particular – indicate significant trading links across quite wide areas (lead and silver mining being best known from the Mendips and Derbyshire, and gold from Dolaucothi in Wales, perhaps with added sourcing from the continent). But above all, it is the presence of the names of tribal kings – often otherwise unknown – which indicates the shifting nature of political alliances during the period before AD 43. They are a powerful indication of the key importance of individual rulers in 'the changing social and political situation within Britain . . . writing . . . allows the permanent recording and public display of prescriptions, commands, and claims, in many different places at once. His name, power, and person once inscribed, the king may be ubiquitous, his title absolute . . . writing is also a technology which, amongst other things, facilitates the exercise of power over the ruled and the expression of adherence to the ruler through the public exposition of monumental inscriptions.'[2]

The find-spots of the coins gives an indication of the territories controlled by different individual rulers. In this sense they assist us in exploring the relationship between details about tribes and their kings provided by Caesar and the accounts of post-invasion writers. It seems that some kings ruled over only a part of what

---

1 Jonathan H. C. Williams, 'Pottery stamps, coin designs, and writing in late Iron Age Britain', in A. E. Cooley, ed. *Becoming Roman, Writing Latin? Literacy and Epigraphy in the Roman West*, (JRA Supp. Series 48, Portsmouth, RI, 2002), 135–149, at p. 135.

2 Williams, 'Pottery Stamps', p. 147.

was later regarded as a *civitas* or 'administrative canton' when Roman authority was imposed on the south of the island. Elsewhere, other kings may have been successful in bringing together several smaller groups under the authority of a single ruler. Above all, the overriding impression is of a state of flux, with rulers holding authority for a while and their realms then being divided up. The picture which emerges from coins is supported by Dio's account of the expulsion of *Berikos* which provided the justification for Claudius' invasion in AD 43 (LACTOR 11. E3.1).

The coins most often bear the king's name in an abbreviated form; some also mention his father's name with the abbreviation 'f' for the Latin 'filius' and affirm their title 'rex' (king). It seems that dynastic considerations played a large part in legitimising an individual's right to rule. A few examples also include abbreviated details of the place where they were minted.

Some of the detail provided on the coins matches the occasional mentions of British kings which we find in ancient authors. According to Augustus (*Res Gestae* 32.1, LACTOR 11 B4.1), two British kings, Dumnobellaunus and Tinco[marus], had 'fled to me as suppliants'. The latter may be identified with Tincomarus (**A2** below); in addition, Cunobelinus (**A8** and **A9** below) is called 'king of the Britons' and father of Adminius in Suetonius *Caligula* 44.2 (LACTOR 11 D1). In all probability, many of these British rulers were probably recognised by Augustus and his successors as Roman allies or client kings.

The reference numbers used in this section refer to the British Museum's website which students at all stages are encouraged to explore:

http://www.britishmuseum.org/research/collection_online/collection_object_details.aspx

This updates R. Hobbs, *British Iron Age Coins in the British Museum* (British Museum Press London, 1996), which also contains photographs and descriptions of most known British coin types then available. For a brief introduction to Iron Age coinage in Britain, see P. de Jersey, *Celtic Coinage in Britain*, Shire Publications, Princes Risborough, 2001, and D. Nash, *Coinage in the Celtic World*, B.A. Seaby, London, 1987. A compendium of known legends on British Iron Age coins, with accompanying commentary, is given by M. Mays, Inscriptions on British Celtic coins, *Numismatic Chronicle* 1992, 57–82. See also R. Reece, *The Coinage of Roman Britain* (Tempus, 2002), D. Holman, 'Iron Age Coinage and Settlement in East Kent', *Britannia* XXXVI (2005), pp. 1 – 54. J. Creighton, Coins and Power in late Iron Age Britain (Cambridge University Press, 2009) discusses the relationship between British rulers and Rome as reflected by their coins and other archaeological evidence.

Note: the coins which follow are not reproduced in actual size, but the diameter of each coin illustrated is given in the descriptions of them.

Christopher Grocock (with thanks to Prof. Colin Haselgrove for numerous comments, suggestions and corrections in the summary above and in the descriptions of coins which follow.)

A1 Anonymous gold staters

(i) A stater from Ringwood, Hampshire ?80–60 BC

[*BM* 1980, 0634.45. Found in 1979. Diameter 19mm, weight 6.37 g.]

This example demonstrates how the original designs could become very fragmented and stylised. The abstract wreath design on the obverse ultimately derives from the head of a classical deity – possibly Apollo – on fourth century BC gold coins of Phillip II of Macedon, whilst the crude representation of a horse on the reverse is derived from the chariot design on Philip's coins. Like the majority of finds of this type, this coin was found far to the south of its supposed territory of origin in the regions bordering the Thames, and the actual place where it was minted is unknown: the supposed North Thames origin for the type is based on 19th century finds.

(ii) A coin of the English East Midlands ?60–30 BC

[*BM* 1990,0541.1. Diameter 18.5 mm, weight 5.93 g.]

This example typifies the designs of many anonymous British coins, with the degraded head of Apollo on the obverse, and a very stylised horse on the reverse. It is possibly the product of the Corieltavi, a people whose territory was focused on modern Lincolnshire and the surrounding areas of the East Midlands.

(iii) A coin of central southern England *c.* 60–20 BC

[*BM* 1978,0108.8. Diameter 17.5 mm, weight 5.64 g.]

This coin, found in 1975 in a hoard of coins at Waltham St Lawrence, Berkshire, shows the stylised head of Apollo, facing right on its obverse, while the reverse again depicts a stylised horse, facing to the right, with a triple tail; there is a (?chariot) wheel below the horse.

A2 Gold stater of Tincomarus *c.* 20–10 BC

Obv: TINC(OMARUS)
Rev: Horseman.
C(OMMI) F(ILIVS)

[*BM* 1996,1022.58. Diameter 17 mm, weight 5.41 g.]

The titulature runs continuously from obverse to reverse; “Tincomarus son of Commius”.

For many years, this ruler’s name was expanded to Tincommius, but in 1996 coins found in a hoard at Alton (Hampshire) at last confirmed the correct reading. The fine lettering and well-cut horseman on this particular type suggest a classically trained die cutter who copied the design from a Roman *denarius*. Cruder copies of this coin also exist (e.g. BM 770). Tincomarus probably succeeded Commius *c.* 30 BC, and the adoption of Roman models in the later stages of his coinage suggests that he was among the British rulers who concluded treaties of friendship with the Roman authorities across the channel during Augustus’s reign. He is later seemingly recorded by Roman sources as having sought the protection of the emperor and we must assume that at the end of the 1st century BC he was ejected from his kingdom south of the Thames by a rival. Other coins in the collection show triple-tailed horses and an abstract wreath design based on the head of Apollo.

Note that the abbreviated name in this and **A4** below are contained in a cartouche; Jonathan Williams, 'Pottery Stamps', 137 has put forward a persuasive case for pottery stamps on amphorae and *terra* sigillata being the origin of this design, which is 'quite unprecedented on either Roman or Gaulish coinage.'

A3 Gold coins of Addedomaros *c.* 30–10 BC

(i) Gold stater

Obv: Abstract wreath design in the form of a six-armed spiral.
Rev: Horse, right.
ΑΘΘΙΙ(DOMAROS) (Addedomaros)

[BM 1995,1014.32. Diameter 17 mm, weight 5.42g]

(ii) Gold quarter-stater

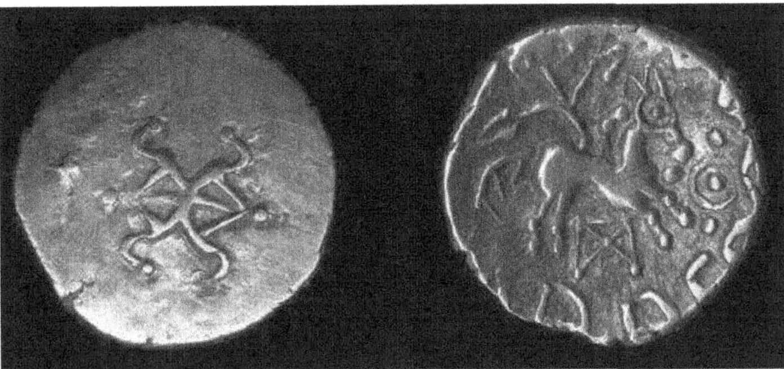

Obv: Two opposed crescents
Rev: A horse.
ΑΘΘΙΙ(DOMAROS) (Addedomaros)

[*BM* 1995,1014.36. Diameter 13 mm, weight 1.33g]

Earlier coins from the north Thames area, such as this gold stater of Addedomaros, king of the Trinovantes or Catuvellauni, make use of Gallo-Roman script rather than Latin, writing the king's name with the *theta* for the –d- or –th- sound. The writing is extremely poor in quality. Both coins are metal-detector finds from Essendon.

A4 **Gold stater of Tasciovanus** *c.* 20 BC–AD 10

Obv: TASCIO(VANVS)
Rev: Horseman.
To the right, SEGO.

[*BM* 1919,0213.323. Diameter 17 mm, weight 5.42 g.]

Tasciovanus was a contemporary of Tincomarus. He ruled a kingdom centred to the north of the Thames, and some of his coin types also show traces of Roman influence. There have been finds of his coins at Essendon and Tring, and in Epping. Many coins attributed to Tasciovanus bear the mintmark VER or VERLAMIO, confirming that a British centre of importance preceded the Roman city at St Albans. The horseman on some of his coins wears a coat of mail similar to the example found among the contents of the rich mid-first-century AD tomb excavated in 1990 at Folly Lane, just across the river from St Albans. As with **A2** above, the king's name is contained in a cartouche, this time a tablet with concave sides.

A5 **Silver coin of Eppillus** *c.* 10 BC–AD 10

Obv: Crescent between two stars.
REX CALLE(VA) above and below crescent.
Rev: Eagle.
Behind, EPP(ILLVS).

[*BM* 1988,0627.176. Diameter 13 mm, weight 1.26 g.]

The titulature runs continuously from reverse to obverse: "Eppillus, king of Calleva".

Eppillus was another ruler who described himself on his coinage as a son of Commius. His reign probably overlapped that of Tincomarus and the mintmark CALLEVA bears out the evidence of recent archaeological excavations, which demonstrate that there was an important British settlement on the site of Roman Silchester from the mid-1st century BC onwards. Eppillus appears to be the first British ruler to use the Roman title REX on his coinage.

A6 Silver coin of Esuprastus *c.* AD 30–40

Obv: Head, facing left.
Around the edge, SVB ESVPRASTO.
Rev: Stylised horse, with a crescent above.
ES[ICIO] FECI. (I, Esicio, made (this) under (authority) of Esuprastus)

[*BM* 2000,.0301.7. Diameter 13 mm, weight 0.95 g]

This coin was probably minted in the territory controlled by the Iceni. It was found as part of a hoard at Fincham, Norfolk. The 'Prasutagus' whose name the inscription recalls may be the ancestor of the better-known king of that name whose fame largely rests on his widow Boudica. See J. H. C. Williams 'The Silver Coins from East Anglia Attributed to King Prasutagus of the Iceni' (*Numismatic Chronicle* 2000, pp. 276–281). Prof. Colin Haselgrove has helpfully commented that 'The recent Oxford D Phil on the coinage of the Iceni by John Talbot attributes this coin type to the period just before the Claudian invasion. He argues that the designs are derived from a later silver coin type of Cunobelin (Hobbs, *British Iron Age Coins in the British Museum* (1996), no. 1871).' The issuing of coins in Icenian territory is an interesting indication of how far continental influence was spreading by this early date following the invasions of Caesar. This 'rare but celebrated' example adds the name of the maker as well as the authority for doing it: 'I, Esicio, made (this) under (authority) of Esuprastus.'

A7 Gold staters of Verica *c.* AD 10–40

Obv: VIRI(CA), split by vine-leaf.
Rev: Horseman.
Around, CO(MMI) F(ILIVS) (Son of Commius).

[*BM* 1919,.0213.165. Diameter 17 mm, weight 5.42 g.]

The titulature runs continuously from obverse to reverse, "Virica, son of Commius".

This coin, part of the Alresford Hoard, found in Hampshire in 1880, may be the work of a Roman-trained engraver, and the vine-leaf on the obverse has been suggested as symbolising the pro-Roman outlook of Verica's kingdom. Verica, the third southern ruler to style himself 'son of Commius', probably succeeded Eppillus as the ruler of Calleva sometime in the early 1st century AD.

(ii)

Obv: COM(MI) F(ILIVS). (Son of Commius)
Rev: VIR(ICA) REX (king Virica)

[*BM* 1919, 0213.179. Diameter 17.5 mm, weight 5.32 g.]

Verica is undoubtedly synonymous with the British ruler called Berikos by the Roman historian Cassius Dio (see LACTOR 11, E3.1), writing in Greek. The subsequent ousting of this ruler (in civil war?) was used by Claudius as a pretext for the Roman invasion in AD 43.

A8 Gold stater of Cunobelinus *c.* AD 10–40

Obv: Ear of wheat.
CA and MV(LODVNVM) on either side.
Rev: Horse.
Below, CVNO(BELINVS).

[*BM* 1977,0434.11. Diameter 16.5 mm, weight 5.36 g.]

Between *c.* AD 10 and 40 much of south-east England, north and south of the Thames, was ruled over by Cunobelinus, whose capital was at Camulodunum, the British predecessor of Roman Colchester, where this coin was apparently minted. Some 15 other gold staters issued by Cunobelin are available to view on the British Museum website.

The ear of unimproved wheat (probably spelt – it is 'bearded' which accounts for its earlier misidentification as barley) on the obverse of Cunobelinus's gold stater is evidently a counterpart to the vine-leaf on Verica's issues. Although the precise significance of this emblem is unclear, wheat was one of the principal exports from Britain at this time according to Strabo 4.5.2 (LACTOR 11 B3.2) and it may therefore be a symbol of the kingdom's wealth and indicate its trading links with the continent.

A9 Bronze coins of Cunobelin *c.* AD 10–40

(i)

Obv: Bearded head, facing forward
Rev: Image of a boar, (a symbol of strength.)
CVN (Cunobelinus) below the boar on the reverse.

[*BM* R.8527. Diameter 14.5 mm, weight 2.12 g.]

(ii)

Obv: Pegasus, facing to the right;
CVNO (Cunobelinus)
Rev: Victory sacrificing a bull, both facing right;
TASCI (Tasciovanus)

[*BM* 1919,0213.408. Diameter 15 mm, weight 2.58 g.]

This bronze coin clearly states Cunobelinus' dynastic claims by appealing to his lineage as a descendant from Tasciovanus.

(iii)

Obv: Head (perhaps intended for that of Cunobelinus).
Around, CVNOBELINVS REX (King Cunobelinus)

Rev: Bull butting. Below,
TASC(IOVANI FILIVS) (Son of Tasciovanus)

[BM 1925,1201.1. Diameter 17 mm, weight 2.42 g.]

Copper alloy coin. The titulature runs continuously from obverse to reverse. R. Hobbs, *British Iron Age Coins in the British Museum* (British Museum Press London, 1996) no. 1944, p.133.

This is the only issue of Cunobelinus to bear the title REX and belongs to the later stages of his coinage. Unlike his coin types which carry the mintmark CAMV, those with the legend TASCIOVANI F(ILIVS) are thought to have been issued from a second mint, possibly at Verulamium (St Albans). There is no independent evidence to indicate whether Cunobelinus was actually a son of Tasciovanus, or whether he simply laid claim to the relationship to legitimate his succession to the domains previously ruled over by Tasciovanus. See also F. M. Morris, 'Cunobelinus' Bronze Coinage', *Britannia* 44 (2013), pp. 27 – 83.

SECTION B

THE FIRST CENTURY (AD 43–98)

(a) THE CLAUDIAN INVASION (AD 43–47)

B1 Claudia Prima tombstone — Claudian or Neronian

Tiberius Claudius Seleucus, freedman of the emperor, ship's captain, erected this monument to Claudia Prima his freedwoman.

[*CIL* 13. 3542 = EDCS 10600310. Boulogne (Bononia)]

A stone plaque found in the 18th century near the Porte Gayole. In the Haigneré-Vaillant Museum.

This is perhaps the oldest inscription from Boulogne, the port from which the Claudian invasion force set sail. Gaius had built a lighthouse here and it is the site of a first-century fort, probably the headquarters of the *classis Britannica* (Brulet in Maxfield 1989). Boulogne has a number of tombstones of naval personnel, suggesting that it was early (and continued to be) an important base for the fleet. Seleucus was freed by Claudius (whose names he took), which sets a limit on the date of the epitaph.

B2 Longinus Sdapeze (ala I Thracum) — AD 43–49

Longinus Sdapeze, son of Matygus, *duplicarius* in the *ala prima Thracum* from the district of Sardica, aged 40, of 15 years' service, lies buried here; his heirs had this set up under his will.

[*RIB* 201 add. Colchester (Camulodunum)]

Tombstone found in 1928 near no. 18. Now in Colchester Museum

The relief shows a cavalryman in scale armour on a richly caparisoned horse, riding over a crouching naked barbarian. Above this relief is a winged sphinx flanked by lions; round each lion is twined a snake. Thracians are known to have served in the Roman army prior to the creation of the province of Thrace (the area now southern Bulgaria and northern Turkey) in AD 46 (Tac. *Ann.* 4.46), so the *ala I Thracum* could have come over with the initial invasion force in AD 43 and been stationed at Colchester some time between then and the creation of the colony in the winter of AD 49–50. Two military bases are known at Colchester: a fortress below the later city and, to the south, at Gosbecks, a fort. This unit perhaps occupied the fort, whether before, after, or at the same time as legion XX occupied the fortress is not known. The stone is in good condition but is defaced. This led to the suggestion that it had been overthrown, soon after erection, in the Boudican rebellion. Excavations in 1996 on the site of the tombstone recovered the face and cast doubts on the theory of deliberate damage (Crummy 1997, 50). An alternative reading of the name is "Longinus son of Sdapezematygus". The *duplicarius* was second-in-command of a cavalry *turma* (troop); his rank reflects his pay grade – he received double pay.

B3 Dannicus (ala Indiana) — Claudian-early Flavian

Dannicus, cavalryman of the *ala Indiana*, from the troop of Albanus, served for 16 years, a citizen of the Raurici, lies buried here; Fulvius Natalis and Fl[avi]us Bitucus *(set this up)* according to his will.

[*RIB* 108. Cirencester (Corinium)]

A tombstone found in 1835 at Watermoor near the south gate of Corinium, beside Ermin Street. Now in Corinium Museum.

The relief shows a cavalryman poising his lance over his prostrate enemy (photo in *RIB* online). The Raurici lived in the area around Augst (Augusta Raurica) on the upper Rhine. The *ala Indiana* was originally raised in Gaul; it was named after Julius Indus, a tribesman of the Treveri (from the Trier region), who led a band of native cavalry loyal to Rome in the suppression of a native uprising in AD 21 (Tac. *Ann.* 3.42). Subsequently the band was incorporated as a regular unit of the Roman army and was stationed in upper Germany, where Dannicus was recruited. Dannicus died in service, so if the unit came to Britain in AD 43, he cannot have lived beyond the year AD 58. However, the stone may be later in date than this – AD 69 at earliest – if the name of one of Dannicus's heirs is correctly restored as Fl[avi]us; in this case the unit cannot have come over to Britain as early as AD 43. The fort at Cirencester was occupied from *c.* AD 45 to *c.* AD 75. On Julius Indus see also **B18.**

B4 Sex. Valerius Genialis (ala Thracum) — Claudian-early Flavian

Sextus Valerius Genialis, cavalryman of the *ala Thracum*, a citizen of the Frisiavones, in the troop of Genialis, aged 40 years, of 20 years' service, lies buried here; his heir had this set up.

[*RIB* 109. Cirencester (Corinium)]

*A tombstone found in 1836 near **B3**. Now in Corinium Museum.*

A gabled tombstone with a relief which shows a cavalryman brandishing his lance above a fallen enemy. He carries a shield and also an enigmatic item which is probably a standard (photo *RIB* online). The Frisiavones lived in the area of the lower Rhine, close to its mouth, so it is probable that Genialis was recruited to the *ala Thracum* when it was serving in Lower Germany, its base before it came to Britain. If that is so, Genialis, with 20 years' service, can have died no later than AD 62. Hence the Thracians may have been based at Cirencester before the *ala Indiana*. This is probably the same cavalry unit (the *ala I Thracum*) as is attested at Colchester (**B2**). Note that Genialis has the *tria nomina* of a Roman citizen.

B5 Rufus Sita (cohors VI Thracum) — Mid-1st century AD

Rufus Sita, cavalryman in the Sixth Cohort of Thracians, aged 40, of 22 years' service, lies buried here; his heirs had this stone erected according to his will.

[*RIB* 121. Gloucester (Glevum)]

A tombstone found in 1824 at Wootton, about a kilometre to the east of the site of the early military base at Kingsholm. Now in Gloucester City Museum.

A relief above this inscription shows a cavalryman with a shield in his left hand, a long sword (*spatha*) at his right side, brandishing a spear over his fallen enemy. Above this scene is a sphinx, guardian of the tomb, flanked by lions, symbols of the consuming power of death (photo in *RIB* online). There is the same combination of motifs on the tombstone of a Thracian cavalryman from Colchester (**B2**). The unit in which Sita served is a mixed unit, a *cohors equitata. Cohors VI Thracum* is thought to have formed part of the garrison of Kingsholm, a military base founded in the 40s and evacuated in the late 60s, predating the Gloucester fortress. It probably shared accommodation here with part of legion XX, commemorated by a fragmentary (and now lost) tombstone (*RIB* 122) and by **B20.** Rufus (like Longinus in **B2**) is a Latin 'given' name. *Exs* in place of *ex* ('according to') also appears on **B2** to which this stone bears several similarities.

B6 Ti. Claudius Tirintius (cohors Thracum) — Before AD 72

Tiberius Claudius Tirintius, cavalryman of the ... Cohort of Thracians, aged 57 years, of [20+] years' service, lies buried here.

[*RIB* 291. Wroxeter (Viroconium)]

Part of a tombstone, found in 1783 just north of the basilica. Now in Rowley's House Museum, Shrewsbury.

The relief above the tombstone shows a cavalryman riding over his fallen enemy (drawing in *RIB* online). The number of the cohort is missing. It may be *cohors VI* (attested at Gloucester, **B5** or *cohors I* which is known to have been in Britain by AD 122 (*CIL* 16.69). Tirintius had probably served at least 25 years since he had already received Roman citizenship. His names, Ti. (Tiberius) Claudius, indicate a grant from either

Claudius or Nero, so this inscription must date no later than early Flavian. A military base was established at Wroxeter in the mid-first century, presumably in connection with Ostorius Scapula's campaign against the Silures. A legionary base, an auxiliary fort and camps are known in the area.

B7 L. Vitellius Tancinus (ala Vettonum) *c.* AD 50–60

Lucius Vitellius Tancinus, son of Mantaius, a citizen of Caurium in Spain, cavalryman of the *ala Vettonum*, Roman Citizens, aged 46, of 26 years' service, lies buried here.

[*RIB* 159. Bath (Aquae Sulis)]

A tombstone found in 1736 in the old market place. Now in the Roman Baths Museum.

The relief above the inscription shows a cavalryman riding over a prostrate enemy. Tancinus probably took the names Lucius Vitellius on receiving Roman citizenship in the year AD 47–48 when L. Vitellius was *censor* with Claudius. It would be typical of Claudius to insist that his colleague should share fully in the censorship, giving his names to some of the new citizens. The award could have been made to Tancinus when he had completed 25 years' service; alternatively he may have gained it on the occasion when the unit in which he was serving, the *ala Vettonum*, received its block grant of citizenship, commemorated in the title which it bears. The dating of the inscription depends on which of these alternatives is correct, lying somewhere between AD 48 and the late 60s. As a Spaniard serving in a Spanish unit, he was probably recruited to the unit before it came to Britain. This tombstone is one of the pieces of evidence suggesting that there may have been a Roman fort at Bath.

B8 C. Gavius Silvanus (cohors Praetoria) Mid-1st century AD

To Gaius Gavius Silvanus, son of Lucius, of the voting tribe Stellatina, formerly senior centurion of the Eighth Legion Augusta, tribune of the Second Cohort of Vigiles, tribune of the Thirteenth Urban Cohort, tribune of the Twelfth Praetorian Cohort, decorated by the deified Claudius in the British war with necklets, armlets, medals and a gold crown. *(Set up)* to the patron of the colony by decree of the decurions.

[*CIL* 5. 7003 = *ILS* 2701 = EDCS 05400255. Turin (Augusta Taurinorum), Italy]

Gavius Silvanus was driven to suicide as a praetorian tribune in AD 65 (Tac. *Ann.* 15.71). Thus at the time of the British war he will have been at a relatively early stage in his career, probably serving as an *evocatus* in the praetorian guard (retained in service while awaiting promotion to a centurionate). The level of his decorations is appropriate to that rank. Details of the early service of senior centurions are often omitted from inscriptions. He will certainly not, by AD 43, have risen as high as *primus pilus* (senior centurion) a post which he held in legion VIII; this inscription does not therefore provide evidence for the participation of legion VIII in the British invasion, as has previously been argued. The *vigiles* functioned as a fire brigade and night watch in Rome and Ostia. The decurions who decreed the inscription are local magistrates, members of the city council of what was Silvanus's home town, as the voting tribe shows. See **F20–22.**

B9 M. Vettius Valens (cohors Praetoria) AD 66

Marcus Vettius Valens, son of Marcus, of the voting tribe Aniensis, soldier in the Eighth Praetorian Cohort, *beneficiarius* on the staff of the praetorian prefect, decorated in the British war with necklets, armlets and medals, (appointed) *evocatus* and awarded a gold crown, centurion of the Sixth Cohort of Vigiles, the *statores*, the Sixteenth Urban Cohort, the Second Praetorian Cohort...

[*CIL* 11. 395 = *ILS* 2648 = EDCS 24600984. Rimini (Ariminum), Italy]

Vettius Valens served in Claudius's British campaign as a member of the emperor's bodyguard (the praetorian cohorts) and was decorated twice, once as an orderly on the staff of the commanding officer of the guard (the prefect) and once after he had been kept on (*evocatus*) beyond the normal 16-year term of service – the same rank and the same scale of award as that at which Gavius Silvanus (**B8**) was decorated in

Britain. He was subsequently promoted centurion, rose high in the military service and went on to serve as a procurator in Lusitania (posts recorded in the latter part of this inscription, not quoted above). The *statores* were based at the Praetorian Camp in Rome: they functioned as military police. A consular date, equivalent to AD 66, is given in the latter part of the inscription.

B10 P. Anicius Maximus (legio II Augusta) Claudian

To Publius Anicius Maximus, son of Publius, of the voting tribe Sergia, prefect of Gnaeus Domitius Ahenobarbus, senior centurion of the Twelfth Legion Fulminata, camp prefect of the Second Legion Augusta in Britain, prefect of the army in Egypt, awarded military decorations by the emperor on account of the expedition, honoured on the occasion of the British War with a mural crown and a ceremonial spear. The city of Alexandria which is in Egypt set this up.

[*CIL* 3. 6809 = *ILS* 2696 = EDCS 28400836. Antioch in Pisidia (Antiochia)]

The career of Anicius Maximus is dated by the references to Domitius Ahenobarbus, who died in AD 40, and to the British War, which must be that of Claudius in AD 43. Gnaeus Domitius Ahenobarbus, Nero's father, was probably an honorary local magistrate at Antioch in Pisidia at an unknown date; if so, he would have served *in absentia* with a 'prefect' acting as his deputy. The camp prefect was a member of the equestrian order, and was third in line of command of the legion, ranking only after the legate and the *tribunus laticlavius*, the senatorial tribune. The prefect of the army in Egypt seems to have been the senior military officer in Egypt, an imperial province where no senators (hence no legate nor laticlave tribune) were permitted to set foot. He served under the prefect of Egypt, one of the highest ranking of equestrian officials. Anicius Maximus was awarded military decorations on two occasions: the cryptic reference to an emperor (unnamed) suggests an award by Gaius. The second occasion was the British War. The award of a crown and a spear is the one appropriate to his rank. Antioch was in the Roman province of Galatia (modern Turkey).

B11 Gaius Saufeius (legio IX) Claudio-Neronian

To Gaius Saufeius, son of Gaius, of the Fabian voting tribe, from Heraclea, soldier of the Ninth Legion, aged 40, of 22 years' service; he lies here.

[*RIB* 255. Lincoln (Lindum)]

Tombstone found in 1865 on the west side of High Street. Now in the British Museum.

Gaius Saufeius, like his comrade in legion IX, Quintus Cornelius **G13,** lacks a *cognomen*. Elsewhere in the empire soldiers without *cognomina* are almost all pre-Claudian, and the few examples in Britain should therefore date to the early years of the conquest, thus giving a *terminus ante quem* for the arrival of the legion at Lincoln (Keppie 1995). The Lincoln fortress (situated in the upper part of the city) is known to date no earlier than *c.* AD 60, so it is probable that there was an earlier military base nearby, probably on the lower ground to the south by the river, nearer to the cemetery area where this inscription was found. Heraclea was in Thrace (northern Turkey).

B12 M. Favonius Facilis (legio XX) AD 43–49

Marcus Favonius Facilis, son of Marcus, of the voting tribe Pollia, centurion of the Twentieth Legion; Verecundus and Novicius his freedmen set this up; here he lies.

[*RIB* 200. Colchester (Camulodunum)]

A tombstone found in 1868 in a Roman burial area on the west side of Colchester. Now in the Castle Museum, Colchester. (Fig.1).

See Fig.1 (page 23) for a drawing of the inscription. Above the text is a relief of the soldier. It shows Facilis in military uniform, wearing a cuirass and a tunic adorned with pendant straps, and carrying a *vitis* (a vinestick), the staff of office of the centurion. The stone was originally painted. Near it was found a lead container with cremated bones inside, and a pottery cup of mid-first-century date.

If Facilis was still a serving soldier at the time of his death (and this is by no means certain, as ex-centurions do not always call themselves veterans), it must have occurred while his legion was still based at Colchester, that is before the winter of AD 49–50, when, it may be inferred from Tacitus (*Ann.* 12.32 = LACTOR 11, F3.4), it moved west. Note that the legion lacks its honorary titles, *Valeria Victrix*, 'Brave and Victorious', which it was probably awarded in AD 61 as a result of its conduct in the suppression of the Boudican rebellion (but cf. **F8** note). This stone, together with **B2**, was thought to have been overthrown in the Boudican rebellion when Colchester was sacked (Tacitus *Ann.* 14.32 = LACTOR 11, F3.4), though doubt has now been thrown on this idea (Crummy 1997, 50).

B13 M. Petronius (legio XIV Gemina) Mid-1st century AD

Marcus Petronius, son of Lucius, of the Menenian voting tribe, from Vicetia, aged 38 years, a soldier of the Fourteenth Legion Gemina, served 18 years, was a standard-bearer and lies buried here.

[*RIB* 294. Wroxeter (Viroconium)]

A tombstone found in 1752 with RIB *293. Now in Rowley's House Museum, Shrewsbury.*

Legion XIV Gemina received the honorary titles *Martia Victrix* in AD 61 in recognition of the part it played in the suppression of the Boudican rebellion. Although the titles are sometimes omitted from inscriptions even after this date, it is more likely that both this inscription and **G12** (also from Wroxeter) date to before AD 61. The absence of a *cognomen* for Petronius is consistent with a date in the early years of the conquest (Keppie 1995, and cf. **B11**). Archaeological evidence for the foundation of the known Wroxeter fortress dates it to the mid-50s. Vicetia is now Vicenza in northeast Italy. Italy continued to provide the majority of recruits to the legions until the early second century when provincials started to dominate.

B14 Aureus of Claudius AD 46–47

Obv: Head of Claudius wearing laurel wreath.
TI(BERIVS) CLAVD(IVS) CAESAR AVG(VSTVS) P(ONTIFEX) M(AXIMVS) TR(IBVNICIA) P(OTESTATE) VI IMP(ERATOR) XI.
(Tiberius Claudius Caesar Augustus, chief priest, in his sixth year of tribunician power, hailed *imperator* eleven times)

Rev: No legend. Triumphal arch surmounted by equestrian statue flanked by two trophies:
DE BRITANN(IS). ((*victory*) over the Britons)

[*RIC Claudius* 33 = *BM* 1863,0501.1]

Gold coin (*aureus*) minted in Rome. For the commemorative arches set up in celebration of Claudius's British victory see **B16**. Gold and silver coins of this same type were also issued in AD 49–50 at Rome. Caesarea in Cappadocia minted silver two-drachma coins, *c.* AD 45 also with the legend DE BRITANNIS, '(triumph) over the Britons', which show Claudius in his triumphal chariot (*RIC Claudius* 122).

B15 Claudius to the athletes AD 46

Tiberius Claudius Caesar Augustus Germanicus Sarmaticus, *pontifex maximus*, in his sixth year of tribunician power, designated consul for the fourth time, acclaimed *imperator* twelve times, father of his country – Greetings to the association of touring athletes. I received with pleasure the gold crown which you sent me on account of the victory over the Britons, as a perpetual symbol of your loyalty to me. The delegates were Tiberius Claudius Hermas; Tiberius Claudius Cyrus; Dio son of Mykkalos, from Antioch.

[*P. Lond. (Greek Papyri in the British Museum)* 3.215]

For the full text in translation see Lewis and Reinhold 1966, 232.

B16 Arch of Claudius AD 51

Tiberius Clau[dius Cai]sar Augu[stus Germani]cus, son of Drusus, *pontifex maximus*, in his eleventh year of tribunician power, consul five times, hailed as im[perator 22 (or 23) times, father] of his country; erected by the Senate and people of Rome because [he received the submission] of eleven British kings, [conquered without] any loss, and because he first brought barbarian tribes [beyond Ocean] into the dom[inion of the Roman people].

[*ILS* 216 = EDCS-00900120*. Rome (Roma)]

Inscription above the arch of Claudius, over the Via Flaminia; still standing in the fifteenth century. Fragments now in the courtyard of the Palazzo dei Conservatori, Capitoline Museum.

Cf. Cassius Dio 60.22.1 (= LACTOR 11, E7.2; LACTOR 15, C11 and note p.219): "The Senate on hearing of his achievement voted him the title *Britannicus*, and gave him permission to hold a triumph. They also voted an annual festival to commemorate the event, and decreed that two triumphal arches should be erected, one in Rome and one in Gaul…." Note also the coin (**B14**) illustrating a triumphal arch. It was in fact Claudius's son who received the title *Britannicus*. The eleven British kings presumably include those who were won over by diplomacy as well as those who submitted to force. The arch in Gaul was perhaps erected at Boulogne whence the invasion army had set sail for Britain (see **B1** above). The achievements of Caesar in Britain seem to have been forgotten or brushed aside. Archaic spellings typical of Claudius's antiquarianism feature on many of his inscriptions, including this one, and the spelling of 'Caisar' reflects this. The arch carried statues of members of the imperial house. See Barrett 1991 for a discussion of the reconstruction of the arch and its inscription.

(b) THE SETTLEMENT OF THE SOUTH (AD 47–69)

B17 Bossington lead pig AD 60

NERONIS AVG(VSTVS) EX K(ALENDIS) IAN(VARIIS) IIII COS BRIT (Of Nero Augustus, from 1 January in his fourth consulship. British).

(on sides): From 1 July, *pontifex maximus,* consul

From the lead and silver works. Under G. Nipius Ascanius

[*RIB* 2.1.2404.2 = BM 1861,0218.1. nr. Bossington]

Found in 1783 nr. Bossington near where Roman road from Old Sarum to Winchester crossed the river Test. Now in British Museum.

This is the earliest 'lead pig' from Britain of certain date. *RIB* 2.1.2404.1, given as no. 23 in previous editions of this volume, though datable to AD 49 is long lost and is not certain to have been an ingot. This example probably came from the Mendips (though Flintshire is possible). It certainly shows early exploitation of Britain's metal resources, and compare Pliny's contemporary praise for British lead-mines (*NH* 34.164 = LACTOR 20.M72).

B18 Tombstone of Julius Classicianus, procurator *c.* AD 61–64

To the spirits of the departed and of Gaius Julius Alpinus Classicianus, son of Gaius, of the Fabian voting tribe, ... procurator of the province of Britain. Julia Pacata I[ndiana], daughter of Indus, his wife, had this built.

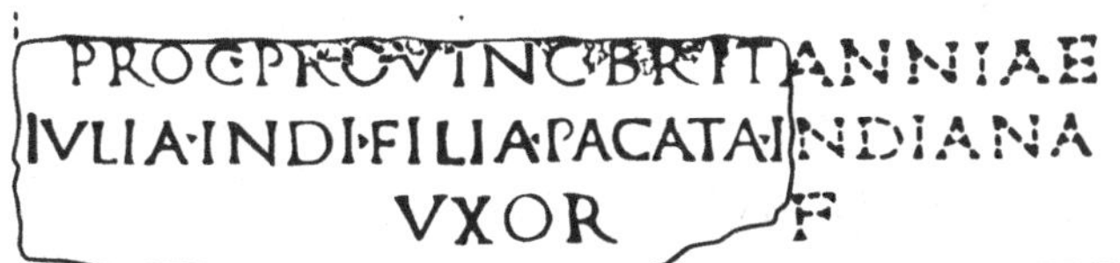

Fig. 5

[*RIB* 12. London (Londinium)]

Fragments of tomb found partly in 1852, partly in 1935 in a bastion of the Roman city wall. Now in the British Museum.

A carved bolster (also found in 1852) probably belongs to this monument. In AD 61 Classicianus succeeded Catus Decianus as procurator (chief finance officer), sent by Nero after the Boudican rebellion. Having the power to report directly to the emperor, he criticised Suetonius Paulinus for his handling of the rebellion, and as a result, after a special commissioner had been sent to investigate, Suetonius was recalled (Tacitus, *Ann.* 14.38–39 = LACTOR 11, F4.1–2). Classicianus was himself a provincial; he almost certainly came from northern Gaul (Birley 2005, 304) and had married the daughter of a Treveran noble (Julius Indus) who had helped to suppress the rebel Julius Florus in AD 21 (Tacitus, *Ann.* 3.42: cf. **B3**). For the date of the Boudican revolt see Syme 1958, Appendix 69, 762ff.

The precise date of Classicianus's death is not known, but assuming a three to four-year period of office as procurator, it probably occurred by the mid-60s. The fact that London was the place of Classicianus's burial suggests that he lived here and hence that London was already the seat of the procurator by the 60s. The form of the tomb from which this inscription comes has been discussed by Grasby and Tomlin (2002).

B19 L. Valerius Geminus (legio II Augusta) — Claudian-Neronian

To the spirits of the departed, Lucius Valerius Geminus, son of Lucius, of the Pollian voting tribe, from Forum Germ(anorum), veteran of the Second Legion Augusta, aged 50(?). He lies here. His heir *(set this up)* according to his will.

[*Britannia* 36 (2005), 478, no 4 = *RIB* 3.3121 = EDCS-05000559. Alchester, Oxfordshire]

Tombstone found in fragments during excavation in 2003. Now with the Oxfordshire Museums Service.

This tombstone of a veteran of *II Augusta* was found in fragments reused in the foundations of the late Roman town wall. The formulae used in the text suggest a Claudio-Neronian date (which is consistent with the archaeological evidence for the date range of the site). It is the first example of a serving soldier or veteran of *II Augusta* belonging to its stay in Britain prior to its move to Caerleon in AD 75. An early military base has been identified at Alchester, and timbers from its annexe have produced a tree-ring date indicating felling in the winter of AD 44/45. Whether Geminus retired while legion II was still at Alchester, settling in the *canabae* (civilian settlement) which may be assumed to have developed outside the base, or whether the unit had already moved on (perhaps to Lake Farm, Dorset or to Exeter, founded *c.* AD 55) and he retired to the town developing at the site of his old base is impossible to determine on the available evidence. (For a full discussion of the stone see Sauer 2005a.) It is probable that Geminus joined the legion when it was based at Strasbourg, in Southern Germany; he was born at Forum Germanorum (or Germanici) which lies in Northern Italy, in the Maritime Alps. The correct form of the town's name is discussed by Sauer (2005b, 202–03).

B20 L. Octavius Martialis (legio XX) Claudian-Neronian

(In memory of) Lucius Octavius Martialis, son of Lucius, of the Pollian voting tribe, from Eporedia, soldier in the Twentieth legion.

[*Britannia* 36 (2005), 476–77, no. 3 = *RIB* 3.3073 = EDCS-44500025. Gloucester (Glevum)]

Tombstone found in fragments on London Road, north-east of Gloucester. In Gloucester City Museum.

Apart from one fragmentary, and now lost, tombstone (*RIB* 122) this is the first inscription of a serving soldier of legion XX from Gloucester. It can be dated stylistically to the Claudio-Neronian period, both in terms of its text – the omission of *Dis Manibus* ('to the spirits of the departed) and the fact that legion XX lacks titles – and of the portrayal of the head of the deceased, carved above. Martialis is shown with projecting ears and hair combed forward in a manner very similar to that of Favonius Facilis, centurion of legion XX, at Colchester (**B12**). Martialis probably served at the early military base at Kingsholm, just north of the later fortress and colonia of Gloucester, which legion XX (or part of it) shared with *cohors VI Thracum* (**B5**). Eporedia is modern Evrea, in northern Italy.

(c) THE FLAVIANS AND NERVA (AD 69–98)

B21 Chester lead water-pipe AD 79

(Made) in the ninth consulship of the Emperor Vespasian and in the seventh of Titus, acclaimed *imperator*, in the governorship of Gnaeus Julius Agricola.

[*RIB* 2.3.2434.1. Chester (Deva)]

Pieces of lead water-piping found in 1899 running east-west in the central range of the fortress, c. 23m. north of Eastgate Street. Now in Grosvenor Museum, Chester.

The date is the first half of the year 79, providing a firm *terminus ante quem* for the foundation of the fortress. The inscription occurs twice on the 5.026 m-long section of pipe which was exposed. The pipe was part of the water-supply put into the legionary fortress at Chester early in the governorship of Agricola. The construction of the fortress may well have begun during the term of office of his predecessor, Julius Frontinus, since a piped water supply is not a primary necessity. A further length of pipe with a similar inscription was found in 1969 below the courtyard of the elliptical building in the central range of the fortress (*RIB* 2.3.2434.3). Schoolteachers may find an easily accessible illustration in the *Cambridge Latin Course*, III, p. 91.

B22 T. Valerius Pudens (legio II Adiutrix) *c.* AD 71–78

Titus Valerius Pudens, son of Titus, of the Claudian voting tribe, from Savaria, a soldier of the Second Legion Adiutrix Pia Fidelis, in the century of Dossennius Proculus, aged 30 years, of [6] years' service; his heir set this up at his own expense; here he lies.

[*RIB* 258. Lincoln (Lindum)]

Tombstone found in 1849. Now in the British Museum

In a gable above the text are two opposed dolphins and a trident; below it an axe.
Legion II Adiutrix was raised at the time of the Civil Wars of AD 69, from sailors of the Ravenna fleet. The dolphins and trident are presumably an allusion to this origin. It came to Britain in AD 71 with the new governor, Cerealis, presumably replacing legion IX at Lincoln, and was transferred to Chester, forming its original garrison, in about AD 78. Dossennius was still in service when he died and was buried at Lincoln, so his years of service (one Roman numeral is lost before 'I') are more likely to have been six (VI) than eleven (XI) which would take us to AD 80. Savaria, a Claudian colony in Pannonia Superior, is modern Szombathely in Hungary.

B23 C. Calventius Celer (legio II Adiutrix) AD 78–87

Gaius Calventius Celer, son of Gaius, of the Claudian voting tribe, from Apri, soldier of the Second Legion Adiutrix Pia Fidelis, in the century of Vibius Clemens [...]

[*RIB* 475. Chester (Deva)]

Tombstone found in 1891 built into the north wall of the fortress. Now in the Grosvenor Museum, Chester.

Legion II Adiutrix was based at Chester from about AD 78 until its move from Britain to the Danube in about AD 87 to take part in Domitian's Dacian War. Apri is a Claudian colony in Thrace (in northern Turkey).

B24 Verulamium forum AD 79 or 81

[To the Emperor Titus Caesar] Ves[pasian Augustus], son [of the deified] Vespa[sian, *pontifex maximus*, in his ninth? year of tribunician power, hailed *imperator* 15? times, consul 7? times], desi[gnated consul for the 8th time, censor, father of his country, and Caesar Do]mi[tian, son of the deified Vespas]ian, [consul 6 times, designated consul for the 7th time, *princeps iuventutis* and priest of] all [the colleges, through Gnaeus Julius A]gric[ola, go]ver[nor, the city of] Ve[rulamium to mark the bui]lding [of the basilica].

[*JRS* 46 *(1956)*, 146–7 no.3 = *RIB* 3.3123 = EDCS-13600218. St Albans (Verulamium)]

Fragments of an inscription found during excavation in 1955. Now in the Verulamium Museum.

Only five small fragments (containing about 21 letters of Latin) survive of this large (4.06 m x 0.71 m) inscription and so the detail of the wording is not absolutely certain beyond the standard imperial titles. As restored above, lines 2–3 give a date of AD 79; an alternative restoration giving a date in AD 81, is also possible (Birley 2005, 82). The third and fourth lines which mention Domitian were erased after his death in AD 96, when his memory was officially damned. The inscription was found during excavations in the forum/basilica complex, and it is on this basis that the word *basilica* has been restored in line 5, assuming that the inscription commemorates the dedication of the building. The restoration *[... basilica or]nata* – 'the building of the basilica' is far from certain. The surviving VE in the last line can be restored equally well as *[municipium] Ve[rulamium]* (as above – 'the city of Verulamium') or *[civitas Catu]ve[llaunorum]* – the settlement of the Catuvellauni, so the inscription cannot be used as independent evidence to confirm Tacitus's statement, in his account of the Boudican rebellion, that Verulamium was a *municipium* (Tac. *Ann.* 14.33 = LACTOR 11, F3.4). This is the only inscription attesting the sort of building activity alluded to by Tacitus (*Agr.* 21). For a fragment from Bath, attesting building activity in AD 76 during the governorship of Agricola's predecessor, see *RIB* 172.

B25 Classicus, prefect of the Sixth Cohort of Nervii AD 65/70–80

[…] to Classicus, prefect of the Sixth Cohort of Nervii.

[*Bloomberg WT* 33 = EDCS-69100073. London *(*Londinium)]

An incomplete silver fir writing tablet with two lines of a page preserved on the inner face.

The Classicus mentioned here is probably the same man as the Treveran noble Julius Classicus who is recorded as commander of a cavalry *ala* in AD 70, and he was probably a kinsman of Julius Classicianus, procurator of Britain (see **B18**), who was also a Treveran noble. Previously not attested in Britain before a diploma of AD 122, the Sixth Cohort of Nervii now appears to have been one of the eight cohorts of auxiliary troops brought over to Britain in AD 61 to strengthen the British garrison after the Boudiccan rebellion (Tacitus, *Annals* 14.38). See also other evidence from the Bloomberg site, *WT* 48, *WT* 55 and *WT* 62 = **G31, H47** and **B26.**

B26 Cavalry present in London *c.* AD 80–90/5

[. . .], troop of [. . .] ; Longinus, troop of Mar[. . .]; Agrippa, troop of Silvanus; Verecundus, troop of Silvanus.

[*Bloomberg WT* 62 = EDCS-69100102. London *(*Londinium)]

An incomplete silver fir writing tablet with extensive traces of about six lines of writing in two columns on the ungrooved inner (recessed) face.

This appears to be a loan-note, to which the members of the various cavalry-troops would have been witnesses; there were usually seven such. The names are common *cognomina*, and appear to be imperial mounted guards, seconded from cavalry units in the provincial armies. They may have been members of the part-mounted cohorts (*cohortes equitatae* – see *WT* 48 and *WT* 55 = **G31** and **H47**) or the governor's mounted guards. There are subtle differences in the writing of each line, suggesting that each witness wrote his own name against his seal. This is also the case in *WT* 55 = **H47**.

B27 Evidence of occupation in Iceni territory *c.* AD 80–90/5

. . . was with the Iceni at the fort of Epocuria, and Julius Suavis has accepted it for himself . . . nor he . . .

[*Bloomberg WT* 39 = EDCS-69100079. London (Londinium)]

An incomplete silver fir writing-tablet with five lines of text legible on the face.

This seems to be part of a letter rather than a legal document, and it is interesting for its reference to the Iceni; its date, some 60 years or more after the Boudiccan revolt, would support the view that the area was garrisoned, here by an otherwise unknown fort (*castellum*) named 'Epocuria'. Tomlin comments that 'both **epo-s* and *curia* (defined by Rivet and Smith (1979, 318) as 'court, ward, assembly' or 'centre of a *pagus*') are well-attested place name elements, but there is no (other) instance of their being combined. Still, the combination is plausible, and hardly any names are known from the canton of the Iceni.'

B28 A casualty of war Late 1st to early 2nd century AD?

To the sprits of the departed, T. Annius ..., centurion of the First Tungrian Cohort, (killed?) in the ... war ... His heir(s) had this set up.

[*Britannia* 29 (1998), 435–36 no. 7 = *RIB* 3.3364 = EDCS-11800970. Chesterholm (Vindolanda)]

Part of a grave slab, found in 1997, re-used in the fourth-century praetorium. Now in Vindolanda Museum.

A.R. Birley attempts a bolder restoration, with supporting arguments, in *Britannia* 29 (1998), 299–305. He proposes: "centurion of legion ..., temporarily in charge of the First Tungrian Cohort, died in the British war, killed by the enemy". The centurion clearly has the *tria nomina* (three names) of a Roman citizen, but some auxiliary centurions are attested as citizens while still serving. The context suggested for a British war is the troubles at the accession of Hadrian (cf. **C41**). This is a strong possibility, but earlier problems under Domitian, or a war elsewhere in the empire, cannot be discounted. The surviving T is interpreted by Tomlin, *Britannia* 29 (1998), 436, as possibly equivalent to the Greek letter theta, used to mean "died in action". The use of the formula D(is) M(anibus) in abbreviated form and the writing out in full of *stipendiorum* suggest a late first-century date. The first fort at Vindolanda was founded somewhere between AD 85 and AD 90, and the Tungrians are known to have formed the garrison of the site in Period I, AD 85/90-*c.* 95 and again in Period IV/V, AD 105-*c.* 125 (information from R.E. Birley).

SECTION C

THE SECOND CENTURY (AD 98–192)

(a) TRAJAN (AD 98–117)

C1 Caerleon stone of Trajan AD 100

For the Emperor Caesar Nerva Trajan Augustus, son of the deified Nerva, Conqueror of Germany, *pontifex maximus*, with tribunician power, father of his country, consul for the third time, the Second Legion Augusta.

[*RIB* 330 add. Caerleon (Isca Silurum)]

A marble commemorative slab found in 1928. It had been reused on the site of a stone–built exercise hall in the rear part of the fortress. Now in the Caerleon Legionary Museum.

Cos II was altered to *cos III*, suggesting that the stone was drafted in AD 99 and was brought up-to-date in AD 100. The inscription is made from imported Tuscan marble. Traces of the red paint which highlighted the letters still survive. It is not known which building it originally came from, though the internal bath-house was certainly undergoing important construction work at about this time.

C2 Rebuilding at York AD 107–8

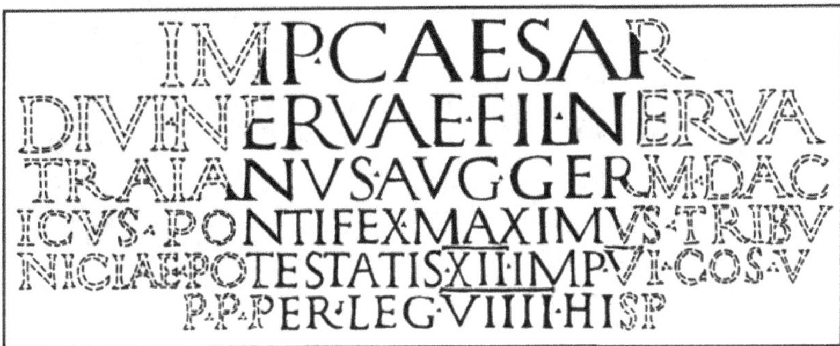

Fig. 6

[*RIB* 665 add. York (Eboracum)]

The Emperor Caesar Nerva Trajan Augustus, son of the deified Nerva, Conqueror of Germany, [Conqueror of Dacia], *pontifex maximus*, in his twelfth year of tribunician power, acclaimed *imperator* six times, [consul five times, father of his country], by the Ninth Legion Hispana.

Part of a commemorative tablet found in 1854 in King's Square near the Roman south-east gateway. Now in the Yorkshire Museum.

Trajan's twelfth year of tribunician power ran from 10 December AD 107 to 9 December AD 108. This is the last dated reference to legion IX Hispana in Britain. Some time thereafter it was replaced at York by legion VI Victrix, which probably came to Britain in AD 122. The restoration of the inscription given in Fig. 3 is based on the suggestion (in *RIB* 665 add.) that *p(ater) p(atriae)* – 'father of his country' – be transferred to the last line which is centred to balance line 1. This last line is sometimes restored to read: *portam per leg VIIII Hispanam fecit*, 'had the gate made by the ninth Legion Hispana,' on the assumption that the inscription referred to the rebuilding of a gate. However, in inscriptions of this date it is rare to specify what is being built; see for example the Caerleon inscription, **C1**. If the fragmentary inscription *RIB* 464 is correctly restored to record building at Chester in AD 102–117, there is evidence from inscriptions for construction work going on under Trajan at all three legionary bases in Britain.

C3 Gelligaer dedication AD 103–111

For the [Emperor] Caesar Nerva Trajan Augustus, son of the deified Nerva, Conqueror of Germany, Conqueror of Dacia, *pontifex maximus*, with tribunician power, father of his country, five times consul, [acclaimed *imperator* four times, the Second Legion Augusta *(built this)*.]

[*RIB* 397 + *JRS* 52 (1962), 193 no.10. Gelligaer]

Found 21 kilometres north of Cardiff (Roman name unknown). A commemorative tablet found in 1909, near the south-east gate of Gelligaer fort. Now in the National Museum of Wales, Cardiff.

"Five times consul" = AD 103–111. The stone is broken off at the bottom, but the name of legion II Augusta is restored on the assumption that it is normally the legions who were responsible for building work at this period, and legion II, based at nearby Caerleon, is the likeliest candidate. The stone fort at Gelligaer, whose building is commemorated by this inscription, was laid out adjacent to its Flavian timber predecessor.

(b) HADRIAN (AD 117–138)

C4 *As* of Hadrian AD 119

Obv: Bust of Hadrian wearing laurel-wreath.
IMP(ERATOR) TRAIANVS HADRIANVS AVG(VSTVS) (Imperator Trajan Hadrian Augustus)

Rev: Britannia seated with right foot resting on a rock. Shield stands beside her.
PONT(IFEX) MAX(IMVS) TR(IBUNICIA) POT(ESTATE) CO(N)S(VL) III. S(ENATVS) C(ONSVLTO). BRITANNIA (*pontifex maximus*, holding tribunician power, three times consul. By decree of the Senate. Britannia).

[*RIC* Hadrian 577*a*]

The Britannia motif is thought to be an allusion to the successful resolution of the problems Hadrian faced in Britain at the beginning of his reign (SHA *Hadrian* 5.1 = LACTOR 11 J1.1).

C5 A military diploma AD 122

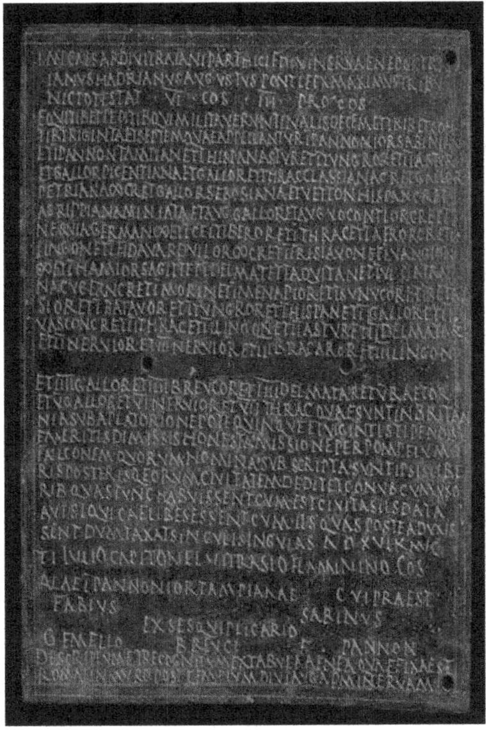

The Emperor Caesar Trajan Hadrian Augustus, son of the deified Trajan Parthicus, grandson of the deified Nerva, high priest, in his sixth year of tribunician power, three times consul, proconsul:

To the cavalrymen and infantrymen who served in the 13 *alae* and 37 cohorts here named:
(1) I Pannoniorum Sabiniana, (2) I Pannoniorum Tampiana, (3) I Hispanorum Asturum, (4) I Tungrorum, (5) II Asturum, (6) Gallorum Picentiana, (7) Gallorum et Thracum Classiana civium Romanorum (8) Gallorum Petriana milliaria civium Romanorum (9) Gallorum Sebosiana, (10) Vettonum Hispanorum civium Romanorum (11) Agrippiana Miniata (12) Augusta Gallorum (13) Augusta Vocontiorum civium Romanorum.

(1) I Nervia Germanorum milliaria, (2) I Celtiberorum, (3) I Thracum, (4) I Afrorum civium Romanorum, (5) I Lingonum, (6) I Fida Vardullorum milliaria civium Romanorum, (7) I Frisiavonum, (8) I Vangionum milliaria, (9) I Hamiorum Sagittariorum, (10) I Delmatarum, (11) I Aquitanorum, (12) I Ulpia Traiana Cugernorum civium Romanorum, (13) I Morinorum, (14) I Menapiorum, (15) I Sunucorum, (16) I Baetasiorum. (17) I Batavorum, (18) I Tungrorum, (19) I Hispanorum, (20) II Gallorum, (21) II Vasconum civium Romanorum, (22) II Thracum, (23) II Lingonum, (24) II Asturum, (25) II Delmatarum, (26) II Nerviorum, (27) III Nerviorum, (28) III Bracarorum, (29) III Lingonum, (30) IIII Gallorum, [(31) IV Lingonum] (32) IIII Breucorum, (33) IIII Delmatarum, (34) V Raetorum, (35) V Gallorum, (36) VI Nerviorum, (37) VII Thracum;

which are in Britain under Aulus Platorius Nepos, who have served twenty-five years, been given honourable discharge by Pompeius Falco, whose names are written below, citizenship for themselves, their children and descendants, and the right of legal marriage with the wives they had when citizenship was granted to them, or, if any were unmarried, with those they later marry, but only a single one each.

17 July in the consulship of Tiberius Julius Capito and Lucius Vitrasius Flamininus. To Gemellus, son of Breucus, a Pannonian, formerly *sesquiplicarius* of the *ala I Pannoniorum Tampiana*, commanded by Fabius Sabinus.

Copied and checked from the bronze tablet set up at Rome on the wall behind the temple of the deified Augustus near *(the statue of)* Minerva.

[Witnessed by] Tiberius Claudius Menander, Aulus Fulvius Justus, Tiberius Julius Urbanus, Lucius Pullius Daphnus, Lucius Nonius Victor, Quintus Lollius Festus, Lucius Pullius Anthius.

[*CIL* 16. 69 = BM 1930,0419.1 = EDCS-12300273*. O-Szöny, Hungary (Brigetio)]

Now in the British Museum. This is the text of the outer faces of the two leaves of a military diploma. I have followed the editors of diplomas by adding (in parentheses) numbers for the 13 *alae* and 37 cohorts, where the Latin text simply writes 'et' (and). *Cohors IV Lingonum* was omitted in error from the outer faces, but appears on the inner. These inner faces repeat the text (minus the names of the seven witnesses), but are less well inscribed and contain a number of errors. The two leaves of a diploma were wired together and sealed with the seals of the witnesses. This example was still wired together when found.

The inclusion of *proconsul* in the titles of Hadrian implies that he was away from Italy at the time of issue; he was probably in Britain. This diploma establishes, to within a few months, the date of arrival of Platorius Nepos as governor of Britain, for the soldiers whose grant is recorded had been discharged by Nepos's predecessor, Pompeius Falco. (For Platorius Nepos see **F138**). The 50 units named on this diploma may represent a nearly complete tally of the auxiliary garrison of Britain in July AD 122.

A *sesquiplicarius* is a junior officer who received pay-and-a-half; he was third in command of a cavalry troop. Note that the recipient of this diploma was a Pannonian, who served in a Pannonian unit and who returned to the area of his birth after discharge – the document was found at the site of Brigetio, a frontier fort on the Danube in the province of Pannonia Superior (northern Hungary).

C6 Altars to Neptune and Oceanus — Early 120s AD

(i) To Neptune, the Sixth Legion Victrix Pia Fidelis *(set this up)*.

(ii) To Ocianus, the Sixth Legion Victrix Pia Fidelis *(set this up)*.

[*RIB* 1319 and 1320. Newcastle upon Tyne (Pons Aeli)]

A pair of altars found in 1875 (a) and 1903 (b) in the river Tyne by the site of the Roman bridge (by the present Swing Bridge) at Newcastle. Now in the Great North Museum, Hancock.

The centrepiece of the inscription to Neptune is a dolphin entwined around a trident, of that to Ocianus (= Oceanus) an anchor (drawings in *RIB* online). These two altars are thought to have been set up in a shrine on the bridge constructed across the Tyne by Hadrian at Newcastle *(Pons Aeli)*, the lowest bridging point of the river. Legion VI Victrix came to Britain from lower Germany in AD 122, along with the new governor, A. Platorius Nepos (see **F1**); the "marine" dedications of these two altars may allude to the sea-crossing which the legion had undertaken in travelling to Britain. Dedications to Neptune are commonly found in contexts associated with the sea in Britain: note **F16** (Chichester), **G44** (Lympne) and **H25** (York). Note also the curse tablet invoking Neptune, found on the foreshore of the Hamble Estuary (*Britannia* 28 (1997), no. 1.)

C7 Milecastle 38 building inscription *c.* AD 122–125

(In honour of) the Emperor Caesar Trajan Hadrian Augustus, the Second Legion Augusta *(built this)* under Aulus Platorius Nepos, governor.

[*RIB* 1638 add. Hadrian's Wall]

A dedication slab found between 1751 and 1757 at Hotbank milecastle, No. 38. Now in the Great North Museum, Hancock.

This is one of three surviving inscriptions recording the building of the milecastles of Hadrian's Wall, dating their completion (and probably their construction) to the governorship of Platorius Nepos (AD 122 to at least AD 124: see **F1**). Hill (1991) considers that this inscription and *RIB* 1634, 1637 and 1666 were all produced by the same person. The milecastles were part of the original scheme for Hadrian's Wall, and were built by the three legions, II Augusta (this one), VI Victrix and XX Valeria Victrix; each legion designed its milecastles slightly differently (Breeze and Dobson 2000, chap. 2).

C8 Halton Chesters dedication *c.* AD 122–125

For the Emperor Caesar Trajan Hadrian Augustus, the Sixth Legion Victrix [Pia Fidelis] *(built this)* under Aulus Platorius N[epos], governor.

[*RIB* 1427. Halton Chesters, Northumberland (Onnum)]

A dedication slab, found in 1936 at the west gate of Halton Chesters fort. Now in the Great North Museum, Hancock

Platorius Nepos was governor from AD 122 to at least AD 124. This inscription shows that the forts, though structurally secondary to Hadrian's Wall, were nevertheless added soon after the building began, and still within the governorship of Nepos.

C9 Benwell *classis Britannica* building inscription *c.* AD 122–125

For the Emperor Caesar Trajan Hadrian Augustus, a detachment of the British f[leet] *(built this)* under the governor Aulus Platorius N[epos].

[*RIB* 1340. Benwell (Condercum)]

A building inscription found in 1937, in the portico of the granaries of Benwell fort. Now in the Great North Museum, Hancock.

This (and **C14**) are the earliest building inscriptions recording a unit other than a legion being involved in building work in Roman Britain (though note that 'fleet', is a restoration for '*c[lassis]*').

C10 Great Chesters dedication AD 128–138

For the Emperor Caesar Trajan Hadrian Augustus, father of his country.

[*RIB* 1736. Great Chesters, Northumberland (Aesica)]

A dedication slab found shortly before 1851, near the east gate of Great Chesters fort. Now in Chesters Museum.

Hadrian took the title *pater patriae* – 'father of his country' – in AD 128; assuming that this title is correctly used (and this is not invariably the case, cf. **F25**) this inscription dates the construction of Great Chesters fort to the latter part of the reign. The fort was built entirely to the south of the Wall instead of projecting across it as was the case with the early forts such as Halton Chesters and Benwell. Cf. also Carrawburgh (**C11**), built in *c.* AD 130–132.

C11 Carrawburgh dedication c. AD 130–132

[... under Julius Se]verus as governor, the First Cohort of Aquitanians built this under [...]ius Nepos, prefect.

[*RIB* 1550. Carrawburgh, Northumberland (Brocolitia)]

Part of a dedication slab found in 1838 in the north-east corner of Carrawburgh fort. Now in Chesters Museum.

This fragmentary text dates building work at Carrawburgh fort to a governorship, almost certainly that of Julius Severus, later than that of Platorius Nepos. (Julius Verus is virtually ruled out as the First Cohort of Aquitanians was at Brough-on-Noe during his governorship (**C35**)). This is consistent with the fact that Carrawburgh fort, like Great Chesters, is not built straddling the line of Hadrian's Wall (as is the case with all of the clearly early forts, where topography permitted), but is attached to its south side. This (together with **C13** and possibly **C14**) is one of the earliest building inscriptions set up by an auxiliary unit in Britain, though it is known from one of the Vindolanda tablets (*Tab. Vindol.* 1.1) that auxiliary soldiers were engaged in construction work in the early Trajanic period (c. AD 95–105).

C12 Netherby dedication AD 122–128

For the Emperor Caesar Trajan Hadrian Augustus, the Second Legion Augusta built this.

[*RIB* 974. Netherby, Cumbria (Castra Exploratorum)]

An inscription seen in 1601, built into the house at Netherby. Now lost.

This inscription from the outpost fort of Netherby is not sufficiently closely datable to indicate whether the outposts formed part of the initial scheme for Hadrian's Wall, or whether they were part of the secondary plan when forts were built on the line of the Wall. The terminal date of AD 128 is based on the absence of 'father of his country' in the emperor's titles (but see comment on **C10**). Inscriptions from the other two Hadrianic outpost forts provide dates of before 128 for Birrens (*Transactions of the Dumfries and Galloway Natural History and Antiquarian Society* 38 (1959–60), 142 ff) and ?AD 124/30 for Bewcastle (*RIB* 995).

C13 Bowes dedication c. AD 130–132

For the Emperor Caesar Trajan Hadrian Augustus, son of the deified Trajan [Parthicus], grandson of the deified Nerva, *pontifex maximus*, [in his ... year of tribunician power], three times consul, father of his country, the Fourth Cohort of B[reuci under the governor Sextus Jul]ius Sev[erus] *(built this)*.

[*RIB* 739. Bowes, Yorkshire (Lavatrae)]

A dedication slab seen before 1600 in the church at Bowes, where it had been used as an altar slab. Recorded by Camden (1600). Now lost.

Camden gave the name of the unit as *IIII F[....]*. There is no likely candidate in Britain so Birley (cited in *RIB*) suggested it should read *IIII B[reucorum]*. *IIII Delmatarum*, another possibility, was stationed at this time at Hardknott (below, **C14**).

C14 Hardknott fragments c. AD 119–38

[For the Emperor Ca]esar Trajan [Hadria]n [Augustus], son of the deified [Trajan] Parthicus, [grandson of the deified] Nerva, *pontifex maximus* [... three times consul, ...] governor, the Fourth Cohort of Delmatians [built this].

[*JRS* 1965, 222, no.7 = *RIB* 3.3219 = EDCS-11800714. Hardknott, Cumbria (Mediobogdum)]

*Fourteen scattered fragments of a dedication slab, found in 1964 at the south-east gate (*porta praetoria*).*

This inscription probably dates the original construction of the fort at Hardknott (though some have argued for a Trajanic foundation). Hadrian took his third consulship in AD 119; he did not take a fourth. The name of the governor is not recoverable. The Fourth Cohort of Delmatians is first attested in Britain on a diploma of AD 103 (*RIB* 2.1.2401.1 = *CIL* 16. 48).

C15 Moresby dedication AD 128–38

(In honour) of the Emperor Caesar Trajan Hadrian Augustus, father of his country, the Twentieth Legion Valeria Victrix *(built this)*.

[*RIB* 801. Moresby, Cumbria]

A sandstone tablet in three parts found in 1822 near the east gate of Moresby fort. Now at BM 1970,0102.2

The date is given by the title *pater patriae* taken by Hadrian in AD 128. The construction of Moresby was presumably linked with the extension of the Hadrianic frontier down the Cumberland coast.

C16 Maenius Agrippa statue base Mid-2nd century AD

Marcus Maenius Agrippa Lucius Tusidius Campester, son of Gaius, of the voting tribe Cornelia, host of the deified Hadrian, father of a senator, prefect of the Second Flavian Cohort Equitata of Britons, chosen by the emperor Hadrian and sent on an expedition to Britain, tribune of the First Cohort Equitata of Spaniards, prefect of the Ala Catafractata of Gauls and Spaniards, imperial procurator, prefect of the British fleet, procurator of the province of Britain, *equo publico*, patron of his city; the people of the village of Censorglacum erected this in recognition of the privileges they obtained by favour of the excellent and all-powerful emperor Antoninus Augustus Pius as a result of his intervention, privileges which are a perpetual source of strength and comfort. The site was given by decree of the decurions.

[*ILS* 2735 = *CIL* 11. 5632 = EDCS-23000300. Camerini (Camerinum) Italy]

A statue base found in the 17th century.

The expedition to Britain in which Maenius Agrippa took part is either the war which Hadrian waged against the Britons at the start of his reign or another campaign later within the reign. The existence of this later campaign depends to a large extent on the disputed dating of this inscription and that of **C19** (for the various views cf. Birley 1961, 26–29; Jarrett 1976, 145–51; Dobson 1978, 236; Maxfield 1981, 196–97; S. S. Frere, 'M. Maenius Agrippa, the *expeditio Britannica* and Maryport', *Britannia* XXXI (2000), pp. 23–28; Breeze 2003). *Equo publico* means that Agrippa had been granted the honour of taking part in the ceremonial ride-past in Rome, a relic of the days when the equestrian nobility were Rome's cavalry force.

C17 Maenius Agrippa altar Hadrianic

To Jupiter, Best and Greatest, the First Cohort of Spaniards commanded by Marcus Maenius Agrippa, tribune, set this up.

[*RIB* 823. Maryport, Cumbria (Alauna)]

Altar found before 1725 outside the Roman fort at Maryport. Now at the Senhouse Museum, Maryport.

This altar is one of a remarkable collection of dedications to Jupiter Optimus Maximus (seventeen have now been found), set up by the *cohors I Hispanorum equitata.* These altars were found, buried in several pits around the parade ground at the Maryport fort. It seems probable, as Wenham suggested (1939, 28), that these altars were a record of the annual oath of allegiance of the soldiers, and as they all show so little weathering the previous year's altar was buried as the new one was set up. Alternatively, it was thought that they might have been buried in batches having stood under shelter, but re-excavation of the archaeological context from 2011 onwards showed that they were in fact used as packing in post pits; in addition, two more undisturbed pits were also found, one of which contained another almost complete altar (**J5 (iii)** and see also **J5 i, ii, iv**). Notes by Pete Wilson in *Britannia* 44 (2013), pp. 290 ff.

Cohors I Hispanorum was resident at Maryport in the Hadrianic period, the first of five different units to occupy the site (which remained in use from c. AD 122 to c. AD 400). Some of the commanding officers named on these altars are tribunes (as here), others prefects (as **C18**); the former commanded units 1000-strong, the latter 500-strong. This indicates that *I Hispanorum* changed in establishment strength during its sojourn at Maryport, and the fact that the fort appears originally to have been built for a large unit, suggests that the unit was reduced in size (Jarrett 1976; Breeze 1997).

C18 Maryport altar — Hadrianic

To Jupiter Best and Greatest, the First Cohort Equitata of Spaniards commanded by Lucius Antistius Lupus Verianus, son of Lucius, of the tribe Quirina, prefect, from Sicca in Africa *(set this up)*.

[*RIB* 816. Maryport, Cumbria (Alauna)]

*Altar found with **C17** and **J5 (i)**. Now at the Senhouse Museum, Maryport.*

Antistius Lupus Verianus held the rank of prefect when he commanded *I Hispanorum*. Sicca Veneria lay in the province of Africa Proconsularis (in modern Tunisia), about 120 km inland from Carthage. For other Maryport altars, see **J5**.

C19 Titus Pontius Sabinus — Hadrianic

Front: Titus Pontius Sabinus, son of Titus, of the voting tribe Palatina, *primus pilus II*, procurator of the province of Narbonensis, magistrate, priest and patron of the city. (Erected by) Valeria Procula, daughter of Lucius, his wife. The site was given by decree of the decurions.

Back: Titus Pontius Sabinus, son of Titus, of the voting tribe Palatina, prefect of the First Cohort Equitata of Pannonians and Dalmatians, Roman citizens, tribune of the Sixth Legion Ferrata, decorated on the Parthian expedition by the deified Trajan with a ceremonial spear, a standard and a mural crown, centurion of the Twenty-Second Legion Primigenia, centurion of the Thirteenth Legion Gemina, senior centurion of the Third Legion Augusta, in command of detachments of a thousand men from each of Legions VII Gemina, VIII Augusta and XXII Primigenia on the British expedition, tribune of the Third Cohort of Vigiles, tribune of the Fourteenth Urban Cohort, tribune of the Second Praetorian Cohort, *primus pilus II*, procurator of the province of Narbonensis, magistrate, priest, patron of the city.

[*ILS* 2726 = EDCS-20500054. Ferentini (Ferentinum) Italy]

A statue base inscribed front and back. Found in 1851. Now in the museum at Ferentini.

The front of the inscription gives the high spots of Sabinus's career; the reverse gives the full details. After starting service as an equestrian military commander, Sabinus obtained a direct commission into the legionary centurionate and rose from there into the ranks of the procurators. (On career changes of this sort see Dobson 1972). The three legions which sent detachments to the British war were based in Spain (VII Gemina) and Upper Germany (VIII Augusta and XXII Primigenia). Sabinus's career can be approximately dated by the reference to the Parthian War which began in AD 114 and in which Trajan was engaged at the time of his death in AD 117. The date of the British expedition depends on the length of time Sabinus is estimated to have taken to advance from tribune of legion VI (the post he held in AD 117) to the senior centurionate and his appointment in charge of the detachments sent to Britain. Estimates vary considerably, allowing for participation in the troubles at the start of Hadrian's reign or in a campaign anywhere up to the mid-120s. The nature of the post *primus pilus II* is obscure.

C20 Sestertius of Hadrian AD 134–138

Obv: Bust of Hadrian wearing a laurel wreath.
HADRIANVS AVG(VSTVS) CO(N)S(VL) III P(ATER) P(ATRIAE) (Hadrian Augustus, three times consul, father of his country)

Rev: Britannia seated with right foot resting on a rock, holding a spear in crook of left arm. Shield stands beside. Below S(ENATVS) C(ONSVLTO) (by decree of the Senate)

[*RIC* Hadrian 845. *Sestertius*]

A large series of coins issued at the end of Hadrian's reign recapitulated his provincial tours and commemorated the armies of the provinces visited. (PJC).

C21 Carvoran altar AD 136–137

To the Fortune of the Emperor for the welfare of Lucius Aelius Caesar, Titus Flavius Secundus, prefect of the First Cohort of Hamian Archers, because of a vision, fulfilled his vow willingly and deservedly.

[*RIB* 1778. Carvoran, Northumberland (Magnis)]

An altar, found in 1831 in the bathhouse at Carvoran fort. Now in the Great North Museum, Hancock.

Lucius Aelius was adopted Caesar in AD 136 and died on January 1, AD 138. This, together with the following inscription, date a rebuilding of the fort rampart at Carvoran to *c.* AD 136–137, indicating that construction work on the Hadrianic frontier was continuing right down to the end of the reign. Dedications to the goddess Fortuna are not uncommon finds in bath-houses where their presence is often associated with the practice of using the bath-house for gambling; it is as likely to be due to the need to avert the evil eye from the naked soldiers.

C22 Carvoran building-stone *c.* AD 136–138

The century of Silvanus built 112 feet of rampart under the command of Flavius Secundus, prefect.

[*RIB* 1820. Carvoran, Northumberland (Magnis)]

A building-stone found in 1940 near Carvoran fort. Now in the Great North Museum, Hancock.

This stone is dated by the reference to Flavius Secundus, known from **C21** (above) to have been in command when Lucius Aelius was Caesar. The verb *vallare* to build a *vallum*, a rampart, occurs in Britain only on this and two other stones from Carvoran, *RIB* 1816 and 1817, which are therefore almost certainly contemporary.

(c) ANTONINUS PIUS (AD 138–161)

C23 Corbridge, probably from the west granary AD 139

For the Emperor Titus Aelius Antoninus Augustus Pius, consul for the second time, under the charge of [the governor], Quintus Lollius Urbicus, the Second Legion Augusta built this.

[*RIB* 1147. Corbridge, Northumberland (Coria?)]

A dedication slab found in 1935 reused as a paving-stone in the west granary at Roman Corbridge. Now in Corbridge Museum.

The mason incorrectly inscribed ANIONINO, LOLII and VRBIC·I. The stone is dated by the consulship. Together with **C24** it points to the rebuilding of the fort at Corbridge, at the very beginning of Pius's reign, in connection with the move forward into Scotland and the construction of a new frontier across the Forth-Clyde isthmus. For Lollius Urbicus as governor of Britain cf. SHA, *Antoninus Pius* 5.4 (LACTOR 11 K1.1). His name appears also on an inscription recording the building of a fort on the Antonine Wall (**C27**) and on one from the area between Hadrian's Wall and the Antonine Wall (**C26)** The governor is not named on the distance slabs from the Wall itself (cf. **C28–C30**).

The Roman name for Corbridge, formerly taken to be *Corstopitum* (Rivet and Smith 1979), now appears, from evidence in the Vindolanda tablets, to be *Coria* (**G191**; Bowman and Thomas 1991, 71; 1994, 96–97).

C24 Corbridge, probably from the east granary AD 140

For the Emperor Caesar Titus Aelius Antoninus Augustus Pius, in the year of his third consulship, father of his country, under the charge of the governor, Quintus Lollius Urbicus, the Second Legion Augusta built this."

[*RIB* 1148. Corbridge, Northumberland (Coria?)]

Part of a dedication slab found in 1907 reused as a paving-stone in the east granary at Roman Corbridge. Now in Corbridge Museum.

Note that *III cos* – 'third consulship' has been altered from *II cos* – 'second consulship' (cf. **C1** from Caerleon).

C25 Sestertius of Antoninus Pius AD 143–144

Obv: Head of Antoninus Pius wearing laurel-wreath.

ANTONINVS AVG(VSTVS) PIVS P(ATER) P(ATRIAE) TR(IBVNICIA) P(OTESTATE) CO(N)S(VL) III. (Antoninus Augustus Pius, father of his country, having tribunician power, three times consul)

Rev: Victory standing on globe, holding wreath in extended right hand and palm-branch in left hand over left shoulder.

IMPERATOR II. BRITAN(NICA) (twice hailed *imperator*. British (Victory))
Below: S(ENATVS) C(ONSVLTO) (by decree of the Senate)

[*RIC* Antoninus Pius 719. *Sestertius* = BM R. 13600]

Pius's second imperial salutation was no doubt on account of his British victory, alluded to here by the figure of Victory. The earliest dated reference to Pius's salutation as *imperator II* is in AD 142 (*CIL* 10. 515 = *ILS* 340).

C26 High Rochester building slab AD 139–*c*.143

For the Emperor Caesar Titus Aelius Hadrianus Antoninus Augustus Pius, father of his country, under Quintus Lollius Urbicus, governor, the First Cohort Equitata of Lingones built this."

[*RIB* 1276. High Rochester, Northumberland (Bremenium)]

A dedication slab found in 1852 reused in the floor of a water-tank in front of the headquarters building; original position unknown. Now in the Great North Museum, Hancock.

High Rochester lies on Dere Street, a day's march north of Corbridge. Between Corbridge and High Rochester lies Risingham, where a new fort was constructed in the Antonine period.

C27 Balmuildy slab AD 139–*c*.143

[For the Emperor Caesar Titus Aelius Hadrianus Antoninus Augustus Pius, father] of his country, the Second Legion Au[gusta built this under] Quintus Lollius Ur[bicus], governor.

[*RIB* 2191. Balmuildy, Lanarkshire]

Part of a commemorative tablet found built into a byre at Balmuildy. Now in the Hunterian Museum, Glasgow.

The fort of Balmuildy lies on the Antonine Wall but was constructed before it. Urbicus does not appear on any of the distance slabs (cf. **C28–C30**) and may not have been involved in the construction. Auxiliaries, as well as legionaries, are attested building forts on the Antonine Wall: cf. *RIB* 2145 (Rough Castle), 2155 (Castlecary) and 2170 (Bar Hill).

C28 The Bridgeness slab Early 140s AD

For the Emperor Caesar Titus Aelius Hadrianus Antoninus Augustus Pius, father of his country, the Second Legion Augusta built 4,652 paces.

[*RIB* 2139. Bridgeness, West Lothian]

A dedication slab found in 1868 on Windmill Hill immediately overlooking the Firth of Forth and the site of the end of the Antonine Wall. Now in the Museum of Scotland, Edinburgh. (There is also a cast in the Hunterian Museum Glasgow.)

There is a relief on either side of the inscribed central panel, each in a pillared niche. On the left, representing the campaigning which preceded the building of the Wall, is a helmeted cavalryman with spear and shield, thrusting at four naked enemies. One is headless, one falling dead, one crawling and one sitting defenceless. On the right is a representation of the *suovetaurilia* – a ceremonial sacrifice of a pig *(sus)*, sheep *(ovis)* and bull *(taurus)* – which inaugurated the construction of the Wall. The animals move towards a seated figure. In the background are five figures, one plays a double flute, one is holding a *patera* over the altar, and one holds a *vexillum* inscribed LEG II AVG (photo in *RIB* online).

This is one of a series of inscriptions (20 are now known) recording lengths of the Antonine Wall built by the three legions involved in its construction. On these inscriptions legion II is recorded as complete (as here), the other two only as detachments. Note that this text records the building length in paces *(passus)*; compare **C29** and **C30** where the unit used is feet *(pedes)*. For a text and commentary on this and all the other distance-slabs from the Antonine Wall see Keppie 1998.

C29 Duntocher distance-slab — Early 140s AD

For the Emperor Caesar Titus Aelius Hadrianus Antoninus Augustus, father of his country, a detachment of the Sixth Legion Victrix Pia Fidelis built 3,240 feet of rampart.

[*RIB* 2200 add. Duntocher, Lanarkshire]

A commemorative tablet, found in 1812 on the line of the Antonine Wall at Braidfield Farm. Original position must have been 1.1 km south-east of Duntocher fort. Now in the Hunterian Museum, Glasgow.

The inscribed panel is supported by two winged Victories in relief, each standing on a globe. They are flanked left by Mars Victor (the victorious god of war) and right by Virtus Augusta (the valour of the emperor), who holds in her left hand a sheathed ceremonial sword inverted, and in her right a *vexillum* inscribed *Virtus Aug(usta)* (photo in *RIB* online). Note that the 'wall' is here described as a rampart (*opus valli*). The distance recorded here (and on **C30** and on all other slabs from the westernmost four miles of the Wall) is recorded in feet, contrasting with the paces used further east. This is perhaps a reflection of the dislocation caused by the change in plan when it was decided to add extra forts to the Wall line.

C30 Duntocher distance-slab — Early 140s AD

For the Emperor Antoninus Augustus Pius, father of his country, the Second Legion Augusta built 3271 feet.

[*RIB* 2204. Duntocher, Lanarkshire]

A commemorative tablet found before 1699 on the line of the Antonine Wall near the farm of Carleith, about 1.6 km west of Duntocher fort. Now in the Hunterian Museum, Glasgow.

The tablet is adorned with a Capricorn, a Pegasus and rosettes (drawing in *RIB* online). Note that this seems to record building by a whole legion and not a detachment; contrast **C28**.

C31 Altar from Newstead — Antonine

To Diana the queen, on account of successful ventures, Gaius Arrius Domitianus, centurion of the Twentieth Legion Valeria Victrix, fulfilled his vow joyfully, willingly and deservedly.

[*RIB* 2122. Newstead (Trimontium)]

Altar found in 1909 in the fort. Now in the Museum of Scotland, Edinburgh.

Arrius Domitianus dedicated three altars at Newstead (this and *RIB* 2123–4). His presence, together with that of another legionary centurion (L. Maximus Gaetulicus, *RIB* 2120) suggests that a detachment of legion XX was in residence at Newstead in the early Antonine period, together with a cavalry unit, the *ala Vocontiorum*. Newstead lies on Dere Street (near Melrose) and is a key fort in the occupations of Scotland.

C32 Graffiti on a Samian bowl before *c.* AD 155

(property) of Materna

[*Britannia* 31 (2000), 445.49 = EDCS-20500225. Mumrills, Stirlingshire]

Two conjoining sherds of a Samian bowl, found in the outer ditch of the fort, backfilled by the Romans in c. *AD 155: scratched after firing above the foot ring. Now in the Falkirk Museum*

This and a similar fragment found in the same context are illustrations of the simple ways in which literacy pervaded the Roman army, here used as signs of ownership.

C33 Dupondius of Antoninus Pius AD 154–155

Obv: Head of Antoninus Pius, wearing a radiate crown.
ANTONINVS AVG(VSTVS) PIVS P(ATER) P(ATRIAE) TR(IBUNICIA) P(OTESTATE) XVIII (Antoninus Augustus Pius, father of his country, in his eighteenth year of tribunician power.)

Rev: Britannia seated on a rock. Shield and spear stand beside her.
Around, BRITANNIA; below, S(ENATVS) C(ONSVLTO) (By decree of the Senate)

[*RIC* Antoninus Pius 930.]

Dupondii and *asses* of this type are found only in Britain, and are common on military sites. They appear to be a special donative given only to the army of Britain. (PJC).

C34 Newcastle, Julius Verus slab *c.* AD 158

For the Emperor Antoninus Augustus Pius, father of his country, the detachment(s) of the Second Legion Augusta, the Sixth Legion Victrix and the Twentieth Legion Valeria Victrix for the armies of the two Germanies, under Julius Verus, governor, *(set this up).*

[*RIB* 1322 add. Newcastle upon Tyne (Pons Aeli)]

A dedication slab found in 1903 in dredging the north channel of the Tyne below the Swing Bridge. Now (2009) in the Great North Museum, Hancock.

Fig. 7

Though well-preserved, abbreviations and mistakes make the translation and interpretation of this inscription uncertain. 'VEXILATIO' (note the ligature in carving TI as a cross) would normally have two LLs and may be singular or an abbreviation of the plural. 'CON{T}R{I}BVTI' (lines 6–7) has lost two letters. 'EX GER DVOBVS' (lines 7–8) has been explained as 'ex Germaniis duabus' (from the two Germanies) or 'ex exercitibus Germanicis duobus' (from the two German armies), both implying that the troops had come *to* Britain *from* Germany; or as 'exercitibus Germanicis duobus' (for the two German armies – as in the translation given above), implying that the troops are being sent *from* Britain *to help* the German armies. There is no clear way of deciding between these possibilities. This inscription has been used (with troops coming from Germany to Britain) as evidence for a "Brigantian revolt" in the AD 150s. The case for the "revolt" is far from proven; for a discussion contrast Breeze and Dobson 2000, 118 with Frere 1987, 135–137. If the troops are actually leaving Britain this would argue against the notion of a revolt.

C35 Brough-on-Noe dedication *c.* AD 158

For the Emperor Caesar Titus Aelius Hadrianus Antoninus Augustus Pius, father of his country, the First Cohort of Aquitanians under Julius Verus, governor, under the charge of Capitonius Pricus, prefect, *(built this).*

[*RIB* 283 add. Brough-on-Noe, Derbyshire (Navio)]

A commemorative slab found in 1903 in the strongroom of the fort's headquarters. Now in Buxton Museum.

The fort was rebuilt on a deserted Flavian site. This reoccupation has been linked to the "Brigantian revolt", on which see above, under no. 61. For Capitonius Priscus cf. *AE* 1982, 850.

C36 Birrens rebuilding AD 157–158

"For the Emperor Caesar Titus Aelius Hadrianus Antoninus Augustus Pius, *pontifex maximus,* in his twenty-first year of tribunician power, four times consul, the Second Cohort of Tungrians, *milliaria, equitata,* C. L., *(set this up)* under Julius Verus, governor."

[*RIB* 2110. Birrens, Dumfriesshire (Blatobulgium)]

A dedication slab found in 1895 in the fort's headquarters building. Now in the Museum of Scotland, Edinburgh.

The Tungrians lived around Tongres, in Belgium. Pius's 21st tribunician power lasted from 10 December AD 157 to 9 December AD 158, The Ravenglass diploma (*Britannia* 28 (1997), 463–64 no. 28) shows Verus in Britain in February AD 158, so his governorship must have included 157. The letters C L cannot be expanded with confidence. The frequently suggested C(IVIVM) L(ATINORVM), "Latin citizens", would be unique and has no evidence to justify it. C(ORAM) L(AVDATA), "publicly praised" i.e. in the presence of the emperor, has been suggested, but this is also unparalleled for a unit, though known for an individual, *AE* 1956, 124. This inscription has been linked to the "Brigantian revolt"; see above under **C34**.

C37 Heddon-on-the-Wall stone (Legio VI Victrix) AD 158

The Sixth Legion Victrix Pia Fidelis rebuilt this in the consulship of Tertullus and Sacerdos; S(...) F(...).

[*RIB* 1389. ?Near Heddon-on-the-Wall, on the line of Hadrian's Wall]

A building-stone found in 1751. Now lost.

S F. are presumably the initials of the centurion in charge of the work. The consuls give the date. This attests repair or reconstruction to the curtain of Hadrian's Wall in AD 158, implying possibly an intention to return to it; cf. **G41** from the same area, which also refers to rebuilding.

(d) MARCUS AURELIUS (AD 161–180)

C38 Corbridge rebuilding *c.* AD 161–166

For the Emperors [Caesars] Marcus Aurelius A[ntoninus Augustus, in his seventeenth? year of] tribunician power, [three? times] consul, [and Lucius Aurelius Verus Augustus, Conqueror of] A[rmenia, in his third? year of tribunician pow]er, twice consul, [a detachment of the Twentieth Legion] Valeria Victrix built this under the charge of [Sextus Calpurnius] Agricola, governor.

[*RIB* 1149. Corbridge, Northumberland (Coria?)]

A dedication slab, part of which was found before 1702 and parts in 1912, 1937 and 1938 at Corbridge. Now in Corbridge Museum.

The inscription is restored as in *RIB* for AD 163, between autumn and 9 December, but is only certainly dated between Verus's second consulship in AD 161 and his third in AD 167. Calpurnius Agricola's governorship of Britain is attested by SHA *Marcus* 8.7–8 (LACTOR 11, L1.1), where he is said to have been sent specifically to deal with a threat of war in Britain. For the possibility that the Roman name of Corbridge was Coria see under **C23**. For other inscriptions of Calpurnius Agricola see **C39** (also Corbridge), **C40** (Carvoran), *RIB* 1703 (Vindolanda), *RIB* 589 (Ribchester) and note also *RIB* 793 (Hardknott) as a possible example.

C39 Invincible Sun-god (Legio VI Victrix) — *c.* AD 161–166

~~To the Invincible Sun-god~~, a detachment of the Sixth Legion Victrix Pia Fidelis set this up, under the charge of Sextus Calpurnius Agricola, governor.

[*RIB* 1137. Corbridge, Northumberland (Coria?)]

A dedication slab found in 1911 incorporated in the roadway south of Site XI. Now in Corbridge Museum.

Flanking panels which once carried the figures of Victory are now lost (drawing in *RIB* online). Line 1 was later erased, possibly after the death of Elagabalus in AD 222. Elagabalus identified himself with the Sun-god, and erasure of his name might extend to monuments to that god. Sun-worship came from the East, but is rare in Britain, except when later associated with the cult of Mithras.

C40 Carvoran Dea Syria altar — *c.* AD 161–166

To the Syrian Goddess, under Calpurnius Agricola, governor, Licinius Clemens, prefect of the First Cohort of Hamians, *(set this up).*

[*RIB* 1792 add. Carvoran, Northumberland (Magnis)]

Altar seen in 1599 at Melkridge, about 8 kilometres east of Carvoran. Now in Museum of Archaeology and Ethnography, Cambridge.

The altar has a decorated capital (drawings in *RIB* online). The Hamians were a unit of Eastern archers. They came from Syria, and brought with them the worship of their homeland goddess. This special type of unit appears to have continued to recruit from the original homeland *(contra* Haynes 1993, 145 but the evidence referred to is unpublished, so difficult to assess). Note that the same unit was at Carvoran in *c.* AD 136–137 (**C21**) and at Bar Hill on the Antonine Wall under Pius *(RIB* 2172).

C41 Ilkley Lucanus dedication — AD 161–169

[For the welfare of the Emper]ors Caesars, the Augusti, Antoninus and Verus, beloved by Jupiter, Caecilius Lucanus, prefect of the cohort, *(set this up).*

[*RIB* 636 add. Ilkley, Yorkshire]

A dedication found in, or before, 1603 built into the parish church. Later destroyed, perhaps during repair work.

Dedication perhaps to Iovi Dilect(ori), otherwise unknown (Birley 1978, 19). The common identification of Ilkley with Olicana is rejected by Rivet and Smith 1979, 430f. They suggest Verbeia (493) but there is no evidence that this river-name was also used for the fort. Further inscriptions recording activity under Marcus and Verus are known from Stanwix (AD 167, *RIB* 2026) and Great Chesters (AD 166–169, *RIB* 1737).

C42 Anociticus altar *c.* AD 177–180

To the god Anociticus. Tineius Longus *(set this up)* having, while prefect of cavalry, been adorned with the *(senatorial)* broad stripe and designated quaestor by the decrees of our best and greatest Emperors, under Ulpius Marcellus, consular governor.

[*RIB* 1329. Benwell (Condercum)]

An altar found in 1862 in a Roman temple outside the fort. Now in the Great North Museum, Hancock.

The fortunate discovery of a diploma (*RMD* III, 184), showing Ulpius Marcellus as governor in AD 178, has cleared up an old problem. Ulpius Marcellus was sent against the Britons by Commodus (Dio 72.8.2 = LACTOR 11, M1). This seemed to imply that Commodus as sole emperor had appointed him as governor. The inscription however refers to Marcellus as governor under the joint reign of Marcus and Commodus, AD 176–180. The designation as quaestor would have been on 23 January, so AD 177–180 are the possible years. Now that it is clear that Ulpius Marcellus was already governor under Marcus and Commodus, a fact obscured by Dio, there is no need to argue for a second governor called Ulpius Marcellus in order to explain the inscription. Jarrett 1978 discusses the problem as it existed before the discovery of the diploma. *RIB* 1327 and 1328 give the god's name as Antenociticus. His life-sized stone statue stood in the temple, and fragments including the notable head survive (*CSIR* I.1, no.231). The portrayal is Celtic rather than classical. He is an interesting example of a local god worshipped by a commanding officer, a legionary centurion (1327) and an auxiliary unit (1328).

(e) COMMODUS (AD 180–192)

C43 Chesters aqueduct *c.* AD 178–184

Water brought for the Second Cavalry Regiment of Asturians under Ulpius Marcellus, governor.

[*RIB* 1463. Chesters, Northumberland (Cilurnum)]

A dedication slab found in 1897 in the south-east part of the fort. Now in the Chesters Museum

The presence of the *ala II Asturum* (originally raised in north-west Spain) under Ulpius Marcellus is significant, as the regiment continues to be stationed at Chesters throughout the third century and is still there *c.* AD 400, if that date for the Wall section in the *Notitia Dignitatum* is accepted. At this Wall fort at least there appears to be continuity of unit from the 180s. At Old Carlisle the *ala Augusta ob virtutem appellata* is found in AD 188, AD 191, AD 197 and AD 242 *(RIB* 893–5, 897).

C44 Sestertii of Commodus AD 184

(i)

Obv: Head of Commodus wearing laurel-wreath. Around,
M(ARCVS) COMMODVS ANTON(INVS) AVG(VSTVS) PIVS BRIT(ANNICVS). (Marcus Commodus Antoninus Augustus Pius Britannicus)

Rev: Britannia standing, holding sword.
Around, P(ONTIFEX) M(AXIMVS) TR(IBVNICIA) P(OTESTATE) VIIII IMP(ERATOR) VII CO(N)S(VL) IIII P(ATER) P(ATRIAE). *(pontifex maximus,* in his ninth year of tribunician power, hailed *imperator* for the seventh time, consul for the fourth time, father of his country)
S(ENATVS) C(ONSVLTO) on either side of Britannia, BRITT(ANNIA) below.

[*RIC* Commodus 437]

These two coins commemorate Commodus's victory in Britain, won by Ulpius Marcellus (cf. comment under **C42**). Another sestertius of AD 184 (*RIC* Commodus 440) has the same obverse and a reverse showing Victory seated on a pile of weapons, holding a shield in left hand and a palm-branch in right hand, with the legend 'British Victory'. For a medallion of AD 185 still celebrating this victory see Frere 1987, Pl. 31, 5.

C45 Kirksteads altar — Later 2nd century AD

To ..., Lucius Junius Victorinus Flavins Caelianus, commander of the Sixth Legion Victrix Pia Fidelis, *(set this up)* because of successful achievements beyond the Wall.

[*RIB* 2034 add. Kirksteads, Cumbria]

An altar found in 1803 near Kirksteads Farm. Now in the British Museum, BM 1970,0102.6

The inscription clearly belongs to a period when Hadrian's Wall was the frontier, and is probably later than Hadrian. It names the Wall as the VALLVM, strictly "rampart" as does the Ilam pan **(C47)** and the *Notitia Dignitatum* (LACTOR 11, Z2.1, line 32). Junius Victorinus is probably to be identified with a man of that name who was governor of Upper Germany in 166/208, a post he will have held prior to coming to Britain. The suggestion of military activity north of Hadrian's Wall may be compared with *RIB* 946, from Carlisle, which has been restored to refer to "the slaughter of a band of barbarians". The findspot may have been a wayside shrine.

C46 Legio VI at Castlecary — *c.* AD 175–190?

To the god Mercury, soldiers of the Sixth Legion Victrix Pia Fidelis, being citizens of Italy and Noricum, set up this shrine and statuette, gladly, willingly and deservedly fulfilling their vow.

[*RIB* 2148. Castlecary]

Altar found in or before 1845 between the west rampart of Castelcary fort and the Red Burn. Now in the Museum of Scotland, Edinburgh.

The significance of this inscription depends upon its dating. The argument may be summarised thus: a mixture of Italians and Noricans would be only likely to occur in a legion newly-raised in Italy and stationed in Noricum. The only possibility is *legio II Italica,* and it must be assumed that a detachment of that legion has been transferred into *legio VI Victrix.* The dating given here is that in Mann 1969, 92, cf. Jarrett and Mann 1970, 194, being the period when *legio II Italica* would have contained such a mixture of original Italian recruits and local Norican recruits. The inscription would then show activity on the Antonine Wall at a time when it is generally thought to have been abandoned.

C47 The Ilam pan 2nd century AD

MAIS COGGABATA VXELODVNVM CAMMOGIANNARIGOREVALI AELIDRACONIS

Mais Co(n)gabata Uxelodunum Cam(b)og(l)anna rigore val(l)i Aeli Draconis

Bowness on Solway, Drumburgh, Stanwix, Castlesteads, on the line of the Wall [*or* the Aelian Wall] (the product *or* property) of Aelius Draco [*or* of Draco].

[*Britannia* 35 (2004), 344–45, no. 24. Ilam, Staffordshire]

Copper alloy vessel. Found in 2003 by a metal-detectorist. Acquired jointly by the British Museum, the Potteries Museum and Art Gallery (Stoke-on-Trent) and the Tullie House Museum and Art Gallery (Carlisle).

The vessel, a skillet missing its handle, is elaborately decorated with a 'Celtic' curvilinear design, richly inlaid with coloured enamels. The text is incised in a continuous band around its circumference, on a plain field just below the rim. The engraver miscalculated the spacing, crowding in part of the text with no gaps between words. This text indicates that Hadrian's Wall was referred to as a *vallum* (or rampart); cf. the Kirksteads altar (**C45**). This is the word also used in the late Roman *Notitia Dignitatum* (LACTOR 11, Z2.1, line 32), confirming that it is its common name. It is unclear whether *Aeli* attaches to the Wall, which precedes it, or to the personal name which follows. If the latter, it implies that Draco was awarded citizenship under Hadrian or Antoninus Pius. He was, perhaps, a retired auxiliary soldier who had the vessel 'personalised' for him as a souvenir of his military service. Alternatively, he may be the craftsman who made it. The four place names are those of forts at the west end of Hadrian's Wall, listing eastwards from the western terminus at Bowness on Solway, but omitting Burgh by Sands (Aballava). This vessel is one of three known which list forts at the western end of the Wall. The other two are the Rudge Cup (*RIB* 2.2415.53), found in Wiltshire, and the Amiens Patera (*JRS* 41 (1951) 22–24), from northern France. The table below compares the names given to the sites listed on each and in the equivalent section of the entry *'per lineam valli'* of the *Notitia Dignitatum*.

ILAM PAN	RUDGE CUP	AMIENS PATERA	*NOTITIA DIGNITATUM*	MODERN NAME
MAIS	MAIS	MAIS		Bowness on Solway
COGGABATA			CONGAVATA	Drumburgh
	ABALLAVA	ABALLAVA	ABALLABA	Burgh by Sands
VXELODVNVM	VXELODVM	VXELODVNVM	PETRIANIS	Stanwix
CAMMOGIANNA	CAMBOGLANS	CAMBOGLANS	AMBOGLANNA	Castlesteads
	BANNA	BANNA		Birdoswald
			MAGNIS	Carvoran
		ESICA	AESICA	Great Chesters

SECTION D

SEVERUS AND THE THIRD CENTURY (AD 193–284)

(a) SEVERUS (AD 193–211)

D1 Denarius of Clodius Albinus AD 196–7

Obv: IMP(ERATOR) CAE(SAR) D(IDIVS) CLO(DIVS) SEP(TIMIVS) ALB(INVS) AVG(VSTVS) (The Emperor Caesar Didius Clodius Septimius Albinus Augustus)

Rev: Legionary eagle between two standards.
Around FIDES LEGION(VM) CO(N)S(VL) II (The fidelity of the legions, twice consul)

[*RIC* Albinus 19 = BM R.15196 Mint of Lugdunum]

On Clodius Albinus, governor of Britain at the time of Commodus's assassination and self-proclaimed emperor, see Dio 73.14.3–15.2, 75.4.1 (= LACTOR 11, N1.1–3). Severus' activities in Britain are discussed in N. Hodgson, 'The British Expedition of Septimius Severus', *Britannia* 45 (2014), pp.31–51. On the circulation and hoarding of denarii during the Roman occupation of Britain, see J. Creighton, 'The Supply and Movement of Denarii in Roman Britain', *Britannia* 45 (2014), pp. 121 – 163.

D2 Brough-under-Stainmore rebuilding AD 197

For the Emperor Caesar Lucius Septimius Severus Pius Pertinax Augustus and for [Marcus Aurelius Anto]ninus Caesar ... in the consulship of [Later]a[nus] and Rufinus.

[*RIB* 757. Brough-under-Stainmore, Cumbria (Verterae)]

A dedication slab found in 1879 in restoring the church. Now built into the porch.

The consuls are for AD 197. Marcus Aurelius Antoninus Caesar was Septimius's son, the future emperor Caracalla. It has been suggested that there was a disaster in AD 197, when the governor Clodius Albinus was defeated at Lyons by Severus. The assumption was that when Albinus withdrew troops from Britain the northern barbarians broke into the province. Building activity under the early governors of Severus, (e.g. **D2–D8** and **D10–D13**, and even **D16–D17** (from Wales)), has then been explained as repairs to damage caused by this. There was trouble in the north at this time, cf. Dio 75.5.4 (= LACTOR 11, N3.1), but this is not necessarily the reason for all, or indeed any, of the rebuilding. Some at least may be simply part of a normal repair programme, which carries on at least into the 240s AD (**D25–D32 and D34–D35).** Repairs of ageing buildings are referred to specifically in **D10, D16, D17, D28, D32 and D39.**

D3 Ilkley rebuilding AD 197–198

[The Emperor Caesar Lucius Sept]im[ius] Severus [Pius Pertinax] Augustus and Antoninus Caesar destined (to be emperor) restored this under the charge of Virius Lupus, governor.

[*RIB* 637. Ilkley, Yorkshire]

A dedication slab found before 1600 near the church. Now lost.

See **C41** *note* for doubts on the Roman name of Ilkley. IMP after ANTONINVS CAESAR was apparently omitted by a mason's error. This is dated between the defeat of Clodius Albinus on 19 February AD 197, and Caracalla becoming Augustus on 28 January AD 198.

D4 Bowes bath-house AD 197–198

To the goddess Fortuna, Virius Lupus, governor, restored this bath-house, burnt by the violence of fire, for the First Cohort of Thracians; Valerius Fronto, prefect of the Vettonian Cavalry Regiment, had charge of the work.

[*RIB* 730. Bowes, Yorkshire/Durham (Lavatrae)]

An altar found before 1600 at Bowes. Now at the Museum of Archaeology and Ethnography, Cambridge.

The dating is based on the fact that Lupus refers to himself as legate for one emperor, Severus, cf. **D3** above. Dedications to Fortuna commonly appear in fort bath-houses (cf. **C21** and note). The *ala Vettonum*, originally recruited in west-central Spain, appears to be at Binchester during the third century. It is not clear why its commander is in charge here. For Virius Lupus see also **D3** and *RIB* 1163 (Corbridge).

D5 Bainbridge barracks AD 205

For the Emperor Caesar Lucius Septimius Severus Pius Pertinax Augustus and for the Emperor Caesar Marcus Aurelius Antoninus Pius Felix Augustus and for Publius Septimius Geta most noble ~~Caesar~~, in the consulship of ~~Our Lords~~ the Emperor Antoninus (for the second time) and Geta Caesar, the Sixth Cohort of Nervians built these barrack-blocks, under the charge of Gaius Valerius Pudens, most illustrious consular governor, overseen by Lucius Vinicius Pius, prefect of the said cohort.

[*JRS* 51 (1961), 192 = *RIB* 3.3215 = EDCS-13400111. Bainbridge, Yorkshire (Virosidum?)]

Dedication slab found in 1960 in the east gateway of the fort. Now at the School of Classics, University of Leeds.

The text is flanked by reliefs, reading downwards: on the left panel a Capricorn, Victory on a globe holding palm-branch in left, and wreath in right hand, an eagle on a thunderbolt with wreath in its beak; on the right panel a "lunula", a draped Genius holding over his left arm a cornucopia and in his right hand a wreath above a small altar, a bull facing left (CSIR I.3, no. 106). 'Caesar' and 'Our Lords' have been erased (indicated above by the double strikethrough: Geta's name and/or titles were erased after his murder by Caracalla in 212, though not consistently, see **D6–11, D12, D13, D16, D17**). CENTVRIAM (barrack-block) has been altered to CENTVRIAS (plural). The Nervii, from whom the cohort was originally raised, came from modern Belgium, around Bavay.

D6 Bainbridge defences *c.* AD 205–208 (206?)

For the Emperor Caesar Lucius Septimius Severus Pius Pertinax Augustus and for the Emperor Caesar Marcus Aurelius Antoninus Pius Felix Augustus and for Publius ~~Septimius Geta, most noble Caesar,~~ the Sixth Cohort of Nervians [built this rampart] with annexe-wall of uncoursed masonry under the charge of Lucius Alfenus Senecio, most illustrious [consular governor]; Lucius Vi[nici]us Pius, prefect [of the said cohort, had direction] of the work. [...]ecio [...]

[*RIB* 722 add. Bainbridge, Yorkshire (Virosidum?)]

A dedication slab found shortly before 1600 at the Roman fort. Now lost, though drawing was made (see RIB online)

The slab was flanked on both sides by a panel carrying a winged Victory. The name Geta and his title were erased. The name of the prefect is restored on the analogy of **D5**, as read by Alföldy in *JRS* 1969, 246. It may be possible to restore in the last line the consuls for AD 206, Senecio and Aemilianus cf. Birley 1988, 170 and 254 fn. 2. For the Nervii see under **D5.**

D7 Bowes rebuilding *c.* AD 205–208

For the Emperors Caesars Lucius Septimius Severus Pius Pertinax, Conqueror of Arabia, Conqueror of Adiabene, Most Great Conqueror of Parthia and Marcus Aurelius Antoninus Pius, both Augusti, and ~~for the most noble Caesar Publius Septimius Geta,~~ on the order of Lucius Alfenus Senecio, governor, the First Cohort Equitata of Thracians *(set this up).*

[*RIB* 740. Bowes, Yorkshire/Durham (Lavatrae)]

A dedication slab found in 1929 outside the vicarage. Now in north transept of Bowes church

Compare **D4** and **D8** note for erasure of Geta's name. The three new titles of Severus were gained from his victories in the East (AD 197–201). Adiabene was a small vassal-kingdom of Parthia, east of the Upper Tigris. For the origins of Thracian units see under **B2.**

D8 Greta Bridge building *c.* AD 205–208

For the Emperors Caesars Lucius Septimius Severus Pius Pertinax and Marcus Aurelius Antoninus Pius, both Augusti, and for ~~Publius Septimius Geta~~, most noble Caesar, under the charge of Lucius Alfenus Senecio, governor.

[*RIB* 746. Greta Bridge, Yorkshire]

A dedication slab found in 1793 near north gate of fort. Now in the Bowes Museum, Barnard Castle.

The sides of the slab are decorated. Geta's names have been erased, but his title remains.

D9 The Greetland Victoria Brigantia AD 208

To the goddess Victoria Brigantia and to the Divine Powers of the two Emperors, Titus Aurelius Aurelianus gave and dedicated *(this altar)* for himself and his family, while he himself was master of the sacred rites, in the third consulship of Antoninus and the second of Geta.

[*RIB* 627. From Greetland, 3 kilometres south of Halifax]

An altar found in 1597. Now at Museum of Archaeology and Ethnography, Cambridge.

(Drawing in *RIB* online) For Brigantia see also **G14**, **J15**, **J51** and notes. This victory, if it refers to Britain, may be one won by a Severan governor, cf. Dio 76.10.6 (= LACTOR 11, N3.2). For 'Divine Powers' (*Numina*) of the Emperors see the introduction to the section on Religion.

D10 Risingham rebuilding AD 205–8

[For the Emperors Caesars Lucius Septimius Severus Pius Pertinax, Conqueror of Arabia, Conqueror of Adi]abene, Most Great Conqueror of Parthia, three times consul, Augustus, and Marcus Aurelius Antoninus Pius, twice consul, Augustus, ~~and for Publius Septimius Geta, most noble Caesar~~, the First Cohort of Vangiones, *milliaria, equitata,* restored from ground-level this gate with its walls, which had fallen in through age, on the order of Alfenus Senecio, of senatorial rank and consular governor, under the charge of Oclatinius Adventus, procurator of our Emperors, together with its own tribune Aemilius Salvianus.

[*RIB* 1234 add. Risingham, Northumberland (Habitancum)]

Dedication slab found in 1844 at south gateway. Now in Museum of Antiquities, Newcastle upon Tyne.

The inscription is inside a circle with patterned rim; on left side Mars (?), on right Victory (?) with globe at feet. The top of the relief has been lost, including heads of both figures (drawing and photo in *RIB* online). Caracalla was consul for the second time in AD 205, and for the third time in AD 208. **D11** may be the same tribune. The unit of Vangiones was originally raised in Germania Superior, around Worms. The description "collapsed through old age" is not uncommon, and there is no reason not to take it literally, cf. above under **D2**.

D11 A *numerus* at Risingham *c.* AD 205–207??

To Jupiter Best and Greatest, the detachment of Raetian javein-men under the command of Aemilius Aemilianus, tribune of the First Cohort of Vangiones, *(set this up).*

[*RIB* 1216. Risingham, Northumberland (Habitancum]

Altar found about 1751. Now lost. Drawing of 1753, reproduced in RIB, shows several mistakes either down to the original inscription or the 18th-century drawing.

There was a knife and axe on the right-hand side of the altar (drawing in *RIB* online). AEMILIANVS could have been miscopied from an original SALVIANVS, and the inscription refer to the same officer as **D10**. The *gaesati Raeti* from Switzerland took their name from their homeland, Raetia and the particular sort of Celtic javelin their used, and were definitely at Risingham in AD 213: *RIB* 1235.

D12 Birdoswald granary *c.* AD 205–208

For the Emperors Caesars Lucius Septimius Severus Pius Pertinax and Marcus Aurelius Antoninus, both Augusti, ~~and for Publius Septimius Geta, most noble Caesar~~, the First Aelian Cohort of Dacians and the First Cohort of Thracians, Roman citizens, built this granary under Alfenus Senecio, consular governor, through the agency of Aurelius Julianus, the tribune.

[*RIB* 1909 add. Birdoswald, Cumbria (Banna)]

A dedication slab found in 1929 reused in the floor of a barrack-block in the fort. Now in Tullie House Museum, Carlisle.

There is a curved Dacian sword on the left, a palm-branch on the right (drawing in *RIB* online) cf. the stone of Modius Julius *RIB* 1914. The Roman name of Birdoswald is now thought to be Banna, not Camboglanna (Rivet and Smith 1979, 261f, and see **E5**). Geta's name is erased. The title "Roman citizens" marks an occasion on which the unit's men at the time were granted citizenship *en masse* for valour; it was retained as a battle-honour. There appears to have been more than one *cohors I Thracum,* and this unit is not necessarily the same as **D4** and **D7** both at Bowes.

D13 Corbridge granary *c.* AD 205–208

The Emperor Caesar Lucius Septimius Severus Pius Pertinax Augustus and the Emperor Caesar Marcus Aurelius Antoninus Pius Augustus and Publius Septimius Geta Caesar built this granary through the agency of a detachment [of the ... Legion under *(name lost)*, governor].

[*RIB* 1151 add. Corbridge, Northumberland (Coria)]

A dedication slab, part of which was found in 1725 reused as a roofing slab in the crypt of Hexham Abbey, where it still is, and part in 1907 among the foundations of the south-west tower, now built into north wall of the nave.

Geta's name is damaged in a fairly half-hearted attempt at erasure but still clearly readable. The governor whose name is lost may be L. Alfenus Senecio (as in **D6–D8, D10, D14**), C. Valerius Pudens (**D5**), or Virius Lupus (Birley, 2005, 211). For the Roman name of Corbridge see **C23**.

D14 Benwell dedication *c.* AD 205–208

To the Victory of the Emperors while Alfenus Senecio was consular governor, the Fortunate First Cavalry Regiment of Asturians *(set this up),* when ... M(...) was prefect.

[*RIB* 1337 add. Benwell, Northumberland (Condercum)]

A dedication slab found c. 1669 among ruined walls of the fort. Now lost.

Birley 2005, 189 suggests that the letters near the end may give a possible extra title of the unit, perhaps 'praetorian' rather than the name of a prefect. A winged Victory flanked both sides of the slab (drawing in *RIB* online). The emperors were Septimius Severus and his son Caracalla. The victory may be one of those won in Britain before the arrival of Severus, referred to by Dio 76.10.6 (= LACTOR 11, N3.2), but it need not be one in Britain. Alfenus Senecio also appears on **D6–D8, D10,** *RIB* 723 (Bainbridge), *RIB* 1462 (Chesters) and *Britannia* 8 (1977), 432 (Vindolanda). *RIB* 1277 (High Rochester) and *RIB* 1612 (Housesteads), both of AD 198–209, may also belong to this governor. The *ala I Asturum* was originally raised in north-west Spain.

D15 Quarrying inscriptions AD 207

(i) A detachment of the Second Legion Augusta; the working-face of Apr(...), under Agricola, the optio.

[*RIB* 1008. Cumbria quarries]

An inscription seen c. 1604 cut on the rock-face about 9 metres above the river on the north side of the river Gelt, 1 kilometre south-east of Low Gelt Bridge.

Above the inscription is a naively drawn face ☺ (see drawing in *RIB* online)! Roman quarries were usually state-owned; this one was under military control. An *optio* was the second-in-command of a century.

(ii) In the consulship of Aper and Maximus, the working-face of Mercatius.

[*RIB* 1009. Cumbria quarries]

An inscription seen before 1607 c.30 cm beyond the end of RIB 1008.

The consuls are those of AD 207.

D16 Caerleon rebuilding AD 198–209

[The Emperors] Caesars Lucius Septimius [Severus Pius Pertinax Augustus and Marcus Aurelius Antoninus A]ugustus ~~and Publius~~ Septimius [Geta, most noble Caesar, restored the building] ruined [by age].

[*RIB* 333. Caerleon, Gwent (Isca)]

Fragments of a block forming a medial part of a frieze found between 1845 and 1850 in the churchyard, perhaps from the head quarters building of the fortress. Now in Caerleon Museum.

It has been suggested in the past that, 'ruined by age', masked destruction by the enemy, but this view is no longer given credence. There was much rebuilding, beginning under Severus and continuing into the third century, cf. **D17**, **D28**, **D32**, **D39**. The fact that legion II Augusta spent much of its time in the north in the second century (cf. **C12 C23, C24, C27, C28, C30)** may account for some dilapidation at Caerleon, cf. **D38**. Geta's *praenomen* was erased, his *nomen* left intact. The rest of his name and title is lost.

D17 Caernarfon aqueduct AD 198–209

[The Emperors Caesars Lucius] Septimius Severus Pius Per[tinax Augustus and Marcus A]urelius Antoninus [Pius Augustus] ~~and Publius Septimius Geta most noble Caesar~~, [restored] the channels of the aqueducts fallen in through age for the First Cohort of Sunicians ...

[*RIB* 430 add. Caernarfon (Segontium)]

Fragments of a commemorative slab, reused in the Roman fort as cover-slabs in a hypocaust, found partly in 1845, partly in 1852, in Llanbeblig Vicarage garden. Now in National Museum of Wales, Cardiff.

The Sunici, better Sunuci, originated in Lower Germany. Casey, Davies and Evans 1993, 72f., discuss a large drain near the find-spot of the inscription, which they think might be overflow from the *castellum aquae*, the collecting-point from which the water of an aqueduct is distributed.

D18 An unknown soldier AD 208–209

To the departed: […]ius Se[…], soldier of [the *(perhaps Twenty-Second Primigenia)* Legion]... Pia Fidelis, soldiers of the detachment of the same legion going on the British campaign had this memorial erected out of their own funds.

[*ILS* 9123 = EDCS-10600264*. Amiens, northern France (Samarobriva)]

Limestone slab found in 1848 reused on the road to Nazon. Now in the Mowat Museum.

The style of the lettering of this inscription makes it probable that the *expeditio Britannica* referred to is that begun in AD 208 by Severus and his sons Caracalla and Geta. The soldier commemorated was a member of a legionary detachment, perhaps from Legion XXII Primigenia, based at Mainz, western Germany. Herodian 3.14.3 (= LACTOR 11, N3.4) says that troops came from everywhere for the campaign; cf. **D21**. It has been suggested that the centurion of *legio I Italica,* who set up an altar at Old Kilpatrick on the Antonine Wall while temporarily in command of an auxiliary cohort (*Britannia* 1 (1970), 310f. n.20), had come to Britain on the Severan *expeditio.* (The legion was stationed in Lower Moesia, modern Bulgaria) (Birley 1983, 73–77). An earlier date was suggested in Breeze and Dobson 1969–70, 120 fn. 48.

D19 A Corbridge granary officer AD 209–211

[...]norus [...] officer in charge of the granaries at the time of the most successful expedition to Britain, gladly and deservedly fulfilled his vow.

[*RIB* 1143. Corbridge, Northumberland (Coria?)]

An altar, found in 1908, in the west granary. Now in the Corbridge Museum.

"Granaries" seems more likely than "granary" (the Latin word is abbreviated) This is most probably the campaign under Severus. For the Roman name of Corbridge see **C23**.

D20 Caracalla's "Setting-out"

(i) *Denarius* AD 208

Obv: Head of Caracalla wearing laurel-wreath.
ANTONINVS PIVS AVG(VSTVS) (Antoninus Pius Augustus)

Rev: Caracalla on horseback. Captive on the ground in front of the horse.
PONTIF(EX) TR(IBVNICIA) P(OTESTATE) XI CO(N)S(VL) III (*pontifex,* in the eleventh year of his possession of tribunician power, consul for the third time). PROF(ECTIO) (setting-out).

[*RIC* Caracalla 108 = BM R.15399. *Denarius*]

(ii) *As* or medallion AD 209

Obv: Bust of Caracalla wearing laurel-wreath.
ANTONINVS PIVS AVG(VSTVS) (Antoninus Pius Augustus)

Rev: Bridge of boats, with soldiers crossing.
PONTIF(EX) TR(IBVNICIA) P(OTESTATE) XI (or XII) CO(N)S(VL) III (*pontifex,* in the eleventh (or twelfth) year of tribunician power, consul for the third time)
TRAIECTVS (Crossing)

[*RIC* Caracalla 441 = BM R.16588]

This coin is sometimes interpreted as a literal reference to bridge building during the campaigns in Scotland (e.g. Robertson 1980; Hanson and Maxwell 1983, 206); a more elaborate structure, with triumphal arches at each end, is depicted on an *as* of Severus (*RIC* 786; Frere 1987, pl. 31.8). Elsewhere TRAIECTVS is used on the coinage as an alternative form of PROFECTIO, the setting forth from Rome of an imperial expedition. In the present case the bridge is an alternative symbol for a journey in place of the more usual ship. (PJC)

D21 Tombstone of Cesennius Senecio — *c.* AD 209–211

To the departed: Gaius Cesennius Senecio, centurion of the Second Praetorian Cohort Pia Vindex, trainer of the praetorian cavalry: erected by Gaius Cesernius Zonysius his freedman and heir: Zoticus brought his body from Brittania.

[*ILS* 2089 = EDCS-18800400. Rome (Roma)]

A marble urn, found near St. Peter in Vincola. Now at Palermo.

Cesennius could have come to Britain with Severus in AD 208. The date is suggested by the fact that a Caes. Senecio was a centurion of the *vigiles* in AD 205 *(CIL* 6.1057). Promotion of centurions of the *vigiles* to centurions of the urban cohorts and then to centurions of the praetorian cohorts is well attested. The titles *pia vindex* were given to the praetorian cohorts by Severus. The inscription is inconsistent in spelling (e.g. the freedman should be Cesennius not Cesernius, Britain is 'Brittania'), and reflects the spoken language.

(b) SEVERUS'S SUCCESSORS (AD 211–284)

D22 Building at Carpow — AD 212–?

The Emperor and Our Lord Marcus Aurelius Antoninus Pius Felix ...

[*JRS* 55 (1965), 223f., no.10 = *RIB* 3.3512; *cf. Wright 1974.* Carpow]

Two portions of a monumental dedication found in 1964 on the south roadway of the east gate of the base. Now in Dundee Museum.

The left-hand sculptured panel, which includes the I of IMP (Emperor), carries the emblems of the Legion II Augusta, a Capricorn and two Pegasi (*CSIR* I.4, no.171). The restoration is controversial, cf. Wright 1974. If correct it would indicate work still in progress at Carpow after the death of Severus and before the presumed withdrawal from the lands which Severus had conquered (Dio 77.1.1 = LACTOR 11, O1.2; Herodian 3.15.6 = LACTOR 11, N4.6). Over 200 tiles from Carpow of the Legion VI Victrix give it the title *B(ritannica),* only otherwise attested at York by a single example (*RIB* 2.4.2460.71–74, Carpow; *RIB* 2.4.2460, 75, York). The title was presumably taken in AD 210 when the three emperors took the title BRITANNICVS, and dropped not long afterwards.

D23 High Rochester declaration of loyalty — AD 213

[For the Emperor Caesar, son of Lucius Septimius Severus Pius Pertinax Augustus, Conqueror of Arabia, Conqueror of Adiabene, Most Great Conqueror of Parthia, grandson of the deified Antoninus, Conqueror of Sarmatia, great-grandson of the deified Antoninus Pius, great-great-grand son of the] dei[fied Hadrian, great-great-great-grandson of the deified] Tr[ajan, Conqueror of Parthia, and of the dei]fied N[erva, Marcus] Aure[lius Antoninus Pi]us Felix [Augustus, M]ost Great [Conqueror of Parthia, Most Great Conqueror of Britain], *pontifex* [*maximus,* in his] sixteenth [year of tribunician power, twice] acclaimed *imperator,* [father of his country, proconsul, out of their joint] dut[y and devotion ...]

[*RIB* 1278. High Rochester (Bremenium)]

Fragment, found in 1852, at the fort. Now in the Great North Museum, Hancock.

It would appear that the loyalty of the army in Britain was suspect after the murder of Geta by Caracalla at the end of AD 211. Geta had acted as civil governor in Britain during the campaigns of Severus and Caracalla in AD 208- AD 211. Protestations of loyalty to Caracalla and his mother Julia Domna are found at Risingham *(RIB* 1235), Vindolanda *(RIB* 1705), Old Penrith *(RIB* 928), Whitley Castle *(RIB* 1202), Newcastle *(Britannia* 11 (1980), 405 no. 6) and South Shields *(Britannia* 16 (1985) 325f. no. 11), hence the restorations above of the very meagre fragment. The *damnatio memoriae* of C. Julius Marcus, governor in AD 213, see under **D24** may be linked to unrest in the army of Britain.

D24 Netherby declaration of loyalty AD 213

For [our?] Julia Augusta, mother of our em[peror Marcus Aur]elius Antoninus and of the army and senate and country, our of their [common duty] and devotion to his Divine Power, [under the charge of Gaius Julius] Marcus, gov[ernor], the First Aelian Cohort of Spaniards, *milliaria, equitata,* set this up.

[*RIB* 976 add. Netherby (Castra Exploratorum)]

The jamb of a doorway, of perhaps the shrine of the headquarters building, found in 1609 in building Arthuret Church. Since lost.

Daniels (in Daniels and Habottle 1980, 71) suggests n(ostrae), 'our', for the *n* in line 1 of text. The first half of the text, recording Caracalla and his full style, may have been on the corresponding jamb. The name of C. Julius Marcus seems to have been erased on a number of these inscriptions, cf. *RIB* 1202, 1235, *Britannia* 11 (1980), 405 no. 6; 16 (1985), 325f., no. 11. *RIB* 2298 (Welton milestone) gives his name as governor in AD 213. It is not clear how much of Britain he was governing. Herodian asserts that Severus divided Britain into two provinces in or shortly after AD 197 (3.8.2 = LACTOR 11, N1.5). The governors mentioned under Severus operating in the north are still consular (**D3–D8**, **D10**, and **D11–D14**), so if the province is divided the senior governor is in the northern province. Shortly after the situation was reversed, with the senior governor in the southern province. For full discussion see Birley 2005, 333–6.

D25 High Rochester rebuilding AD 216

For the Emperor Caesar Marcus Aurelius Severus Antoninus Pius Felix Augustus, Most Great Conqueror of Parthia, Most Great Conqueror of Britain, Most Great Conqueror of Germany, *pontifex maximus,* in his nineteenth year of tribunician power, twice acclaimed *imperator,* four times consul, proconsul, father of his country, the First Loyal Cohort of Vardulli, Roman Citizens, *equitata, milliaria, Antoniniana,* built this under the charge of ..., governor.

[*RIB* 1279. High Rochester (Bremenium)]

Dedication slab, found in 1744, at High Rochester. Now in the Great North Museum, Hancock.

The governor's name has been erased. This is probably Gordianus, later the emperor Gordian I; see *RIB* 1049 (Chester-le-Street), AD 216: (line 6). Note the difference between honorary titles given to units (e.g. AELIA), formed usually from the emperor's *nomen,* and given when the unit was raised or decorated, and the third-century and later practice of adding to the unit's name a title derived from the emperor's *cognomen* (e.g. ANTONINIANA) which was replaced at the end of that emperor's reign by one derived from the new emperor's *cognomen.* The Vardulli originated in northern Spain.

D26 Troops from the two Germanies *c.* AD 217

To Jupiter Dolichenus Best and Greatest, for the welfare of the detachments of the Sixth Legion Victrix and the armies of both the Germanies, under the charge of Marcus Lollius Venator, centurion of the Second Legion Augusta, the members of the detachments willingly and deservedly fulfilled their vow.

[*JRS* 57 (1967), 205 no. 16 = *RIB* 3.3253 = EDCS-09800199*. Piercebridge]

Statue base, found in 1966 in the field east of Piercebridge fort. Now in Bowes Museum, Barnard Castle.

A centurion from Germania Superior dedicated to Dolichenus at Piercebridge in AD 217 *(RIB* 1022). *RIB* 1026 is the undated tombstone of a further centurion from Germania Superior, and *Britannia* 17 (1986), 438 no. 20 seems to refer to a soldier from the same province.

D27 High Rochester artillery AD 220

For the Emperor Caesar Marcus Aurelius ~~Antoninus~~ Pius Felix Augustus, in his ~~third~~ year of tribunician power, in his ~~third~~ consulship, proconsul, father of his country, the First Loyal Cohort of Vardulli, ~~*Antoniniana*~~, built this *ballistarium* from ground-level under the charge of Tiberius Claudius Paulinus, governor, under the direction of Publius Aelius Erasinus, tribune.

[*RIB* 1280 add. High Rochester (Bremenium)]

Two parts of a dedication slab found by 1810 and in 1855 respectively, outside the fort. Now at Museum of Antiquities, Newcastle upon Tyne.

The conjunction of TRIB POT III and COS III (just visible despite the erasure) fits Elagabalus giving the date AD 220. Part of his names and the honorific ANTONIANA have also been erased. The traditional interpretation of *ballistarium* as artillery-platform has been challenged, and artillery-shed suggested (Donaldson 1990, 210–213).

D28 Chesters rebuilding October AD 221

The Emperor Caesar Marcus Aurelius ~~Antoninus Pius Felix~~ A~~ugustus~~, ~~most honourable priest of the Invincible Sun-God Elagabalus~~, *pontifex* [*maximus*], in his fourth year of tribunician power, three times consul, father of his country, son of the deified [Antoninus], grandson of the deified Severus, and Marcus [Aur]elius ~~Alexander, most noble~~ Caesar, ~~partner of empire~~, ~~...~~ for the Second Cavalry Regiment of Asturians, ~~*Antoniniana*~~, rest[ored (this building), fallen in] through age, through the agency of Marius Valerianus, [governor], under the direction of Septimius Nilus, prefect [of cavalry]: dedicated on 30 October in the consulship of Gratus and Sele[ucus].

[*RIB* 1465 add. Chesters (Cilurnum)]

A dedication slab, found in 1798 in Chesters fort, in four pieces, with small parts lost. Now in Chesters Museum.

Parts of the names and titles of Elagabalus and Severus Alexander and the honorific ANTONINIANA have been erased. The gap of about 11 letters, erased and illegible, after 'partner of empire' may have indicated the building which was restored, through Mann (cited in *RIB* add.) suggests *imper*[*i et sacerdoti(i) consors*], "partner of empire and priesthood".

D29 Netherby drill-hall AD 222

For the Emperor Caesar Marcus Aurelius Severus Alexander Pius Felix Augustus, *pontifex maximus,* with tribunician power, consul, father of his country, the First Aelian Cohort of Spaniards, *milliaria, equitata,* devoted to his Divine Power and majesty, built a cavalry drill-hall, whose foundations were already laid, and completed it, under the charge of Marius Valerianus, governor, under the direction of Marcus Aurelius Salvius, tribune of this cohort, in the consulship of our Lord the Emperor Severus Alexander Pius Felix Augustus.

[*RIB* 978. Netherby (Castra Exploratorum)]

A dedication slab, found in 1762 in use as a drain-cover at Netherby. Now in Carlisle Museum.

For AELIA see **D25**.

D30 South Shields aqueduct AD 222–223

The Emperor Caesar Marcus Aurelius Severus ~~Alexander~~ Pius Felix Augustus, grandson of the deified Severus, son of the deified Antoninus the Great, *pontifex maximus,* with tribunician power, father of his country, consul, brought in this supply of water for the use of the soldiers of the Fifth Cohort of Gauls, under the charge of Marius Valerianus, governor.

[*RIB* 1060 add. South Shields (Arbeia)]

A dedication slab, found in 1893, in South Shields fort. Now in Arbeia Fort Museum, South Shields

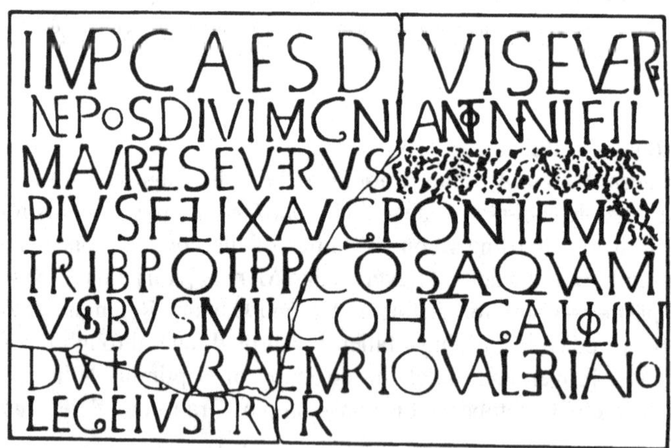

Fig. 8

ALEXANDER was erased when the emperor's memory was damned. Cf. *RIB* 1049 (Chester-le-Street) for an aqueduct built in AD 216, and **C43** and **D17**. See *RIB* add. for further references to the cohort at South Shields.

D31 Chesterholm gate with towers AD 223–225

[... the Fourth Cohort] of Gauls, ~~*Severiana Alexandriana*~~, devoted to his Deity, restored from the foundations this ga[te with its to]wers under Claudius Xenephon, [governor of Lower Britain], under the charge of [...]

[*RIB* 1706. Chesterholm (Vindolanda)]

A dedication slab, found before 1702, at Vindolanda fort. Since lost.

The titles SEVERIANAE ALEXANDRIANAE have been erased, cf. **D25** and **D30**. The first part of the text, recording the names and titles of Severus Alexander, must have been on a corresponding stone (*CSIR* I.6, no. 248).

D32 Great Chesters granary AD 225

The Emperor Caesar Marcus Aurelius Severus Alexander Pius Felix Augustus; the soldiers of the Second Cohort of Asturians, *Severiana Alexandriana,* restored from ground level this granary fallen in through age, while the province was governed by [...] Maximus, governor, [under the charge of] Valerius Martialis, centurion of the ... Legion, in the consulship of Fuscus for the second time and Dexter.

[*RIB* 1738. Great Chesters (Aesica)]

A dedication slab, found in 1767 in Great Chesters fort. Now in the Great North Museum, Hancock.

This translation differs slightly from the translation offered in previous editions of LACTOR 4 and *RIB*. The difficulty, noted in *RIB* is that the inscription carefully gives the name *Severus Alexander* in full as the nominative subject, but ends with a plural verb *RESITVERVNT*, which therefore ought to make the abbreviated *MIL COH II ASTVRVM*, 'soldiers of the Second Cohort of the Asturians,' the subject. As can be seen from the inscriptions above at **D29** and **D30** both forms of expression – work done *for* the emperor by others (**D29**) or written as though the emperor did work in person (**D30**) can be adduced in support of one interpretation over another; it may be that a change in policy, changing the amount of involvement or responsibility attributed to the emperor in such work, caused confusion in the composition of the inscription. See further nos. **D35, D37,** and **D38.**

D33 The Reculver inscription 3rd century AD

[...For]tunatus [dedicate]d the shrine of the headquarters building, together with the basilica, under the consular governor, ...r...ius Rufinus.

[*RIB* 3.3027 = EDCS-13400109. Reculver (Regulbium)]

A dedicatory tablet, found in 1960 in a cellared room below the shrine of the headquarters building of the fort.

A. Triarius Rufinus was restored in the original publication, but he was *consul ordinarius* in AD 210, a socially elevated person not likely to have governed one of the emperor's provinces; Q. Aradius Rufinus, consul a little later, has also been suggested. The date could in fact be considerably later in the third century, as few consuls are known in this period, and Rufinus is not an uncommon name: see further Mann 1977 and Birley 2005, 353–4. The first part of the text, on a separate slab, never recovered, must have indicated the emperor for whom the building was set up. The inscription nevertheless may confirm archaeological indications of an earlier date for Reculver (and Brancaster) than the other Saxon Shore forts (Maxfield 1989, 136–139). This is the first inscription ever to mention the term AEDES PRINCIPIORVM, 'headquarters building', where it can be identified with the official shrine of the headquarters building. For literary references to such shrines, see Herodian, *Histories* 4.4.5 (in Greek) and Statius *Thebaid* 10.176–7. This inscription is also the first certain application of the term BASILICA to a military cross-hall, though in form it resembles a civil basilica.

D34 Lanchester baths and basilica AD 238–244

The Emperor Caesar Marcus Antonius Gordianus Pius Felix Augustus erected from ground level this bath-building with basilica through the agency of Egnatius Lucilianus, governor, under the charge of Marcus Aurelius Quirinus, prefect of the First Cohort of Lingones, *Gordiana.*

[*RIB* 1091. Lanchester (Longovicium)]

A dedication slab, found before 1700 just outside Lanchester fort. Now in the Old Fulling Mill Museum, Durham.

The name of the unit is expanded from *RIB* 1075, LING(ONVM). The unit was originally raised from the *Lingones* of the Langres area of eastern France.

D35 Lanchester headquarters and armouries AD 238–244

The Emperor Caesar Marcus Antonius Gordianus Pius Felix Augustus restored the headquarters building and armouries, which had fallen in, through the agency of Maecilius Fuscus, governor, under the charge of Marcus Aurelius Quirinus, prefect of the First Cohort of Lingones, *Gordiana.*

[*RIB* 1092 add. Lanchester (Longovicium)]

A dedication slab, found in 1715 inside Lanchester fort. Now in the Old Fulling Mill Museum, Durham.

See Bishop and Coulston 1993, 199–201, on the meaning of *armamentaria* (armouries).

D36 Egnatius Lucilianus altar AD 238–244

To the *Genius* of our Lord and of the Standards of the First Cohort of Vardulli and of the Unit of Scouts of Bremenium (High Rochester), *Gordianus,* Egnatius Lucilianus, governor, *(set this up)* under the charge of Cassius Sabinianus, tribune.

[*RIB* 1262. High Rochester (Bremenium)]

An altar, found in 1852, in the strong room of the headquarters building of the fort. Now in Museum of Antiquities, Newcastle upon Tyne.

Place-names are not infrequently found as part of the title of irregular units, cf. **F36, J21, J28 (ii)** and *venatores Bannienses, RIB* 1905, from Birdoswald (Banna).

D37 Nonius Philippus altar AD 242

To Jupiter Best and Greatest, for the welfare of the Emperor Marcus Antonius Gordianus Pius Felix Invictus Augustus and for his wife Sabinia Furia Tranquillina and for their whole Divine House, the Cavalry Regiment styled *Augusta* for valour, *Gordiana,* set this up, when commanded by Aemilius Crispinus, prefect of cavalry, born in the province of Africa, at Thysdrus, under the charge of Nonius Philippus, governor, in the consulship of Atticus and Praetextatus.

[*RIB* 897. Old Carlisle (Maglona?)]

An altar, found about 1550. Now at the Museum of Archaeology and Ethnography Cambridge.

Thysdrus (now El Djem in Tunisia), spelt TVSDRVS in the inscription, was where Gordian III was proclaimed emperor. Maglona is suggested as the Roman name for Old Carlisle by Rivet and Smith 1979, 407; cf. **F40** In the *Notitia Dignitatum* (LACTOR 11, Z2.1, line 28) it is written as *Maglo.*

D38 Caerleon barracks AD 253–257

The Emperors Valerian and Gallienus, Augusti, and Valerian, most noble Caesar, restored from ground-level barrack-blocks for the Seventh Cohort through the agency of Desticius Juba, of senatorial rank, governor, and of Vitulasius Laetinianus, legate of the Second Legion Augusta, under the charge of Domitius Potentinus, prefect of the said legion.

[*RIB* 334. Caerleon (Isca)]

A commemorative tablet, found in or before 1845, outside the east angle of the fortress. Now in Caerleon Museum.

This is the last example anywhere in the empire of a legionary legate. Henceforth all legions were commanded by prefects.

D39 Lancaster baths and basilica Between AD 263 and 268

[For the Emperor ... Postumus ...] on account of the bath-house rebuilt and the basilica restored from ground-level, when fallen in through age, for the troopers of the Sebosian Cavalry Regiment, ~~*Postumiana*~~, under Octavius Sabinus, of senatorial rank, our governor, and under the charge of Flavins Ammausius, prefect of cavalry; dedicated on 22 August, in the consulship of Censor and Lepidus, both for the second time.

[*RIB* 605 add. Lancaster]

A dedication slab, found in 1812 reused in a Roman bath-building inside the late fort. Now in Lancaster City Museum.

POSTVMIANAE is erased but some letters are legible. The consuls were of Postumus' Gallic Empire; the year in which they held office cannot be more closely dated. See *RIB* 2411.88 and 2466.1–2 for a lead sealing and stamped tiles of the *ala Sebosiana* at Lancaster.

SECTION E

CARAUSIUS AND THE FOURTH CENTURY

(a) CARAUSIUS TO CONSTANTIUS (AD 284–306)

E1 ***Antoninianus* of Carausius** AD 290–292

Obv: Busts side by side of Maximian, Diocletian and Carausius, each wearing radiate crown and cuirass.

Around, CARAVSIVS ET FRATRES SVI (Carausius and his brothers)

Rev: Moneta standing with scales and cornucopiae.

Around, MONETA AVGGG = MONETA (TRIVM) AVGVSTORVM (Moneta, the patron goddess of the coinage of the Augusti)

[*Numismatic Chronicle* 1959, 10 = *BM* 1959,0603.1]

The radiate crown is a symbol of autocracy and divinity: it does not occur on the head of a living Emperor before Nero; it comes to indicate a double-unit, and identifies the *antoninianus* as worth two *denarii*.

For ancient historical accounts of the 'usurpation' of Britain by Carausius (AD 287–293) and Allectus (AD 293 – 296), see Eutropius, *Brief History* 9.21–22, and Aurelius Victor, *Caesars* 39. 40–41) (LACTOR 11, R1.1, R1.2.) See also the milestone of Maximian, **E3**. Maximian was the western *Augustus* from AD 286 – 305 as Diocletian's colleague (though Britain was under the control of Allectus until AD 293) and again in AD 307–8. *RIB* 2256 honours him with Diocletian as his colleague, and *RIB* 2301 honours him alone. It is possible, though unlikely, that it was dedicated to Diocletian's successor as *Augustus* in the eastern empire, Gelerius Maximianus but see *RIB* 2293).

E2 Carausius' coins quote Virgil AD 290–292

i) Denarius

Obv: Bust of Carausius wearing laurel-wreath and cuirass.
IMP(ERATOR) CARAVSIVS P(IVS) F(ELIX) AV(GVSTVS)

Rev: Britannia shaking hands with Emperor.
Around, EXPECTATE VENI (come, awaited one)
Below, RSR. (*redeunt Saturnia regna* – the Golden Age returns)

[*RIC* Carausius 555 = BM 1935, 1117.832]

ii) Alloy medallion

Obv: Laureate bust of Carausius, left, wearing consular mantle and holding eagle-tipped sceptre.
VICTORIA CARAVSI AVG (Victory of Carausius Augustus)

Rev: Victory in two-horse chariot or *biga*, right.
Around, IMP C M AV CARAVSIVS P F AVG (Imperator Caesar Marcus Aurelius Carausius Pius Felix Augustus)
Below, I.N.P.C.D.A (*iam nova progenies caelo demittitur alto* – Now a new generation is sent down from high heaven)

[BM 1967,0901.1 = Carson, R.A.G., *Principal coins of the Romans*, Vol. III, 1129. London 1978]

In 1998, Guy de la Bédoyère, *Carausius and the marks RSR and I.N.P.C.D.A.*,The Numismatic Chronicle 158 (1998), pp.79–88, solved 'without a shadow of doubt' (Birley, *RGB* page 376) the puzzle of two abbreviations on Carausius coins – the frequent 'RSR' previously assumed to be a mint mark for Britain, and the unique and unexplained 'INPCDA' – by showing that they form a quotation from Virgil, *Eclogues* 4.6–7, '*redeunt Saturnia regna / iam nova progenies caelo dimittitur alto*' 'the Golden Age returns; now a new generation is sent down from high heaven.' That Carausius should quote Virgil on his coins – the only such example from Roman numismatics – has fascinating implications for our view of literacy and culture in Roman Britain. We might note that rote learning of Virgil was an absolute staple of Latin schooling and that, after the *Aeneid,* the *Eclogues* was the second most frequently quoted work of literature in terms of writing found on the walls of Pompeii (Cooley 2014, appendix 2). *Expectate, veni* itself alludes to Virgil *Aeneid* 2.283 in which Aeneas hails a vision of Hector with the words '*exspectate venis'.*

E3 Milestone of Carausius and two other emperors AD 287–293 and AD 306–307

(i) [~~E~~]m[~~peror~~ …] *RIB* 2290

(ii) To the unconquered Augustus, Emperor and Caesar, Marcus Aurelius Maesaeus Carausius Pius Felix *RIB* 2291

(iii) To the most noble Caesar, Flavius Valerius Constantinus *RIB* 2292

[*RIB* 2290–2 Carlisle (Luguvalium)]

Milestone found in 1894 in the bed of the River Petterill, Gallows Hill, about 11/2 kilometres south of Carlisle. Inscribed three times. Now in Carlisle Museum.

This irregularly shaped stone pillar was carved first with an inscription (*RIB* 2290) just above its centre. This inscription was then erased, leaving only a trace of the title 'IMP'. The stone was turned upside down and *RIB* 2291 carved at the new top (broader) end of the milestone with the inscription to Carausius (AD 287–293). Finally in AD 306–307, the stone was again turned upside down and *RIB* 2292 carved at the narrower end, above where *RIB* 2290 had been. For milestones only bearing the emperor's name and title in the third and fourth centuries see above, *Notes on Roman Epigraphy.*

E4 Five-aureus medallion of Constantius AD 297

Obv Bust of Constantius I facing right, wearing lion-skin headdress.
FL(AVIVS) VAL(ERIVS) CONSTANTIVS NOBILISSIMVS C(AESAR) (Flavius Valerius Constantius, most noble Caesar)

Rev: Constantius standing right, with spear. Victory standing right, behind him, crowns him with a wreath, while he raises Britannia, facing left, from her knees.
PIETAS AVGG (the piety of the Augusti)

[*RIC* 6, *Trier* 32 (Constantius Chlorus). Gold medallion of five *aurei* = *BM* 1928,0208.2]

This commemorates Constantius Chlorus saving Britian from Allectus, in 296, see LACTOR 11, S1–S2. Under the tetrarchy, Constantius was the junior emperor in the West, so credit goes also to the senior emperors, the Augusti. The lion-skin headdress symbolises Hercules.

E5 Birdoswald restorations *c.* AD 296–305

For our [Lords] Dioc[letian] and M[axim]ian, Invincible Augusti, and for Constantius and Maximianus, most noble Caesars, under His Perfection Aurelius Arpagius, the governor, the [...] Cohort restored the commanding officer's house (*praetorium*), which had been covered with earth and had fallen into ruin, and the headquarters building (*principia*) and the bath-house, under the charge of Flavius Martinus, centurion in command.

[*RIB* 1912 add. Birdoswald (Banna)]

Dedication slab, found 1929, reused face downwards as a paving-stone in the floor of a barrack-block in the fort. Now in Carlisle Museum.

Excavations at Haltonchesters and Rudchester, also forts on Hadrian's Wall, have produced just such a picture of decay as is described here. There is therefore no need to explain it as a covert reference to destruction caused by a barbarian invasion in AD 296. This inscription was the first discovered to draw a clear distinction between PRINCIPIA and PRAETORIVM here mentioned as separate buildings. The final building restored appears in Latin abbreviated to BAL. See *RIB* online for reasons for thinking this was a *balneum* (bath house) rather than a *balistarium* (*ballista* platform).

E6 Ribchester (*Bremetennacum*), milestone of Maximian. AD 286–308

To Maximian Augustus

[*Britannia* 45 (2014) 437.7. Ribchester (Bremetennacum)]

A milestone on which only the bottom of the inscribed panel survives, inscribed in poor capitals now badly weathered and used as a gatepost at Stonelands Farm until identified in 2005. It remains in the landowner's possession. The remaining lettering can however easily be read as above.

(b) THE FOURTH CENTURY (AD 306–410)

E7 Visit of Constantine the Great to Britain AD 311–312

Obv: Bust of Constantine facing left, wearing helmet and armour, holding shield and spear.
CONSTANTINVS P(IVS) F(ELIX) AVG(VSTVS)

Rev: Emperor, riding down captive, hand raised in greeting.
Around, ADVENTVS AVG(VSTI) N(OSTRI) (The coming of our emperor)
Below, PLN (Struck at London)

[*RIC* 6, Mint of Londinium 133 *etc.* BM B. 95]

This visit to Britain is associated with the preparations for the civil war fought in Italy in AD 312. The garrisons of the outpost forts of Hadrian's Wall were withdrawn for this campaign. Other visits to Britain are attested by *Adventus* coins issued in AD 307 and AD 314. (PJC)

E8 Gold *solidus* of Magnus Maximus AD 384–385

Obv: Bust of Magnus Maximus wearing diadem and cuirass.
Around, D(OMINVS) N(OSTER) MAG(NVS) MAXIMVS P(IVS) F(ELIX) AVG(VSTVS) (our Lord Magnus Maximus Pius Felix Augustus)

Rev: Two Emperors (Magnus Maximus and Theodosius) on throne, holding a globe. Victory stands behind with outspread wings.
Around, VICTORIA AVGG = VICTORIA AVGVSTORVM (Victory, the patron goddess of the Augusti)
Below, AVG(VSTA) = LONDINIVM (name of mint) and OB(RYZA (purified gold)

[*RIC* 9. Mint of Londinium 2b (Magnus Maximus) = *BM* 1933,0414.17]

This is a specimen of Maximus's fourth issue of gold coins. The mintmark indicates that it was produced by the mint operating at the imperial court which must have been in London at the time. The coinage dates to AD 384/5 and shows that Maximus returned to Britain, presumably to fight the Pictish campaign noted in the Gallic Chronicle. For the suggestion that this was a politically motivated act rather than an actual emergency, see J. Gerrard, *The Ruin of Roman Britain: an Archaeological Perspective* (Cambridge, 2013), p. 25: 'The recorded event may have been little more than a sham concocted as a prerequisite for Maximius' usurpation.'

E9 Ravenscar tower Late 4th century AD

Justinianus, commander; Vindicianus, *magister,* built this tower and fort from ground level.

[*RIB* 721. Ravenscar]

A dedication slab, found in 1774, on site of Roman "signal-station" of Ravenscar (also called Peak). Now in Whitby Museum.

The "signal-stations" of the Yorkshire coast were built in the late fourth century – the Theodosian reorganisation and the time of Magnus Maximus have both been suggested as possible contexts (Casey 1979) – and probably abandoned soon after AD 400. *Magister* is a low rank in the army of the late fourth century. The identification of Justinianus as the man who later became one of Constantine III's generals remains controversial, but more likely if the towers were built during the reign of Maximus (AD 383–88).

E10 Restorations on the Wall by the *civitas* of the Durotriges Dates unknown

(i) The *civitas* of the Durotriges of Lindinis

[*RIB* 1672. Cawfields milecastle (MC 42)]

Building stone found at foot of crags north of Wall. Now in Chesters Museum.

(ii) The *civitas* of the Durotriges of Lindinis

[*RIB* 1673 Housesteads (Vercovicium)]

Uninscribed altar reused as a building stone found in Wall west of fort. Now in Chesters Museum.

The Durotriges were located in Dorset and eastern Somerset. Dorchester (Durnovaria) was the original centre for the *civitas,* which may have been split in the third century AD, with Ilchester (Lindinis) becoming the centre of a separate *civitas* (Stevens 1941, 359).

E11 Restoration of the Wall by the civitas of the *Dumnonii* Date unknown

The *civitas* of the Dumnonii

[*RIB* 1843. Carvoran (Magna)]

Building stone found in or before 1760, near Carvoran. Now in private possession.

The Dumnonii had their centre at Exeter (Isca).

E12 Restoration of the Wall by the civitas of the *Brigantes* Date unknown

The beginning of the length in feet built by the Brigantian *civitas*

[*RIB* 2022. Blea Tarn]

Building stone, recorded before 1794. Now lost.

The Brigantes had their centre at Isurium (Aldborough). For a similar stone referring to the Catuvellauni see *RIB* 1962. *RIB* 1629 and 2053 seem to refer to individuals. None can be dated.

E13 Gold *solidus* of Constantine III AD 407–411

Obv: Bust of Constantine wearing imperial mantle and diadem.

D(OMINVS) N(OSTER) CONSTANTINVS P(IVS) F(ELIX) AVG(VSTVS)

Rev: Emperor standing right, holding labarum and globe, spurning captive at his feet.
VICTORIA AVGGGG = Victoria Augustorum, (Victory of the four emperors)
LD ((minted at) Lugdunum), CON OB (Constantinople purified gold)

[*RIC* 10.1506 = BM 1864,1128.202]

The usurper who usurped the throne in Britain here claims his own legitimacy by associating the three legitimate emperors, Arcadius, Honorius and Theodosius II, with himself in the reverse legend. (PJC).

E14 *Fifth-century purse group containing copper-alloy* **nummi.** After AD 406

[Great Whittington, Northumberland (north of Halton Chesters, Hadrian's Wall)]

Reported by Rob Collins in *Britannia* 39 (2009), pp. 256 ff., this metal-detector find is probably one of coins lost accidentally rather than deliberate deposition. The findspot is located close to the Roman road which ran north-east from Halton Chesters on Hadrian's Wall and south of another Roman road known as the Devil's Causeway. Of the eight copper-alloy *nummi* found, the earliest is an AD 318 Constantine I issue, the latest a House of Theodosius *Gloria Romanorum* issue of AD 406–408. The latter is available to view on the Portable Antiquities Scheme database at https://finds.org.uk/database/search/results/q/NCL--EE2655. For the type, see *RIC* X, no. 142ff. The importance of this find is its indication that even at the end of the Roman occupation period, small denomination coins were still in circulation, including coins which were almost 100 years old. The oldest coin, like three of the others, are from mints in the eastern Mediterranean, and as Collins notes (p. 259) 'provides evidence for direct or indirect contact with people from the Mediterranean in the fifth century that probably post-dates the traditional end date for Roman Britain, *c.* AD 409 or AD 410.' On this, see in particular the collection of papers in F. K. Haarer (ed.), *AD 410: The History and Archaeology of Late and Post-Roman Britain* (Society for the Promotion of Roman Studies, London, 2014), and in particular H. E. M. Cool, 'Which "Romans"; What "Home"? The Myth of the "End" of Roman Britain', at pp. 13 – 22.

SECTION F

GOVERNMENT AND ADMINISTRATION

(a) THE IMPERIAL STAFF

F1 A. Platorius Nepos, governor *c.* AD 125

To Aulus Platorius Nepos Aponius Italicus Manilianus Gaius Licinius Pollio, son of Aulus, of the voting tribe Sergia, consul, *augur*, governor of the province of Britain, governor of the province of Lower Germany, governor of the province of Thrace, legate of the First Legion Adiutrix, quaestor of the province of Macedonia, curator of the Cassian, Clodian, Ciminian and New Trajanic Roads, a candidate nominated by the deified emperor Trajan, military tribune of the Twenty-Second Legion Primigenia Pia Fidelis, praetor, tribune of the plebs, one of the board of three men in charge of capital sentences, patron, by decree of the councillors.

[*ILS* 1052 = EDCS-01600155*. Aquileia, Italy]

Statue base. Now in the Archaeological Museum, Aquileia, north-east Italy.

Inscription on the base of a statue set up in honour of Platorius Nepos, the governor responsible for the building of Hadrian's Wall (see **C7–9**), by the councillors of Aquileia, a city of which he was patron. It gives Nepos's career in reverse order, though the consulate (the supreme magistracy of Rome) and the post of *augur* (a religious official) are highlighted at the start, and there is some mis-ordering of the early posts. The date of Nepos's move to Britain is known very precisely from a military diploma (**C5**); he moved here from Lower Germany, bringing with him legion VI Victrix, formerly based at Xanten *(Vetera)*. The career is typical of that of a governor of an imperial province such as Britain, which, having three legions based within it, was regarded as a senior posting. The governor was appointed by, and was responsible directly to, the emperor.

F2 Governor's headquarters 3rd century AD?

(i) To the deities of the governor's headquarters, Scribonius Demetrius *(set this up)*.

(ii) To Ocean and Tethys, Demetrius *(set this up)*.

[*RIB* 662–3 add. York (Eboracum)]

Two bronze plates, written in Greek and stuck back-to-back, found c. 1840 on the site of the Old Railway Station. Now in the Yorkshire Museum.

Demetrius is often identified with Demetrius of Tarsus, the grammarian who took part in Plutarch's dialogue *De Defectu Oraculorum* in AD 83–4, having just returned from a visit to Britain and having, on imperial orders, joined a voyage to the isles of Scotland. It is thought that he spent some years in York, probably on the staff of Caristanius Fronto, commander of legion IX, subsequently joining Agricola's circumnavigation in AD 83. However at this time the "governor's headquarters" lay at London; there was none at York until the division of Britain into two provinces by Septimius Severus. Hence these dedications may well date to the third century; Demetrius is a common enough name.

F3 **A governor in a divided Britain** 4th century AD

Face: To Jupiter Best and Greatest, his perfection Lucius Septimius [....], governor of B[ritannia Prima] restored (this monument), being a citizen of R[...]

Back: This statue and column erected under the ancient religion,

Left Side: Septimius, governor of the first province, renews.

Right side: *(text missing)*

[*RIB* 103 add. Cirencester (Corinium)]

Base of a Jupiter Column found in 1891 in the garden of 'The Firs', Victoria (or New) Road. Now in Corinium Museum, Cirencester.

Jupiter worship was part and parcel of the official religion of Rome, though the erection of Jupiter columns is something which is particularly characteristic of the Rhineland and Danubian areas where it is most common in the later second to mid-third centuries. The reference to Britannia Prima is generally taken to date the inscription to after the Diocletianic reorganisation of Britain into four separate provinces, each governed by a *praeses*. (For a *praeses* of Britannia Secunda see **E5**.) Birley (2005, 427 note 47) withdraws his previous suggestion that *prima provincia* (first province) could be a third-century, non-technical allusion to Britannia Superior.

F4 **A stilus-tablet** ?1st or 2nd century AD

The imperial procurators of the province of Britain issued (this).

[*RIB* 2.4.2443.2 = BM 1934,1210.100. London (Londinium)]

Wooden stilus-tablet, recessed on one face, found in or near the Walbrook, in or before 1934. Now in the British Museum. On the plain (outside) face, a branded circular stamp:

On the recessed (inside) face there are traces of about five lines of lettering. The original message would have been written with a stilus on wax filling the recess, the traces being left by the stilus penetrating to the wood beneath. The branded stamp authenticates the document. There was the procurator of the province and various procurators concerned with different aspects of the emperor's affairs; it is not clear who is acting together here. Cf. **B18** the tombstone of Julius Classicianus, for a provincial procurator in London by the 60s AD, and **F14** below for an imperial freedman acting as assistant to "procurators" at Combe Down.

F5 Fragments of tile from a Roman temple no date

The procurators of the province of Britain at London.

[*Britannia* 31 (2000), 442., no.39. London (Londinium)]

Four fragments of tile or brick found in 1999 at the site of the possible Roman temple.

The two largest fragments almost certainly fit together, and bear an impressed stamp PPBRLON, *p(rocuratores) p(rovinciae) Br(itanniae) Lon(dini).* For similar stamps, see *Britannia* 16 (1985), 193–196 and *RIB* 2.5.2485. But in this case, R. S. O Tomlin and M. W. C Hassall note that 'autopsy actually suggests PPBRLOA/, (which) would prompt the expansion *Lo(ndini) Au(gustae)*, another testimony to the award of the title *Augusta* to London at some date: for the other evidence, see A. L. F. Rivet and C. Smith, *The Place-Names of Roman Britain* (1979), 260. But difficulties remain.'

F6 A judicial official AD 80s

For Gaius Octavius Tidius Tossianus Javolenus Priscus, legate of the Fourth Legion Flavia, legate of the Third Legion Augusta, *iuridicus* of the province of Britain, governor of the province of Upper Germany, governor of the province of Syria, governor of the province of Africa, priest: Publius Mutilius Crispinus, son of Publius, of the Claudian voting tribe, ordered this to be set up under his will, to his dearest friend.

[*CIL* 3.2864 = *ILS* 1015+add = EDCS-28400116. Nadin (Nedinum, Dalmatia)]

This stone honours Javolenus Priscus, the distinguished jurist, who served as *iuridicus* in Britain in the later first century. *Iuridici* were judicial officials of praetorian status, appointed to help the governor with judicial business. Only seven are at present known for Britain and none is recorded within the province. The restoration of the very fragmentary *RIB* 8 from London to refer to an *iuridicus* is dubious (see Birley 2005, 206 note 62; *RIB* 8 add).

F7 Administration in London *c.* AD 65/70–80

To [...]inus, ?secretary of tribunician rank?, in London.

[*Bloomberg WT* 18. London (Londinium)]

An incomplete larch writing-tablet, on which the last two lines of an address are preserved.

Tomlin in *Roman London's first Voices* p. 94 admits that this tablet is a puzzle, but suggests that the most attractive interpretation is that the addressee was *scr[iba] tr[ibuni] mi[itum]*, a 'scribe' or 'secretary' who would have been given the same grade as the magistrate in whose service they worked.

F8 A *beneficiarius* at Wroxeter ?Before AD 61

Gaius Mannius Secundus, son of Gaius, of the Pollian voting tribe, from Pollentia, a soldier of the Twentieth Legion, aged 52 years, served for 31 years, *beneficiarius* on the staff of the governor, lies here.

[*RIB* 293 add. Wroxeter (Viroconium)]

Tombstone found in 1752 along with no.19 in the Roman cemetery outside the east gate of the city. Now in Rowley's House Museum, Shrewsbury.

The text of this inscription is full of uncertainties. Mannius's rank at the time of his death has been variously restored as *beneficiarius legati pro praetore*, i.e. on the staff of the governor, or as *beneficiarius legati praetorii*, on the staff of the legionary legate. In the former case it can be argued that his presence at Wroxeter does not prove that legion XX was based there since he will have been seconded from the legion to the governor's staff, whence he could have been sent anywhere in the province. In the latter case he is much more likely to be at the legionary base, hence the tombstone can be used as evidence for the garrison of Wroxeter at the time of its erection. This problem is linked with another, the date of the stone. The absence of the honorific *Valeria Victrix* from the legion's name should point to a date before the title was awarded, most probably in AD 61 following the suppression of the Boudican rebellion. At this date, however, legion XIV is thought to have been based at Wroxeter. For a discussion of this problem see Tomlin 1992, where doubt is cast on the idea that the honorific titles relate to the events of AD 61. Other *beneficiarii* appear in **F9–F10, F47**, **G19**, **J12** and **J31.** Above the gable of the inscription is a relief of two lions, one on either side of a pinecone (see drawimg in *RIB* online). Pollentia (modern Pollenza) is in Liguria, in northwest Italy.

F9 A *beneficiarius* at Dorchester — 2nd or 3rd century AD

To Jupiter Best and Greatest and to the Divine Powers of the Emperor, Marcus Varius Severus, *beneficiarius* of the governor, set up this altar with screens from his own funds.

[*RIB* 235. Dorchester, Oxon]

Altar found in 1731 at Dorchester in Court (or Bishop's) Close. Now lost.

As in **F16**, the worship of the Emperor's power is coupled with worship of Olympian gods. For *Numen Augusti* see introduction to the section on Religion.

F10 A *beneficiarius* at Winchester — ?3rd century AD

To the Italian, German, Gallic and British Mother goddesses, Antonius Lucretianus, *beneficiarius* of the governor, restored this.

[*RIB* 88. Winchester (Venta Belgarum)]

Altar found in 1854 near south end of Jewry Street. Now in the British Museum BM 1856,0701.5025 (cast in Winchester Museum).

The governor's *beneficiarii* were sent, not only to military sites (as **F9**), but also to civilian sites. For Mother goddesses see nos **G16** and **J32**. The association here of the German, Gallic and British Mothers may be a reflection of Lucretianus's origin and of the places where he served, or, given the fact that this is the restoration of an earlier dedication, the associations of whoever originally set it up.

F11 A member of Agricola's staff — AD 77–83/4

To [..., trooper] of the *ala Sebosiana, singularis* of Agricola ....

[*Britannia* 29 (1998), 74–75 no. 44. Carlisle (Luguvalium)]

Writing tablet, retrieved from a demolition deposit in a latrine of the mid-Trajanic/early Hadrianic fort. Now in Tullie House Museum, Carlisle

A *singularis* was a member of the mounted bodyguard of a governor. The *ala Sebosiana* was presumably the unit stationed in Carlisle at the time. This is the earliest evidence for its presence in Britain (Jarrett 1994, 41–42). The recipient would have been detached from his unit to serve with the governor, but may have brought the letter back with him when he returned to his unit. The Agricola referred to is undoubtedly Gnaeus Julius Agricola, father-in-law of Tacitus and governor of Britain from *c.* AD 77–83/84. (The archaeological context rules out identification with Sextus Calpurnius Agricola, governor in the AD 160s, and attested on **C38–40.** This fragmentary text joins the Chester lead pipes (**B21**) and the Verulamium forum inscription (**B24**) as the only witnesses to Julius Agricola from archaeological finds.

F12 A *speculator* at London — 1st century AD

To the spirits of the departed, [...]r Celsus, son of Lucius, of the Claudian voting tribe, from [...], *speculator* of the Second Legion Augusta, An[tonius?] Dardanus Cursor, Valerius Pudens [and ...]s Probus, *speculatores* of the legion *(set this up)*.

[*RIB* 19 add. London (Londinium)]

Tombstone found in 1843 in Playhouse Yard, Blackfriars. Now in the British Museum, BM 1855,0804.21.

The head of the deceased is carved in relief in a niche. *Speculatores* functioned as military police, served only on the staffs of governors, and thus are based at provincial capitals. The fact that Celsus's tombstone was set up by his fellow *speculatores* suggests that he died at the base, and hence that London was already the provincial capital by the end of the first century AD, the probable date of this stone.

F13 A *strator consularis* at Irchester — ?3rd century AD

Sacred to the spirits of the departed, Anicius Saturninus, *strator* of the governor, made this memorial to himself.

[*RIB* 233 add. Irchester, Northants]

Slab from a monumental tomb found about 1853, at Irchester, reused at the site of the Roman town. Now in the British Museum, BM 1856,0508.1.

A *strator* was a junior officer in charge of horses. On the strength of this inscription it has been suggested that Irchester was a centre for horse rearing for the Roman army, a notion doubted in the most recent discussion of the site (Burnham and Wacher 1990, 147). The term *equisio cos* is used in one of the Vindolanda tablets (see below, **G8** for a post equivalent to that of *strator cos*). For another example of a *strator consularis*, from Dover, see *Britannia* 8 (1977), 426 no. 4.

F14 Naevius, procurators' assistant — AD 212–217

For the welfare of the Emperor Caesar Marcus Aurelius Antoninus Pius Felix Invictus Augustus, Naevius, imperial freedman, procurators' assistant, restored from ground level these ruined headquarters.

[*RIB* 179 add. Combe Down, Monkton Combe]

Dedication slab found in 1854 near the Roman villa. Now in the Roman Baths Museum, Bath.

Principia here must denote the 'headquarters' of local procuratorial administration, perhaps of an imperial estate, and not, as is more usual, the headquarters building of a fort. Note **F37** for a *centurio regionarius* or 'district officer' with responsibility for policing duties based at Bath. This inscription had been reused as a cover-slab for a coffin.

F15 An *eques singularis* — ?3rd century AD

To the spirits of the departed, Aurelius Macrinus, formerly cavalryman in the emperor's bodyguard.

[*RIB* 714 add. Malton (Derventio)]

Tombstone found in 1753, c. 200 metres north of the Roman fort. Now lost.

The *equites singulares Augusti*, the emperor's bodyguard, were recruited from soldiers in the auxiliary cavalry. Macrinus could have served in this capacity when an emperor (e.g. Severus) was present in Britain, or he could have served abroad and then retired to the fort whence he had originally come. A cavalry unit, the *ala Picentiana*, is attested at Malton in the mid- to late 2nd century (*Britannia* 2, 1971, 291 no.9). An alternative reading for the end of line 2, *'sing. v[ixit]...'* (Davies 1976, 139–40), now given in *RIB* online, would remove the link to the *singulares Augusti.*

(b) LOCAL GOVERNMENT

F16 Togidubnus — 2nd half of 1st century AD

To Neptune and Minerva for the welfare of the Divine House, by authority of Tiberius Claudius [To]gidubnus, great king of Britain, the guild of smiths and those who belong to it gave this temple from their own resources, the site having been given by [...]ens, son of Pudentinus.

[*RIB* 91 add. Chichester (Noviomagus)]

Dedication slab found in 1723 in Lion Street at junction with North Street. Now built into the west face of the council chamber, Chichester.

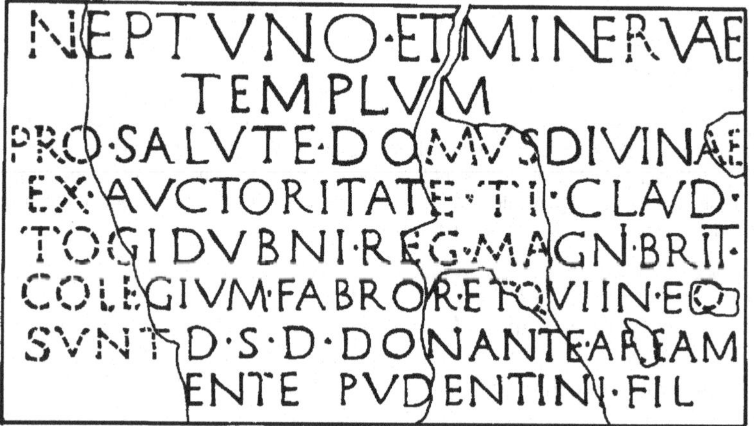

Fig. 9

The name of the British ruler referred to by Tacitus (*Agricola* 14), and who is recorded in this inscription, is now thought more likely to be Togidubnus than Cogidubnus (cf. *Classical Philology* 72 (1977), 339). He is shown by this inscription to have acquired Roman citizenship from Claudius. (See **H2** for another case of a Claudian grant of citizenship from Fishbourne.) His title *rex magnus* ('great king') indicates his eminence (compare Herod the Great); see the discussion in Bogaers 1979. His philo-Roman stance is indicated by the development of the city of Chichester during his reign, when it stood within a friendly kingdom, independent of the authority of the governor of Britain. For a dedication to Nero set up at Chichester during the (assumed) lifetime of Togidubnus see **F17**.

F17 Chichester dedication to Nero AD 59

For Nero Claudius Caesar Augustus, son of the deified Claudius, grandson of Germanicus Caesar, great-grandson of Tiberius Caesar Augustus, great-great-grandson of the deified Augustus, in his fourth year of tribunician power, four times acclaimed *imperator*, consul for the fourth time, by decree of the senate the vow was deservedly fulfilled.

[*RIB* 92. Chichester (Noviomagus)]

Dedication slab found in 1740 on corner of St Martin's Lane and East Street. Now lost.

Here is perhaps an example of the regular annual public vow for the emperor's safety. Compare Pliny's record of a similar vow for Trajan (*Epist.* 10.35). This is one of two major inscriptions erected in Chichester in the middle years of the first century AD, when it still presumably lay in the territory of the allied king Togidubnus. (For the other see **F16**.)

F18 Provincia Britannia Date unknown

To the Divine Power of C[aesar Aug(ustus)], the prov[ince] of Brita[nnia ...]

[*RIB* 5. London (Londinium)]

A slab found in 1850 near Cannon Street. Now lost.

The inscription's abbreviation *C Aug* could refer to any emperor. The cult of the *numina* is a fairly late development, arising out of, but separate from, the official imperial cult (see the introduction to the section on Religion). The provincial council, which is presumably the corporate body intended here, was set up to maintain the official imperial cult. This council increased in importance because it developed rights of access to the emperor.

F19 Tile-stamp of the *res publica* of *Glevum* (Gloucester) ?3rd century AD

Commonwealth (*res publica*) of the people of Glevum, When Naso and [...] were duumvirs

[*Britannia* 31 (2000) 439, no.23. Gloucester (Glevum)]

Tile fragment with an impressed stamp, found in 1983/4 in a 3rd-century context.

The tile fragments bear the impressed stamp [R]PGI[IVIR] / NASOET[...], *[res]p(ublica) G(levensium) (duo)vir(orum) / Naso(nis) et [...]* This is a unique example from the colony of Gloucester, though cf. *RIB* II.5, 2487 for the type of legend. Duumvirs (*duoviri*) were the chief, annually elected magistrates in a self-governing town.

F20 A Gloucester councillor at Bath Date unknown

[...] Decurion of the colony of *Glevum* [....], lived 80 years, Vi[....].

[*RIB* 161. Bath (Aquae Sulis)]

Plinth of a tomb found in 1600 built into the medieval wall of Bath. Now lost.

Glevum (Gloucester) was established as a *colonia* at the time of Nerva (AD 96–97), on the evidence of the tombstone of a soldier named as *M. Ulpio Ner. Quinto Glevi* (*CIL* 6.3346). For the foundation of the colony see Hurst 1988. An earlier (Domitianic) date for the foundation is put forward by Hassall (1999, 183–84).

F21 A councillor of Lincoln

?3rd century AD

(i) To the spirits of the departed: Volusia Faustina, a citizen of Lincoln, lived 26 years, 1 month, 26 days. Aurelius Senecio, decurion, set this up to his deserving wife.

(ii) To the spirits of the departed: Claudia Catiotu[...], lived 60 (or more) years [....].

[*RIB* 250 add.= BM 1862,0423.1 Lincoln (Lindum)]

Tombstone found in 1859 built into foundations of the west wall of the lower city. Now in the British Museum.

Above the inscription are the busts of two women, wearing tunic and mantle; the figure to the left and foreground (Volusia) wears a necklace. The hairstyles of both are consistent with the 3rd-century date proposed for the inscription (Allason-Jones 2005, 132). The name of the second woman is not certain: she may be Claudia Catiotua or Claudia (daughter of) Catiotuus. The relationship of the two deceased women is also unknown: perhaps mother and daughter, or both wives of Aurelius Senecio? Senecio's *nomen*, Aurelius, suggests that he descends from a family which acquired citizenship no earlier than the second half of the second century: he is not, therefore, a descendant of an original colonist. Volusia Faustina could be. In this context (and that of **F20, F22**) a decurion is a member of the city council.

F22 A councillor of York

3rd century AD

To the spirits of the departed (and) of Flavius Bellator, decurion of the colony of York; he lived 29 years ... months ... days.

[*RIB* 674 add. York (Eboracum)]

Stone coffin, with lid, found 1872 at Scarborough Railway Bridge. Now in the Yorkshire Museum.

The skeleton of Bellator had on one finger a gold ring, set with a ruby. The gold ring was the badge of the equestrian aristocracy (cf. **H2**). Unlike the other three colonies in Britain which were veteran settlements, York was a titular colony, the title having been bestowed on the pre-existing settlement which had grown up outside the legionary base. For a sarcophagus of another *decurio coloniae Eboracensis* see *RIB* 3.3203.

F23 A British altar at Bordeaux AD 237

To the goddess Tutela Boudig(a), Marcus Aurelius Lunaris, *sevir Augustalis* of the colonies of York and Lincoln in the province of Lower Britannia *(set up)* the altar which he vowed when he set sail from York; he fulfilled his vow willingly and deservedly in the consulship of Perpetuus and Cornelianus.

[*JRS* 11 (1921), 102 = EDCS-13303053*. Bordeaux (Burdigala)]

Altar found in 1921 at Bordeaux.

The relief above the inscription shows, in the centre, the goddess with the attributes of Cybele; on the left, a bull and above the bull a tree (the sacred pine associated with the cult of Cybele?); far left is a priest wearing a Phrygian cap; to the right is an altar, and beyond the altar the dedicator. On one side of the altar a river god symbolises the Garonne, on which Bordeaux stands; on the other a boar symbolises York (photos on link from EDCS). The name Boudig(a) recalls that of the British queen, Boudica; alternatively the deity honoured may be intended to be Bourdig(a), the tutelary deity of Bordeaux. A *sevir Augustalis* was a member of a board of six men who conducted emperor-worship at chartered towns such as the two colonies of York and Lincoln. The *seviri* were commonly freedmen. This inscription provides the earliest dated reference to York as a colony, and useful evidence for the location of the boundary between upper and lower Britain. The altar is made of millstone grit, from Yorkshire; it was thus conveyed from Britain, presumably with Lunaris, to be set up as an *ex voto* in thanks for a safe journey.

F24 Verecundius Diogenes and his wife Julia Fortunata 3rd or 4th century AD

(i) Marcus Verecundius Diogenes, *sevir* of the colony of York, sea-trader and citizen of the Bituriges Cubi, set this up to himself in his lifetime.

[*RIB* 678 add. York (Eboracum)]

Stone coffin found in 1579 outside York. Lost before 1796.

The restoration *mor(i)t(ex)* is that of J.C. Mann, quoted in Birley (1966, 228) as against the earlier reading of *idem quinquennalis* given in *RIB*. A *moritix* is now known from London (**H24**) and a British trader described as *moritex* is known from Cologne (**H27**). The Bituriges Cubi were located in central Gaul, centred on Bourges. The nature of Diogenes' link with York was probably commercial, with wine as the most likely object of trade between the two cities. The quality of his coffin, and that which he provided for his wife, suggest a degree of affluence, as does his assumption of duty as *sevir* (see **F23**). Like Lunaris in that inscription, he was probably a freedman.

(ii) To Julia Fortunata, from Sardinia, a loyal wife to her husband, Verecundius Diogenes.

[*RIB* 687. York (Eboracum)]

Stone coffin found in 1877, within a few yards of **F24 (i)**. *Now in the Yorkshire Museum.*

F25 Thurmaston milestone AD 119–120

The Emperor Caesar Trajan Hadrian Augustus, son of the deified Trajan Conqueror of Parthia, grandson of the deified Nerva, father of his country, in his fourth year of tribunician power, three times consul, From Ratae 2 miles.

[*RIB* 2244. Thurmaston, Leicestershire]

Cylindrical milestone found in 1771 on the west side of the Fosse Way, two miles from Leicester. Now in the Jewry Wall Museum, Leicester.

Leicester *(Ratae)* is the urban centre of the *civitas* of the Corieltavi (see **F29**) in which this milestone was found and from which its distance was measured. The emperor is here wrongly credited with the title *pater patriae* (father of his country) which he did not assume until AD 128.

F26 Wroxeter forum dedication AD 129–130

For the Emperor Caesar Trajan Hadrian, son of the deified Trajan Conqueror of Parthia, grandson of the deified Nerva, *pontifex maximus*, in his fourteenth year of tribunician power, three times consul, father of his country, the *civitas* of the Cornovii *(set this up)*.

[*RIB* 288. Wroxeter (Viroconium)]

Fragments of a commemorative slab found in 1924 to east of the main entrance to the forum. Now in Shrewsbury Museum and Art Gallery.

This records the building of the forum by the corporate act of the whole community through its government. This is the one Hadrianic civilian public building in Britain whose construction is attested epigraphically, though building activity in the early- to mid-second century is well known from excavation; e.g. the fora at Caerwent, Caistor by Norwich and Leicester, and the replacement in stone of the original (timber) forum at Silchester. The town at Wroxeter developed later than many of the other Romano-British *civitates*, as the site remained that of a legionary fortress until *c.* AD 90. It is one of only two early fortresses (the other is Exeter) to be developed as a *civitas* rather than a *colonia*. The forum was built on the site of an unfinished bath-building. Other forum building inscriptions come from St Albans (**B24**) and possibly Cirencester (*RIB* 114).

F27 Decree of the *civitas* of the Silures Shortly before AD 220

To [Tiberius Claudius] Paulinus, legate of the Second Legion Augusta, proconsul of the province of Narbonensis, governor of the province of Lugudunensis, by decree of the council, the commonwealth of the *civitas* of the Silures *(set this up)*.

[*RIB* 311. Caerwent (Venta Silurum)]

Pedestal found in 1903 on the village green. Now in Caerwent church.

The pedestal probably held a statue of Tiberius Claudius Paulinus, who went on, after the posts named here, to become governor of Lower Britain under Elagabalus. (He is attested in post in AD 220; cf. **D27**). The honour done Paulinus by the council of the Silures presumably stems from connections he had with the city when he was commanding officer of the locally based legion at Caerleon. This inscription, like that of Wroxeter (**F26**), records a corporate act of the community through its elected council. For the career of Paulinus cf. Birley 2005, 47–50.

F28 Kenchester milestone AD 283–284

For the Emperor Caesar Marcus Aurelius Numerianus, the commonwealth of the *civitas* of the Dobunni [...].

[*RIB* 2250. Kenchester (Magnis)]

Milestone found in 1796 on site of north wall of the Roman town. Now in Hereford City Museum.

Milestones, in default of boundary stones, are valuable as evidence for the extent of city territories. The size and prosperity of the city of Cirencester is perhaps not unconnected with the large area of Dobunnian territory, as evidenced by this milestone (Kenchester lies *c.* 80 km from Cirencester).

F29 Tile naming the Corieltavi — Date unknown

... of the *civitas* of the Corieltavi ...

[*RIB* 2.5. 2491.150 = *Britannia* 34 (2003), 382. Caves Inn, Warwicks (Tripontium)]

Tile found in 1965 during excavation.

The first line of a graffito [C]IVITATIS CORIELTAVVOROM[...] of at least four lines (too few letters survive to make any sense of lines 2–4). *Tripontium* lies about 24 kilometres from *Ratae* (Leicester). The graffito gives what may well be a more correct form of what used to be known as the *civitas Coritanorum*. The form *Ratae Coritanorum* was based on Ptolemy's *Geography* (2.3.2: *Coritanoi*), and the Ravenna Cosmography, which records *Ratecorioneltavori*, easily amended to *Rat(a)e Corieltavorum* (Rivet and Smith 1979, 324; Tomlin 1983; Tomlin 1993b, 137–8).

F30 Brougham milestone — AD 258–268

To the Emperor Caesar Marcus Casianius Latinianius Postimus Augustus Pius Felix, the commonwealth of the *civitas* of the Carvetii *(set this up)*.

[*JRS* 55 (1965), 224 no. 11 = *RIB* 3.3525. Brougham, Cumbria (Brocavum)]

Milestone found in 1964 in Frenchfield, beside the Roman Road to Carlisle. Now at Brougham Castle.

Note that the mason has misspelt all three of the 'Gallic' emperor M. Cassianius Latinianius Postumus' personal names! The expansion of *Car* as Carvetii (meaning stag-people) rests on the reading of **F32**, from Old Penrith which refers to the *c. Carvetior*. This new *civitas* is first attested in AD 223 (**F31**), and could have been created when territory, hitherto military, became available for civilian development. The urban centre of the *civitas Carvetiorum* was most probably at Carlisle. For another milestone from the territory of this *civitas*, but not naming it, see **F50**.

F31 Milestone of the civitas of the Carvetii — AD 222–223

For the Emperor Caesar Marcus Aurelius Severus Alexander Pius Felix Augustus, pontifex maximus, in the second year of his tribunician power, consul, proconsul, father of his country, the Community (*civitas*) of the Carvetii (set this up). From Carlisle, 19 miles.

[*Britannia* 36 (2005). 482, no. 11 = *EDCS*-44600269 = *RIB* 3.3526, Langwathby, Cumbria]

The upper half or third of a cylindical milestone cut from yellowish (not local) sandstone, found in 1993 c. 2 km north of Brougham Castle. Remains in the possession of the landowner.

This is the earliest evidence for the *civitas Carvetiorum*, which is attested also on **F30** and **F32** The measurement from Carlisle may be significant, as the likeliest candidate for the centre of government of the *civitas*. The '53 miles' inscribed on *RIB* 2283 (from Kirkby Lonsdale) is probably also a measurement to Carlisle, but no place name is mentioned. Severus Alexander's second tribunate ran from 10 December AD 222 to 9 December AD 223.

F32 A *senator* of the Carvetii — ?4th century AD

To the spirits of the departed (and) to Flavius Martius, a councillor in the *civitas* of the Carvetii, of quaestorian rank, who lived 45 years. Martiola his daughter and heiress had this set up.

[*RIB* 933. Old Penrith, Cumbria (Voreda)]

Tombstone seen c. 1600 by Camden at Old Penrith. Now lost.

The term *senator*, though mainly confined to the Roman senate, is occasionally used in the 4th and 5th centuries as an alternative name for city councillors. The Brougham milestone inscription (**F30**) enables us to expand the *'c'* in line 3 as *civitas*. The *quaestor* was a magistrate with financial responsibilities.

F33 The Catuvellauni repair Hadrian's Wall — Date unknown

From the *civitas* of the Catuvellauni, Tossodio.

[*RIB* 1962. Howgill (Hadrian's Wall milecastle 55)]

Building stone found in or before 1717, built into the wall of farm buildings.

This undated (but broadly "late" inscription) provides the sole specific reference to a *civitas* of the Catuvellauni; but see **B24** (the Verulamium building inscription) for a possible case, and **H10 (ii)** for a woman described as *natione Catuallauna*. For other civilian communities engaged in building repair work on the Wall, see **E10-E12**.

F34 Copper-alloy brooch — Date unknown

Brooch from the *Regio Lagitiensis*

[*Britannia* 32 (2001), 396, no. 39. Alford, Lincolnshire]

A copper-alloy 'knee' brooch found by a metal-detectorist in 2000 in the Alford area, Lincolnshire.

A copper-alloy brooch 29mm long and 13mm wide; triangular in section with two panels of letters moulded in relief, *fibula ex reg(ione) / Lagitiense.* According to R. S. O Tomlin and M. W. C. Hassall, this is Castleford, where 'there was an extensive manufactory including enamel on copper alloy'. This is the first inscription to name explicitly a *regio* in Roman Britain; the existence of others can be inferred from *RIB* 674 (**F22**), 587 (Ribchester, **F35** and *Tab. Vindol.* I. 22. 9–10 (Carlisle).

F35 T. Floridius Natalis, *praepositus* — AD 225–235

... for the welfare of the Emperor [Caesar Al]ex[ander our Augustus and of Julia Mamaea the mo]ther of Our Lord (the Emperor) and of the camp under the charge of Valerius Crescens Fulvianus, governor, Titus Floridius Natalis, legionary centurion in charge of the unit and of the region, restored the temple from ground level as requested [by the god], and dedicated (it) fr[om his own resources].

[*RIB* 587 add. Ribchester (Bremetannacum)]

Part of a dedication slab found in 1811 on the north bank of the river Ribble. Now at Ribchester Museum.

The temple here referred to presumably lay outside the fort. The phrase 'as requested by the god' (*ex responsu*) strongly suggests the cult of Jupiter Dolichenus which was very popular among the third-century soldiery and which reached its high-water mark in the reign of Severus Alexander. Natalis' special command over the region may be connected with its being used for veteran settlement – the Ravenna Cosmography (124) calls Ribchester *Bremetannacum Veteranorum.* For the *numerus* that he commanded see **F36**.

F36 Aelius Antoninus, *praepositus* — AD 238–244

To the holy god Apollo Maponus, for the welfare of Our Lord (the Emperor) and of 'Gordian's Own' Sarmatian cavalry unit of Bremetennacum, [..]lius Antoninus, centurion of the Sixth Legion Victrix, from Melitene, in charge of the unit and the region [....].

[*RIB* 583 add. Ribchester (Bremetennacum)]

Shaft of pedestal found in 1578 at Ribchester; rediscovered in 1814. Now at Ribchester Museum.

The shaft is part of a monument. The right side has a relief of Apollo. On the back two female figures face one another, personifying (on the left) a young, unveiled and undraped *Regio Bremetennacensis* and (on the right) an older, veiled and draped *Britannia Inferior*, who hands an object to the left hand figure. Melitene, on the Euphrates, was the base of legion XII Fulminata. The *numerus* (unit) of Sarmatians has been thought to be descended from the 5,500 Sarmatians sent to Britain in AD 175 (Dio 71.16.2 = LACTOR 11 L1.3). The use of the honorific *Gordiani* at the end of its name dates the inscription to the reigns of the three Emperors called Gordian, since such titles were dropped on the death of the emperor concerned. For Apollo Maponus cf. **J14**. This is one of several examples of a unit being named after the place where it was based: cf. **D36**, **J28 (ii)**, **J21**. The *nomen* of the centurion in line 7 has variously been read as Aelius, Julius and Ulpius, and there is no agreement over the reading of the rest of the inscription from line 11.

F37 A case of vandalism — Date unknown

This holy place, wrecked by insolent people and cleansed afresh, Gaius Severius Emeritus, centurion in charge of the region, has restored to the Virtue and Divine Power of the Emperor.

[*RIB* 152 add. Bath (Aquae Sulis)]

Altar found in 1573 in lower part of Stall Street. Now in the Roman Baths Museum, Bath.

A *centurio regionarius* was a district officer, seconded from his legion for duties presumably connected with security among the civilian population (cf. **F35, F36**). The earliest example in Britain of the title *centurio regionarius* appears at Carlisle in the Trajanic period (*Tab. Vindol.* 2.122). Emeritus probably belonged to the Second Legion at Caerleon. His duties may conceivably have been connected with the imperial estate which has been postulated on the evidence of **F14** from nearby Combe Down.

F38 A *vicus* at Petuaria — AD 139

In honour of the Divine House of the Emperor Caesar Titus Aelius Hadrianus Antoninus Augustus Pius, father of his country, twice consul, and to the divine powers of the emperor, Marcus Ulpius Januarius, councillor of the *vicus* of Petuaria, presented this new stage at his own expense.

[*RIB* 707 add. Brough-on-Humber (Petuaria)]

Dedication slab found in 1937 near west wall of building I (of 1937). Now in Hull Museum.

This stone establishes the status of Petuaria as a *vicus* and one of the few places in Roman Britain known to have possessed a theatre. This stone is dated precisely to AD 139 on the assumption that the reading of line 5 should be *cos II* (as in *RIB* 707 add.) rather than *cos III*, as previously believed (cf. **C23**).

F39 The *vicani* of Carriden — Early to mid-Antonine

To Jupiter Best and Greatest, the people living (*vikani*) at the fort of Velunia, under the charge of Aelius Mansuetus, fulfilled their vow joyfully, freely and deservedly.

[*JRS* 47 (1957), 229–30 no 18 = *RIB* 3.3503. Carriden, West Lothian (Velunia *or* Veluniate)]

Altar, ploughed up in 1956, a short distance east of the site of Carriden fort. Now in the Museum of Scotland, Edinburgh.

As well as pointing to the existence of an organised civilian community at Carriden, the easternmost fort on the short-lived Antonine frontier in Scotland, this inscription is of importance in fixing the location of the site of *Velunia*, thus showing that the ten place-names listed in the Ravenna Cosmography as lying on the Forth-Clyde isthmus run from east to west (Rivet and Smith 1979, 211, 490). The *vicus* in question here will have been subordinate to the authority of the military. *Vici* could also be subordinate to the authority of cities on whose territory they lay. The letter ‘k’ frequently replaces ‘c’ in *vik(ani)*: it is found in both earlier and later inscriptions (see **F40** and **F48**).

F40 The *vicani* of Old Carlisle AD 238–244

To Jupiter Best and Greatest and to Vulkan, for the welfare of our lord Marcus Antonius Gordian Pius Felix Augustus, the people of Maglona dedicated this altar from money contributed by the people.

[*RIB* 899 add. Old Carlisle, Cumbria (Maglona?)]

Part of an altar found in 1842 at Old Carlisle. Now in Carlisle Museum.

The restoration *vik(ani) Mag(lonenses)* (in preference to the *vik(anorum) mag(istri)* given in *RIB*) arises from the re-identification of Old Carlisle as *Maglona* rather than *Olenacum*. For detail see Rivet and Smith 1979, 406–407, *Magis* and *Maglona*. The settlement at Old Carlisle grew up outside a fort and was subject to military authority. For a similar dedication to Vulcan by the inhabitants of a military *vicus* see **F41** from Chesterholm. Vulcan, the god of smiths, was honoured in many places associated with industry.

F41 The *vicani* of Chesterholm 2nd or 3rd century AD

For the Divine House and the Divine Powers of the Emperors, the people of Vindolanda *(set up this)* sacred offering to Vulcan, willingly and deservedly fulfilling their vow under the charge of [...].

[*RIB* 1700 add. Chesterholm (Vindolanda)]

Altar found in 1914 west of the fort. Now on loan to Vindolanda Museum from Chesters Museum.

The inscription's spelling *Vindolandesses* in place of *Vindolandenses* reflects spoken Latin (Mann 1971, 222); cf. the *venatores Banniesses* from Bewcastle (*RIB* 1905). For other dedications to the *Domus Divina* (Divine House) see **F16**, **F38**. For *Numina Augustorum* (Divine Powers) see the introduction to the section on Religion.

F42 The *curia* of the Textoverdi 2nd or 3rd century AD

To the goddess Sattada, the assembly of the Textoverdi fulfilled its vow willingly and deservedly.

[*RIB* 1695. Beltingham, Northumberland]

Altar found in 1835 in Beltingham churchyard. Now in the Great North Museum, Hancock.

The findspot of this inscription, 3 km. south-east of Chesterholm, suggests that the Textoverdi inhabited the area of the South Tyne. This single inscription is the unique evidence thus far found both for the existence of a tribe called the *Textoverdi* and the deity *Sattada* to whom this altar is dedicated. The inscription is particularly interesting for the evidence it provides of the spread of concepts of Roman government to some of the most far-flung parts of the province, though the find-spot's closeness to military bases should equally be noted.

(c) GUILDS

F43 The guild of *peregrini* at Silchester — Date uncertain

[...] of Atticus [... without their offerings] or contributions, [gave from his (or their) own resources, this gift ent]rusted [to him (or them) by the guild of *peregr*]*ini* [dwelling at Calleva].

[*RIB* 69. Silchester (Calleva)]

Dedication slab found in 1907 in the shrine of a Romano-Celtic temple. Now in Reading Museum.

The *peregrini* belonging to this guild at Silchester were probably immigrants, citizens of other cities who have come to Silchester most likely for commercial purposes. Alternatively, they may simply be people lacking in Roman citizenship. This latter alternative assumes that the inscription predates the *constitutio Antoniniana* of AD 212 (which made Roman citizenship almost universal throughout the Empire). Frere and Fulford (2002) suggest a late 1st- or early 2nd-century date for the inscription. For two other practically identical texts, which between them guarantee the restorations to this rather fragmentary inscription see *RIB* 70, 71.

F44 Nonius Romanus statue base — AD 152

To the [god] Mars Lenus otherwise Ocelus Vellaunus and to the Divine Power of the Emperor, Marcus Nonius Romanus, in return for freedom from liability of the college, gave this gift from his own resources, ten days before the Kalends of September, in the consulate of Glabrio and Homulus [23rd August, AD 152].

[*RIB* 309. Caerwent (Venta Silurum)]

Statue-base found in 1904 in house XI. Now in Newport Museum.

The relief on the statue base depicts a goose (*CSIR* 1.5, no. 13). Vellaunus is elsewhere identified with Mercury, one of whose familiars is a goose. A large temple of Mars Lenus is known at Trier in Gallia Belgica, a centre of the cult (where he is known always as "Lenus Mars" rather than, as here, "Mars Lenus"); this may suggest that Nonius Romanus came from Trier. Note that 23rd August is the date of the Roman feast of the Vulcanalia. The nature of the guild referred to is unknown. For *Numen Augusti* see the introduction to the section on Religion.

F45 Two guilds at Lincoln — Date unknown

(i) The .... ward of the guild of Mercury.

[*RIB* 270. Lincoln (Lindum)]

Inscribed plinth from monumental building; found in 1845 in High Street premises. Now lost.

(ii) .... of the guild of Apollo.

[*RIB* 271. Lincoln (Lindum)]

Moulded stone from a portico; found in 1785 on what is now called Lindum Road. Now lost.

Both of these inscriptions appear on building blocks, very probably from guild-rooms. The stones commemorate guilds of worshippers of Mercury and Apollo. The *vicus* referred to in **(i)** is a ward within the colony, whose name is irrecoverable from the recorded reading HRAPO. **(i)** was found with coins of Domitian and Antoninus Pius.

F46 A Lincoln guild treasurer AD 193–211

To the Goddesses of the Fates and to the Divine Powers of the Emperors, Gaius Antistius Frontinus, *curator* for a third time, gave (or dedicated) this altar at his own expense.

[*RIB* 247. Lincoln (Lindum)]

Altar found in 1884 on south side of the lower Roman city. Now in St Swithun's Church, Lincoln.

It is impossible to be certain of what Frontinus had charge (as *curator*); he may, as *RIB* suggests, be a guild-treasurer.

(d) ROADS

F47 Altar to the god who devised roads AD 191

To the god who devised roads and paths, Titus Aurelius Dasso made a vow willingly, joyfully and deservedly. Quintus Varius Vitalis, *beneficiarius consularis* restored the sacred altar, when Apronianus and Bradua were consuls.

[*RIB* 725 add. Catterick (Cataractonium)]

Altar found in 1620 at Thornborough-on-Swale or Catterick Bridge. Now lost.

For *beneficiarius consularis* see **F10**. On the roads leading to Catterick cf. **G9** (*Tab. Vindol.* 2.343, 21), which refers to their bad state of repair (nearly a century before the date of this inscription).

F48 Milestone on territory of Caerhun AD 120–121

The Emperor Caesar Trajan Hadrian Augustus, *pontifex maximus*, in his 5th year of tribunician power, father of his country, three times consul. From Kanovium, 8 miles.

[*RIB* 2265 = BM 1883,0725.1.

Near Llanfairfechan, Gwynedd]

Milestone found in 1888, about 11 kilometres (nearly 7 miles) west of Caerhun fort, buried in a field. Now in the British Museum.

This fine example stands 1.67 m high. The distance is measured from Caerhun, the fort on whose territory it stands. It gives the correct form of the Roman name for Caerhun (Rivet and Smith 1979, 297). Like **F25**, it prematurely credits Hadrian with the title *pater patriae*.

F49 A milestone from Buxton Date unknown

... with tribunician power, twice consul, father of his country, from Navio 11 miles.

[*RIB* 2243. Buxton, Derbyshire, nearly 11 Roman miles SW of Brough-on-Noe (Navio).]

A milestone found in 1862 in Hardwick Square. Now in Buxton Museum.

The distance on this milestone is measured from the fort of Brough-on-Noe in whose territory it was set up. Milestones are also an important source of information on the dates of road building and repair, though in this case the crucial imperial name is missing.

F50 Hesket milestone AD 307–337

For the Emperor Caesar Flavius Valerius Constantinus Pius Felix Invictus Augustus.

[*RIB* 2288 add. Hesket, Cumbria]

Milestone found in 1776 on Roman road between Carlisle and Penrith. Now lost.

This milestone may be assumed to have lain on the territory of the *civitas Carvetiorum* (as the Brougham and Langwathby milestones, **F30** and **F31**)

SECTION G

MILITARY LIFE

(a) GENERAL ADMINISTRATION

G1 One veteran writes to another. *c.* AD 65/70–80

To [...], time-expired veteran of the emperor, time-expired veteran . . .

[*Bloomberg WT* 20 London (Londinium)]

A silver fir writing tablet, incomplete, but with evidence of writing on both sides.

The Latin *emerito*, used twice, is 'a military veteran who has served his time and has been honourably discharged' (Tomlin, ad. loc.). The qualifying word *Aug[usti]*, 'of the emperor', is most odd, other instances being limited to Rome, and Tomlin thinks that the recipient may be 'a veteran of the guard who, like an *euocatus*, has been retained for military service, whether in the provincial administration or in a military training capacity.' The inner face of the tablet is illegible, having been overwritten many times.

G2 A letter from Wroxeter? *c.* AD 80–90/5

... to [...]nor, son of Gessinus; Intervinaris wrote (this) at ?Viroconium.

[*Bloomberg WT* 23 London (Londinium)]

An almost complete outer face of a silver fir writing-tablet.

The name of the recipient has been suggested as a Greek derivation such as *Antenor* or *Nicanor*; while the patronymic *Gessinus* is otherwise unknown, though at least two potters producing Samian ware were called *Gessus*. The place-name is poorly written, but Tomlin writes assuringly ad. loc. that 'in view of Wroxeter's importance in the mid 1st century AD as a legionary base, it is tempting to read *Viroconi* nonetheless, by supposing that the writer misspelled it in some way.'

G3 'Please forward' Late Flavian

At Newstead or Carlisle, for Marcus Julius Martialis.

[*Britannia* 19 (1988), 496–7 no. 31 = *RIB* 2.4.2443.10. Carlisle (Luguvalium)]

Writing tablet found in excavation in a late Flavian context in Castle Street. Now in Tullie House Museum, Carlisle.

The loss of the intervocalic (v) in *Lugu(v)|a[l]io* may indicate unfamiliarity with the name, which is correctly spelt on *Tab. Vindol.* I.22 line 9. This is the earliest attestation of the two place names. Martialis clearly might be found at either of the two forts which lie at the ends of a direct transverse road across the Cheviots. His *tria nomina* suggest that he was either a legionary soldier or centurion, or an auxiliary centurion or decurion. A stilus tablet dated to 7 November AD 83, attests the presence of men of legion XX at Carlisle in the Flavian period (see Tomlin 1992 for a discussion of the text), while **F11** records a cavalry unit, the *ala Sebosiana.* This tablet was subsequently reused (there are traces of a secondary text) before it found its way into the late Flavian deposit.

G4 A military strength report — Last decade of 1st century AD

18 May, net number of the First Cohort of Tungrians, of which the commander is Julius Verecundus the prefect,		752
	including centurions 6,	
of whom there are absent:		
guards of the governor		46
at the office of Ferox		
at Coria		337
	including centurions (?)2	
at London	centurion	1
(lines 10–16 not translated here, though numbers legible)		
total absentees		456
	including centurions 5	
remainder present		296
	including centurion 1	
from these:		
sick		15
wounded		6
suffering from inflammation of the eyes		10
total of these		31
remainder, fit for active service		265
	including centurion 1	

[*Tab. Vindol,* 2.154. Chesterholm (Vindolanda)]

A diptych found in the ditch of the pre-Hadrianic fort of Period 1.

This is one of a handful of records of the actual strength of units, apart from a relatively large number of late date, all referring to the same unit, from Dura Europos. It is the only one found so far in Britain, and the only one anywhere which is not written on papyrus, as it belongs to the enormous number of ink writing-tablets produced by Vindolanda. It is unique in being the actual strength of a *cohors milliaria peditata,* the infantry unit nominally one thousand strong, in this case the *Cohors I Tungrorum*, known from the evidence of other tablets to be at Vindolanda at this time. Oddly it has only six centurions, appropriate for the smaller size unit, the *cohors quingenaria peditata,* not the ten appropriate to the larger unit. This suggests perhaps that the unit is in process of enlargement. A total of 752 would fit the larger unit with a likely theoretical strength of 800 (ten centuries of 80 men). Many men are absent: 46 are detached as guards of the provincial governor; no fewer than 337 are at Coria, which as noted above, **C23**, is thought to be Corbridge on the strength of this and other Vindolanda documents. Of the 296 men present, 31 are unfit for duty, which is not a remarkable percentage for military units, *pace* Bowman and Thomas 1994, 98, who think it is. There is no need to think of the wounded as wounded in battle; accidental injuries are common enough. The number away from the fort shows how real was the problem Trajan saw (Pliny, *Letters*, 10.22): *curandum, ne milites a signis absint,* "Care must be taken that the soldiers be not away from their units" (standards, literally), and how insoluble it was.

G5 British cavalry — *c.* AD 97–*c.* AD 102/3

... the Britons are unprotected by armour (?). There are very many cavalry. The cavalry do not use swords nor do the wretched Britons mount in order to throw javelins.

[*Tab. Vindol.* 2.164. Chesterholm (Vindolanda)]

A diptych found in Room IV, Period 3?

This is apparently "a military memorandum of some kind describing the fighting characteristics and qualities of the native Britons with particular reference to cavalry" (Bowman and Thomas 1994, 106). It may be understood to refer to hostile Britons, or to the suitability for recruitment of native Britons. There is no certain reference to native British cavalry fighting against the Roman army. Bowman and Thomas 1994, 107 cite Tacitus *Agricola* 36 as evidence, but this clearly refers to the Roman cavalry. Formation of Britons into a Roman cavalry regiment seems assured by the existence of an *ala I Britannica,* but Kennedy, 1977 argued that this title only indicated that the regiment had been stationed in Britain. This text is the first definite evidence that Britons fought as cavalry, whether against or for Rome. If it does refer to the quality of native recruits, NIMIVM must be translated with its primary meaning of "too many". This would then mean that too many Britons wanted to be taken on as cavalry, as opposed to infantry (cavalry were better-paid) but they were unsuitable for the reasons stated. BRITTVNCVLI, "wretched Britons", is noteworthy as a term of contempt.

NB 'mount', for Latin *resident,* might better be translated as 'sit back' or 'sit deep'; Roman saddles did not have stirrups, and as reconstruction archaeology has shown, a 'deep seat' was crucial for any rider throwing a spear not to lose his balance completely (CG).

G6 Carpentry and joinery supplies — Last decade of 1st century AD

Metto (?) to his Advectus (?) very many greetings. I have sent you wooden materials through the agency of Saco: hubs, number, 34 axles for carts, number, 38 of them in an axle turned on the lathe, number, 1 spokes, number, 300 planks (?) for a bed, number, 26 seats, number, 8 (?) knots (?), number, 2 (?) boards (?), number, 20+ ..., number, 29 benches (?), number, 6. I have sent you goat-skins, number, 6 (2nd hand) I pray that you are in good health, brother.

[*Tab. Vindol.* 2.309 Inv.no.87.596.d. 20 x 26 mm Chesterholm (Vindolanda)]

This very fragmented tablet is a list of material supplied to the army. The majority are items from a carpenter – axles, planks, and so on – described as 'wooden materials.' Both the man who sent it and the man receiving it seem to have been civilian contractors supplying the army. The numbers of the items would suggest that it is quite a significant contract, and it further indicates the demands placed on the British economy by the Roman army – and the opportunities which it provided for native Britons.

G7 Accommodation needed — Last decade of 1st century AD

Order (accommodation?) to be given to (*name lost*); accommodation moreover where the horses are well housed. Farewell, my dearest brother.

(*Back*) To Flavius Cerialis

[*Tab. Vindol.* 2. 632 Inv.no.93.1246. 94 x 36 mm Chesterholm (Vindolanda)]

This is the right-hand column of a letter to Flavius Cerialis, the prefect or officer-in-charge of the Ninth Cohort of Batavians at Vindolanda, who is perhaps best known from the birthday-party invitation which Claudia Severina wrote to her friend Sulpicia Lepidina, who was Cerialis' wife (**G10** Vindolanda Tablet 2.291). His name is written in large letters known as 'address script' on the back. It seems to be an order in writing from Cerialis to another soldier. The message seems to be less of a request than an instruction to sort accommodation out – for the horses as much as the humans!
See http://vto2.classics.ox.ac.uk/index.php/tablets/search-for-tablets?tablet=632&submit=View for full details.

G8 A soldier's letter — *c.* AD 97–AD 102/3

Chrauttius to Veldeius his brother and old messmate, very many greetings. And I ask you, brother Veldeius – I am surprised that you have written nothing back to me for such a long time – whether you have heard anything from our elders, or about ... in which unit he is; and greet him from me in my words and Virilis the veterinary doctor. Ask him *(Virilis)* whether you may send through one of my friends the pair of shears which he promised me in exchange for money. And I ask you, brother Virilis, to greet from me our sister Thuttena. Write back to us how Velbuteius is (?). *(2nd hand?)* It is my wish that you enjoy the best of fortune. Farewell. *(Back, 1st hand)* (Deliver) at London. To Veldedeius, *equisio* of the governor, from his brother Chrauttius.

[*Tab. Vindol.* 2.310. Chesterholm (Vindolanda)]

A diptych found in Room VIA, Period 3.

VELDEDEIVS seems to be the correct form of the name of the addressee, as VELDEDII occurs on a leather off-cut from Vindolanda, discovered on the floor of a room near to the find-spot of this tablet and identified as belonging to horse equipment, appropriate for an *equisio.* It is the general view that FRATER here, "brother" is simply a term of affection, not of relationship, cf. **G9**, as a true brother would hardly be addressed as an "old messmate". A further difficulty is that Chrauttius seems to be Germanic and Veldedeius seems to be Celtic. This of course means that "parents" also cannot be literal, and that "sister" is simply a term of affection, as in **G10**. An alternative view that could perhaps be considered is that the relation ships were real: if the two brothers had served together for some time, which is not unparalleled, "old messmate" might be used almost playfully. The names of the two brothers would then reflect some oddity in a mixed frontier population. "Parents" could then be taken literally; "sister" remains ambiguous. Thuttena, whatever her relationship to Chrauttius, is one of the few women referred to, other than officers' wives, in connection with the Roman army. Another possible example is in *Tab. Vindol.* 2. 181, *contubernalis Tagamatis,* which it is suggested refers to the unofficial "wife" of a soldier. Bowman and Thomas (1994, 290) argue that LONDINI, a locative, must imply that the letter had been sent to Veldedeius in London, and had simply been received in London and brought to Vindolanda. An ***equisio***, apparently the same as a *strator,* was a groom, but in later contexts *stratores* have the job of inspecting horses bought for the army. Veldedeius could either be accompanying the governor or engaged in official business. Alternatively he could have been detached for service in London as the governor's ***equisio***, and had now returned to his unit at Vindolanda, carrying with him this old letter.

G9 Concerning supplies ?*c.* AD 104–120

Octavius to his brother Candidus, greetings. The hundred pounds of sinew from Marinus – I will settle up. From the time when you wrote about this matter, he has not even mentioned it to me. I have several times written to you that I have bought about five thousand *modii* of ears of grain, on account of which I need cash. Unless you send me some cash, at least five hundred *denarii,* the result will be that I shall lose what I have laid out as a deposit, about three hundred *denarii,* and I shall be embarrassed. So, I ask you, send me some cash as soon as possible. The hides which you write are at Catterick – write that they be given to me, and the wagon about which you write. And write to me what is with that wagon. I would have already been to collect them except that I did not care to injure the animals while the roads are bad. See with Tertius about the eight and a half *denarii* which he received from Fatalis. He has not credited them to my account. Know that I have completed the 170 hides and I have 119 *modii* of threshed *bracis.* Make sure that you send me cash so that I may have ears of grain on the threshing floor. Moreover, I have already finished threshing all that I had. A messmate of our friend Frontius has been here. He was wanting me to allocate (?) him hides, and that being so, was ready to give cash. I told him I would give him the hides by 1 March. He decided that he would come on 13 January. He did not turn up nor did he take any trouble to obtain them since he had hides. If he had given the cash, I would have given him them.

I hear that Frontinius Julius has for sale at a high price the leather ware (?) which he bought here for five *denarii* apiece. Greet Spectatus and ... and Firmus. I have received letters from Gleuco. Farewell.

(Back) (Deliver) at Vindolanda.

[*Tab* . *Vindol.* 2.343, 21. Chesterholm (Vindolanda)]

Room XIV, Period 4. Two complete diptychs.

The ink was still wet when this was folded. It has been written in two columns but beginning with the right-hand one, suggesting that the writer was left-handed. Spectatus and Firmus seem to be military personnel, known from *Tab. Vindol.* 2.180. Firmus had been responsible for issuing supplies to legionaries, and it has been suggested that some or all of the people referred to may be legionary centurions. A number of identifications have been suggested for Candidus, who also seems to be military, including a Candidus on *Tab. Vindol.* 2.180, 181. The tablet comes from the rooms at the end of the barrack, which should be the centurion's quarters. Bowman and Thomas (1994, 322) think some or all of the people might be *optiones*, as concerned with supplies. Who Octavius himself was, is uncertain, whether civilian or military. The sums of money and quantity of goods involved are considerable. It is difficult to be sure what is going on here, in view of the uncertainties about the people involved, and our lack of knowledge on how the army was supplied. It is certainly the procuring of supplies on a large scale, presumably for the army's needs, and quite possibly from a civilian contractor, with some fascinating details. There is archaeological evidence from Catterick for a leather production centre, cf. Burnham and Wacher 1990,111–117; Wilson 2002, 53–54 and Ch. 27. The document is good evidence for the importance of hides and leather in army use, for all kinds equipment and tents. 'Sinew' was a key material used in Roman artillery.

G10 Invitation to a birthday party *c.* AD 97–1 AD 102/3

Claudia Severa to her Lepidina greetings. On 11 September, sister, for the day of the celebration of my birthday, I give you a warm invitation to make sure that you come to me, to make the day more enjoyable for me by your arrival, if you are present (?). Give my greetings to your Cerialis. My Aelius and my little son send him (?) their greetings.

(2nd hand) I shall expect you, sister. Farewell, sister, my dearest soul, as I hope to prosper, and hail.

(*Back, 1st hand)* To Sulpicia Lepidina, wife of Cerialis, from Severa.

[*Tab. Vindol.* 2.291. Chesterholm (Vindolanda)]

Room VIA, Period 3.

Claudia Severa is the wife of Aelius Brocchus. He was a commanding officer, perhaps stationed at Briga, the location of which is not known. She has added a note in her own hand to the birthday invitation, the earliest known example of writing in Latin by a woman. Sulpicia Lepidina is the wife of Flavius Cerialis, prefect of the Ninth Cohort of Batavians at Vindolanda.

G11 A garment or armour sent for cleaning before AD 157?

Century of Domitius Maternus, (property) of Aulius Severus. Smoothed and for (?) darning.

[*Britannia* 42 (2011), 459–60 Caerleon (Isca Silurum)]

Priory Field, within the legionary fortress. Oblong lead tag 85 x 34 mm, with a hole pierced at one end. Found folded up in 2008, but now opened and cleaned.

The lead label is inscribed in cursive letters with a stilus, and is, as *RIB* puts it, 'the Roman equivalent of a laundry label, identifying the owner of the garment attached, and what was to be done to it.' A note of caution is added, however, because craftsmen in a legionary workshop might include *lamnae leviatares* or 'polishers of pieces of armour', so Severus might have been having his armour cleaned or even 'smoothed out' and perhaps 'decorated'; the final Latin words *lev(i)gatam et pingatarem* bear either interpretation. Domitius Maternus may be the same centurion who was discharged with other ranks from the Egyptian Legio II Traiana at Nicopolis in AD 157 after entering service in AD 132/3, but the identification is very tentative.

b) SENIOR AND OTHER RANKS

G12 T. Flaminius, *aquilifer* (legio XIV Gemina) Before AD 61

[Titus] Flaminius, son of Titus, of the Pollian voting tribe, from Faventia, aged 45 years, of 22 years' service, a soldier of the Fourteenth Legion Gemina; I have done my service as *aquilifer* and now am here. *(4 lines of advice on leading a good life follow.)*

[*RIB* 292 add. Wroxeter (Viroconium)]

Base of a sculptured tombstone, found in 1861 in the Roman cemetery on the east side of Wroxeter. Now in Rowley's House Museum, Shrewsbury.

The absence of a *cognomen* suggests an early date, as does the omission of the legion's titles *Martia Victrix* which it was awarded on the occasion of the suppression of the Boudican rebellion in AD 61 (cf. **B13**). Faventia, in Gallia Cisalpina, is now Faenza, northern Italy.

G13 An *eques* of legion IX 1st century AD

(In memory) of Quintus Cornelius, son of Quintus, of the Claudian voting tribe, cavalryman in the Ninth Legion from the century of Cassius Martialis, aged 40 years, served 19 years, lies buried here.

[*RIB* 254. Lincoln (Lindum)]

Tombstone found in 1880, half a mile south of the south gate of the extended colonia. Now lost; sketch in the Society of Antiquaries.

Legionary cavalrymen, unlike auxiliaries, were not organised in separate troops *(turmae)* but were carried on the books of the centuries. For the dating of this stone see **B11**.

G14 Amandus the engineer Antonine

Sacred to Brigantia: Amandus, engineer, by command fulfilled the order.

[*RIB* 2091 add. Birrens (Blatobulgium), Dumfriesshire]

Statue of the goddess Brigantia, found in 1731 in the ruins of a building outside the fort at Birrens. Now in the Museum of Scotland, Edinburgh.

Architectus ('engineer') was attached to a legion but not necessarily a legionary grade, so presumably Amandus was attached to the Sixth Legion based at York. He has been identified with the *Val. Amandus discens (architectum)* (i.e. an apprentice *architectus*) of legion I Minervia attested near Bonn in AD 209; however, archaeological evidence suggests that Birrens had been abandoned in the AD 180s. This dedication to the territorial deity Brigantia suggests that the territory of the Brigantes extended at least as far north as Birrens. The winged figure of the goddess, carved in high relief and standing in a gabled niche, has a gorgon's head on her breast and wears a plumed helmet encircled by a turreted crown. In her right hand she holds a spear, in her left, a globe; to her left stands her shield, to her right an omphalos-stone, associated with Juno Caelestis. These attributes equate her with both Minerva Victrix and Juno Caelestis, consort of Jupiter Dolichenus (see Joliffe 1941). It is said that when first discovered the statuette had traces of gilding (photo in *RIB* online).

G15 A legate of the sixth legion — Late 2nd century AD

To the holy god Serapis, Claudius Hieronymianus, legate of the Sixth Legion Victrix, built this temple from ground level.

[*RIB* 658 add. York (Eboracum)]

A dedication slab found in 1770 near Tanner Row, south-east of the Old Railway Station, York. Now in the Yorkshire Museum.

Hieronymianus may be identified with the senator mentioned in Ulpian, *Digest* 33.7.12.40, and with the governor of Cappadocia at the end of the second and beginning of the third century (Tertullian, *Ad Scapula* 3; Birley 2005, 265). The inscription was found in association with a building thought to be the temple in question, and is one of very few pieces of evidence attesting the worship of this Egyptian deity in Britain. For other Eastern deities, see **J46–J56**.

G16 A pilot of legion VI — ?Severan

To the African, Italian and Gallic Mother goddesses, Marcus Minucius Audens, soldier of the Sixth Legion Victrix, helmsman in the Sixth Legion, willingly, gladly and deservedly fulfilled his vow.

[*RIB* 653 add. York (Eboracum)]

An altar found in Micklegate, opposite Holy Trinity Church, York. Now in the Yorkshire Museum, York.

The helmsman was ranked next below the captain in a Roman warship. Audens is the only legionary helmsman known. His presence at York points to the importance of access to the sea for supplying a legionary base. The dedication to African, Italian and Gallic mother goddesses may be an indicator of the mixed origins of the men then serving at York, very probably in the wake of the Severan campaigns. (For a discussion of men from Africa serving in legion VI cf. Swan 1992).

G17 A camp prefect of legion XX — Early 3rd century AD

To the spirits of the departed, Marcus Aurelius Alexander, camp prefect of the Twentieth Legion Valeria Victrix, a native of Syria Os[roene], lived 72 years, [...]yces and S[... his heirs set this up].

[*RIB* 490. Chester (Deva)]

Fragments of a tombstone found in 1887 in the fortress north wall (east part). Now in the Grosvenor Museum.

The names Marcus Aurelius suggest citizenship acquired after AD 161. Alexander was probably recruited at the time of Marcus' and Verus' Parthian war. This is the latest dated use of the title *praefectus castrorum* which was gradually superseded during the second century by *praefectus legionis*. The reading Syrus Os[roenus] is dubious; Syrus Co[mmagenus] is more probable. This area lay to the west of the Euphrates in northern Syria.

G18 Caecilius Avitus, *optio* ?3rd century AD

To the spirits of the departed, Caecilius Avitus, from Emerita Augusta, *optio* of the Twentieth Legion Valeria Victrix, of fifteen years' service, lived 34 years. His heir had this set up.

[*RIB* 492. Chester (Deva)]

Tombstone found in 1891 in the fortress north wall. Now in the Grosvenor Museum, Chester.

An *optio* served as second-in-command to a centurion. The bearded figure of the *optio* stands in a niche above the inscription. He is holding a tall knob-headed staff in his right hand, and the handle of a square case of writing tablets in his left. His head is bare and he wears over his tunic a heavy cloak *(sagum)*, the ends of which cross and hang down in two tails. A sword with a large round pommel hangs at his right side. For photograph of this tombstone with paintwork restored, see *Cambridge Latin Course* III, page 74. Emerita Augusta, modern Mérida in Spain, was a colony in Lusitania.

G19 Titinius Felix, *beneficiarius* 3rd century AD

To the spirits of the departed, Titinius Felix, *beneficiarius* of the legate of the Twentieth Legion Valeria Victrix, served 22 (?) years, lived 45 years; Julia Similina his wife and heir [set this up].

[*RIB* 505 add. *Chester* (Deva)]

A tombstone found in 1887 in the fortress north wall (east part). Now in the Grosvenor Museum, Chester.

A date in the third century is indicated by the specific mention of the wife of this serving soldier, and also by the absence of a *praenomen*. On the left hand margin of the inscription is a figure facing inwards, dressed in a cloak, tunic and Phrygian cap, identified as an Amazon in *RIB* 505 add. On the right there was probably a corresponding figure (*CSIR* I.9, no. 37). For other *beneficiarii* see **B9**, **F8–F10**, **F47**, **J12**, **J31**.

G20 Eltaominus, veteran, former engineer Date unknown

To Fortune the home-bringer, Eltaominus, veteran and former engineer of the *ala Vettonum*, has paid his vow gladly, willingly, deservedly.

[*Britannia* 45 (2014) 434, no. 4. Binchester (Vinovia)]

County Durham. Sandstone altar found in excavations of the external bath-house on Dere Street in 2013. Now stored in the Bowes Museum.

The altar is carved from buff sandstone, 50 cm by 65 cm and 51 cm deep, with a bull carved in high relief on its left hand side. On the top, there is a shallow round *focus* above a recessed die, with bolsters on either side. The altar is carved in neat almost square lettering 30 mm high. The name *Eltaominus* is unparalleled. This is the first instance of an *architectus* being associated with a cavalry *ala*.

G21 An armourer of legion XX Either first or third century AD

Julius Vitalis, armourer of the Twentieth Legion Valeria Victrix, of 9 years' service, aged 29, by origin a Belga, with funeral at the cost of the guild of armourers. Here he lies.

[*RIB* 156 add. Bath (Aquae Sulis)]

Tombstone found in 1708 near the Fosse Way. Now in the Roman Baths Museum.

The Latin *Natione Belga*, 'by origin a Belga', very probably indicates an origin in the *civitas Belgarum* centred on Winchester, though the possibility of an origin in the province of Gallia Belgica cannot be totally excluded. The armourers of the legion had organised themselves into a guild as was the case with a number of junior ranks and tradesmen within the army. The date of this stone is disputed, as it has both first- and third-century dating indicators.

c) LEGIONARIES

(For further references to legionaries, see the Index)

G22 C. Murrius Modestus (legio II Adiutrix) AD 71–*c.* AD 87

Gaius Murrius Modestus, son of Gaius, of the Arnensian voting tribe, from Forum Iulii, soldier of the Second Legion Adiutrix Pia Fidelis, from the century of Julius Secundus, aged 25 years, served ... years, here he lies.

[*RIB* 157. Bath (Aquae Sulis)]

Rectangular tombstone found (with ***G25****) before 1590 on the Fosse Way, 1.6 kilometres north-east of the baths. Now lost.*

The legion, based at Lincoln when it first arrived in Britain in AD 71, is thought to have been the first unit stationed at Chester, when the fortress was constructed in the late AD 70s (cf. **B23**). It remained there until its withdrawal from Britain in about AD 87. Forum Iulii is most probably the site of that name at Fréjus, in Provence (southern France), though there is another Forum Iulii at Cividale del Friuli in north-east Italy.

G23 C. Juventius Capito (legio II Adiutrix) *c.* AD 77–*c.* AD 87

Gaius Juventius Capito, son of Gaius, of the Claudian voting tribe, from Aprus, soldier of the Second Legion Adiutrix Pia Fidelis, from the century of Julius Clemens, aged 40 years, served 17 years.

[*RIB* 476. Chester (Deva)]

A tombstone found in 1891 in the fortress north wall (west part). Now in the Grosvenor Museum.

Aprus (or Apri) is a Claudian colony in southern Thrace (western Turkey). This is one of three tombstones (the others are *RIB* 475 (**B23**) and 477) from Chester recording soldiers from this city serving in II Adiutrix.

G24 Q. Valerius Fronto (legio II Adiutrix) *c.* AD 77–*c.* AD 87

Quintus Valerius Fronto, son of Quintus, of the Claudian voting tribe, from Celeia, soldier of the Second Legion Adiutrix Pia Fidelis, aged 50 years, served 25 (+) years.

[*RIB* 479. Chester (Deva)]

A tombstone found in 1891 in the fortress north wall (west part). Now in the Grosvenor Museum.

Celeia (modern Celje in Slovenia) was a city *(a municipium)* in the south-east part of Noricum. The numerals giving Fronto's years of service are damaged, but were probably between 25 and 29 years: there certainly were cases, particularly in the first century, where soldiers served more than the normal term of 25 years. Since II Adiutrix was not raised until AD 69, Fronto must have been transferred into it from another unit.

G25 M. Valerius Latinus (legio XX) 1st century AD

To the spirits of the departed, Marcus Valerius Latinus, son of Marcus, citizen of Equestris, soldier of the Twentieth Legion, aged 35 years, of 20 years' service, lies buried here.

[*RIB* 158. Bath (Aquae Sulis)]

Tombstone found with ***G22****. Now lost.*

Latinus came from Colonia Iulia Equestris (Nyon, on Lake Geneva in Switzerland), a colony founded by Caesar for the veterans of legion X Equestris. Stylistically, the stone should date no later than the early second century and, given the absence of the titles *Valeria Victrix*, is likely to be pre- AD 61.

G26 P. Rustius Crescens (legio XX) ?late 1st – early 2nd century AD

To the spirits of the departed and to Publius Rustius Crescens of the Fabian voting tribe, from Brixia, soldier of the Twentieth Legion Valeria Victrix, aged 30 years, served for 10 years; Groma, his heir, had this made.

[*RIB* 503. Chester (Deva)]

A tombstone found in 1887 in the north wall (east part). Now in the Grosvenor Museum, Chester.

Of the figure above the inscription, only the left foot and a trace of the right remain (*CSIR* I.9, no. 34). Brixia is now Brescia in northern Italy. Very few Italians served in the legions after the time of Hadrian.

G27 Gabinius Felix (legio II Augusta) AD 211–222

Sacred to the spirits of the departed, Gabinius Felix, soldier of the Second Legion Augusta *Antoniniana*, lived 40 years; his heir had this set up.

[*RIB* 488. Chester (Deva)]

A tombstone found in 1891 in the fortress north wall (west part). Now in the Grosvenor Museum.

The title *Antoniniana* dates the text to AD 211–222. This stone was incorporated in the north wall when it was reconstructed. II Augusta was stationed at Caerleon; it can only be conjectured why Gabinius was visiting Chester. The two formulae *DMS, D(is) M(anibus) s(acrum)*, and *HPC*, h*(eres) p(onendum) c(uravit)*, do not recur at Chester. For the spelling *vixsit* in place of *vixit*, 'lived', see Mann 1971, 221.

G28 Vivius Marcianus (legio II Augusta) Probably 3rd century AD

To the spirits of the departed and to Vivius Marcianus, centurion of the Second Legion Augusta; Januaria Martina his most devoted wife set up this memorial.

[*RIB* 17 add. London (Londinium)]

Tombstone found in 1669 in St. Martin's Church, Ludgate Hill. Now in the Museum of London.

Below the inscription stands the figure of the centurion in a niche. He holds a scroll in his left hand, perhaps indicating an administrative role (see drawing in *RIB* online). Like **G29** and **G30**, Marcianus has been seconded to the staff of the governor in London. Collingwood (1928, 173) correctly identified the elaborate leaf-stop after the name as a blundered centurion sign. Thus the original reason for the date given by *RIB* – the permission to marry given by Severus to all serving soldiers – is invalid, since at no time did a centurion require such permission. (This error is corrected in *RIB* 17 add.) A third-century date would, however, still appear probable from the style of the inscription.

G29 Flavius Agricola (legio VI Victrix) Probably 3rd century AD

To the spirits of the departed, Flavius Agricola, soldier of the Sixth Legion Victrix, lived 42 years, 10 days; Albia Faustina had this made for her peerless husband.

[*RIB* 11 add. London (Londinium)]

Tomb found in 1787 in Goodman's Fields, the Minories, east of the Roman city wall. Now in the Museum of London on loan from the Society of Antiquaries of London.

The practice of allowing a soldier to marry during his term of service was first allowed by Septimius Severus (AD 193–211). This fact, together with the lack of *praenomen*, indicates a date for the inscription no earlier than the third century. A. Birley suggests that he may be a descendant of a man who was enfranchised when Julius Agricola was governor of Britain, taking the *nomen* of the then imperial family (Flavius) and giving the governor's *cognomen* to his son to pass on to his heirs (Birley 1979, 85).

G30 Julius Valens (legio XX Valeria Victrix) — Date unknown

To the spirits of the departed, Julius Valens, soldier of the Twentieth Legion Valeria Victrix, aged 40 years, lies here; his heir Flavius Attius having the matter in charge.

[*RIB* 13. London (Londinium)]

Tombstone found in 1776 in Church Lane, Whitechapel. Now lost.

Valens had probably been seconded to the governor's staff.

(d) AUXILIARIES

G31 A soldier of the First Cohort of Vangiones — AD 67

In the consulship of Fonteius Capito and Julius Rufus (AD 67), [... *day and month. Writer's name and description* ..., of the First Cohort] of Vangiones, . . . son . . . all . . .

[*Bloomberg WT* 48 London (Londonium)]

A silver fir writing-tablet, complete except for one corner, in two conjoining fragments, with some legible writing in the upper left of the inner recessed face.

The date provided by the consular names is secure, and Tomlin comments that its 'legible text is residual in its archaeological context (*c* AD 80– AD 90/5)', that is period 3 phase 1 (late) in the Bloomberg stratigraphy. The reading *uangio[...]* is also clear, and it must refer to the *Cohors I Vangionum milliaria equitata*, previously first attested in Britain in a diploma of AD 103 (*CIL* 16. 48). It belonged to the garrison of Britain at that time, and this document suggests strongly that it was one of the eight cohorts transferred to Britain from the German tribal area from which it was recruited in AD 61 (cf. Tacitus *Annals* xiv. 38 (LACTOR 11 F4.1). Its fragmentary nature makes it hard to identify precisely but it appears to be a will made by a soldier in favour of his son; it was excavated in a deposit dating to some 20 years after it was made. For another will from Roman Britain see **H36 (i)**.

G32 Ammonius, auxiliary centurion — Flavian

To the spirits of the departed: Ammonius (son of) Damio, centurion of the First Cohort of Spaniards, of 27 years' service (lies here). His heirs had this made.

[*RIB* 2213. Ardoch, Perthshire]

Tombstone found in, or before, 1672, reused in the so-called praetorium *(actually a medieval chapel). Now in the Hunterian Museum, Glasgow.*

The fact that *Dis Manibus*, 'to the spirits of the departed,' is written out in full in this inscription, that the soldier's name *Ammonius* appears in the nominative and that he served more than the standard 25-year term, means that this tombstone must date to the Flavian rather than the Antonine occupation of Scotland. Hence this soldier almost certainly took part in Agricola's campaigns.

G33 An auxiliary standard-bearer — Flavian

To the spirits of the departed, Flavinus, cavalryman in the *ala Petriana*, standard-bearer in the troop of Candidus, aged 25 years, of 7 years' service, lies buried here.

[*RIB* 1172. Hexham, Northumberland]

Tombstone found in 1881 in the foundations of a porch at Hexham Abbey and thought to have been transported there from Corbridge. Now within Hexham Abbey.

Above the inscription is a relief showing a cavalryman carrying a standard which bears a human portrait (an *imago*?), and riding down a naked barbarian (*CSIR* I.1, no 68). The unit appears without the honorary title *c(ivium) R(omanorum)* (attesting a block grant of Roman citizenship) which it had gained by AD 98. It was later doubled in size to become the one *ala milliaria* stationed in Britain.

G34 Missing weapons — Late 1st century AD to before AD 105

Docilis to his prefect Augurinus [...], greetings. As you ordered, we have attached below all the names of lancers who were missing lances, either who did not have fighting lances or who (did not have) the smaller *subarmales*, or who (did not have) regulation swords. Troop of Genialis senior: Verecundus, (one) fighting lance and two *subarmales*.

[*Britannia* 29 (1998), 55–63, no. 16. Carlisle (Luguvalium)]

Writing tablet, retrieved from a demolition deposit from the early Trajanic fort. Now in Tullie House Museum, Carlisle.

This is side one of a wooden writing tablet comprised of two diptychs, together giving four sides of text, all concerned with the loss of arms. This is the first known instance of an inspection leading to a report on missing weapons. Docilis is a decurion (in command of a *turma* or troop), reporting on behalf of the other troop commanders to their commanding officer, Augurinus. He uses conventional military language. This is the earliest occurrence of *lanciarius* (lancer), next known in the early third century. *Lancia pugnatoria* seems to refer to the thrusting spears normally used by the Roman cavalry. The term *subarmalis*, previously unknown in regard to weapons, seems to refer to a smaller throwing spear. *Gladia*, from neuter *gladium* for the more usual masculine *gladius*, is an archaic variant.

G35 Nectovelius — Antonine?

To the spirits of the departed, Nectovelius, son of Vindex, aged 29 years, of 9 years' service, a Brigantian, served in the Second Cohort of Thracians.

[*RIB* 2142 add. Mumrills, Stirlingshire]

Tombstone found in 1834 near the fort. Now in the Museum of Scotland, Edinburgh.

The lettering retains traces of red paint. This stone provides evidence for local recruitment to the *auxilia* in Britain (for the Brigantes, see **E12**). For other examples see Dobson and Mann 1973. E. Birley has argued for a date around AD 100 on the basis of the use of the formula *Dis M.*

G36 A successful boar hunt — Later 2nd or 3rd century AD

To the Divine Powers of the Emperors and to the Unconquered Silvanus, Gaius Tetius Veturius Micianus, prefect of the *ala Sebosiana*, on fulfilment of his vow willingly set this up for taking a wild boar of remarkable fineness which many of his predecessors had been unable to bag.

[*RIB* 1041 add. Bollihope Common, south of Stanhope, in Weardale, Co. Durham]

An altar found in 1747. Its exact findspot is unknown. Now in Stanhope Church.

The fort closest to the findspot of this inscription, Binchester, was occupied in the 3rd century by the *ala Vettonum*; the *ala Gallorum Sebosiana* was then stationed at Lancaster. Neither the garrison of Binchester nor the location of the *ala Sebosiana* is known in the later 2nd century. For *numina Augustorum* see the introduction to the section Religion.

G37 Death at Ambleside fort — 3rd or 4th century AD

To the good spirits of the departed, Flavius Fuscinus, retired from the centurionate, lived 55 years. To the good spirits of the departed, Flavius Romanus, record clerk, lived for 35 years, killed in the fort by the enemy.

[*JRS* 53 (1963), 160 no. 4 = *RIB* 3.3218. Ambleside (Galava)]

A double tombstone found in 1962 about 90 metres east of the fort. It had been reused as part of a modern drain.

The expansion of the 'B' as 'good' in *D(is) B(onis) M(anibus)* at the start of the inscription is speculative as it is unparalleled on a tombstone. The circumstances of Romanus's death are unknown; the stone is not dated but is very unlikely to be earlier than the third century AD. For the spelling *visit* for *vixit*, see Mann 1971, 223 and **G27**.

G38 A doctor at Housesteads — 3rd century AD

To the spirits of the departed (and) to Anicius Ingenuus, *medicus ordinarius* of the First Tungrian Cohort: he lived 25 years.

[*RIB* 1618 add. Housesteads (Vercovicium)]

Tombstone found in, or before, 1813. Now (2009) in the Great North Museum, Hancock.

Medicus ordinarius is most probably a doctor with the rank equivalent to that of a centurion.

e) UNITS

G39 The century of Julius Rufus — Hadrianic

The century of Julius Rufus (built this).

[*RIB* 1356. Between Benwell (Condercum) and Rudchester (Vindovala) on Hadrian's Wall]

The stone was found in 1804 probably near Denton Hall. Now in Denton Hall stable.

Julius Rufus is mentioned on two further inscriptions, *RIB* 1357 and 1386. This stone is assumed to relate to the original construction of the Wall.

G40 A cohort of legion II Augusta — Antonine?

The Fourth Cohort of the Second Legion *(built this).*

[*RIB* 1343. Benwell (Condercum)]

Building stone found before 1873 in Benwell fort. Now in Denton Hall stable.

This inscription is one of a group from the Benwell area which are more ornate than the usual simple building stones (drawing and photo in *RIB* online). They may not be Hadrianic at all, but may relate to a later rebuild. (See Hooley and Breeze 1968, esp. 104–5, discussing Stevens 1966). There is some evidence that Benwell fort remained in occupation when the frontier was moved forward to the Antonine Wall (*RIB* 1330).

G41 A cohort of legion VI Victrix — Antonine

The Tenth Cohort of the Sixth Legion Victrix Pia Fidelis rebuilt this.

[*RIB* 1388. Between Benwell (Condercum) and Rudchester (Vindovala)]

Building stone found in 1751 on the line of the Wall, probably near Heddon-on-the-Wall. Now lost.

This stone is very similar to *RIB* 1389 (**C37**), found at the same place, which has a consular date of AD 158.

G42 The Raeti Gaesati at Great Chesters — 3rd century AD

To the goddess Fortune, a detachment of the Raetian javelin-men, under the command of Tabellius Victor, centurion *(set this up)*.

[*RIB* 1724. Great Chesters (Aesica)]

Altar found in 1908 in the bath building south-east of Great Chesters fort. Now in the Museum of Antiquities, Newcastle-upon-Tyne.

The *Raeti Gaesati* were an irregular unit, a *numerus*, originally raised in Switzerland (see **D11**). On *numeri* in general see Southern 1989. For another dedication to Fortuna from a bath-house see **C21**.

G43 The Raeti Gaesati at Jedburgh — 3rd century AD

To Jupiter Best and Greatest, a detachment of Raetian javelin-men under the command of Julius Severinus, tribune, *(set this up)*.

[*RIB* 2117. Cappuck, Roxburgh, 6 kilometres east of Jedburgh on the line of Dere Street]

Altar, first noticed 1853, forming the lintel over the entrance to the north-west turret of Jedburgh Abbey. Now in the Abbey; cast in the Museum of Antiquities, Newcastle-upon-Tyne.

This inscription (together with *RIB* 2118, a text of *cohors I Fida Vardullorum*) is assumed to have been carried to Jedburgh Abbey from Cappuck, the nearest known Roman fort. The Raeti Gaesati were based at Risingham, together with the *cohors I Vangionum* (see **D11**), a military unit of which Severinus was presumably the tribune. Severinus is attested at Risingham on *RIB* 1212, an altar dedicated to *Fortuna Redux* on completion of the bath-house.

(f) THE FLEET

G44 L. Aufidius Pantera, fleet prefect — Mid- to late 130s AD

To Neptune, Lucius Aufidius Pantera, prefect of the British fleet, *(set up this)* altar.

[*RIB* 66. Lympne (Lemanis)]

Altar found in 1850 in the east gate of the Roman fort. Now in the British Museum, BM 1856,0701.5026

Pantera's command of the British fleet is approximately dated by a diploma of AD 133 (*CIL* 16.76) on which he is named as commander of a milliary *ala*, a post which he will have held shortly before his fleet command. The discovery of this second-century inscription reused in the late Roman fort at Lympne contributes to the evidence that there was an earlier site in the vicinity (cf. Reece 1989, 155). For another prefect of the British fleet see above, **C16** (Maenius Agrippa): for a detachment of the fleet on Hadrian's Wall, see **C9**. For evidence of a pilot, see **G16**.

(g) VETERANS AND THEIR FAMILIES

G45 A veteran of legion II Augusta and his wife 2nd or 3rd century AD

(i) To the spirits of the departed, Julius Valens, veteran of the Second Legion Augusta, lived 100 years; Julia Secundina, his wife, and Julius Martinus, his son, had this set up.

[*RIB* 363. Caerleon (Isca)]

Tombstone found about 1815 at Great Bulmore, 2 kilometres north-east of Caerleon fortress. Now in Caerleon Museum.

This inscription was found, together with seven others (including *RIB* 373, the memorial to Valens' wife, **G45 (ii)**), a coin of Trajan and other remains, suggesting that they may have formed part of a communal tomb.

(ii) To the spirits of the departed and the memory of Julia Secundina, his devoted mother, who lived 75 years; Gaius Julius Martinus her son had this set up.

[*RIB* 373. Caerleon (Isca)]

Tombstone found in 1815, at Great Bulmore. Now in Caerleon Museum.

The mother and son of this inscription are identical with the wife and son of **G45 (i)**

G46 Flavius Natalis, veteran 2nd or 3rd century AD

To the spirits of the departed, Titus Flavius Natalis, veteran, lived 65 years. This was set up by Flavius Ingenuinus and Flavius Flavinus, his sons, and Flavia Veldicca, his wife.

[*RIB* 358 add. Caerleon (Isca)]

Part of a tombstone found in 1909 about 900m west of Caerleon fortress. Now in Newport Museum.

Since Natalis was presumably a legionary, though he makes no mention of his unit, the stone will be post-Flavian in date, an ancestor rather than the veteran himself having been awarded citizenship under one of the Flavian emperors. For another veteran (presumably an auxiliary) who does not mention his unit see **J24**.

G47 Died on active service in Germany 3rd century AD

To the spirits of the departed, Tadia Vallaunius lived 65 years and Tadius Exuperatus, her son, lived 37 years and died on the German expedition. Tadia Exuperata, most devoted daughter, set this up to her mother and brother beside her father's tomb.

[*RIB* 369. Caerleon (Isca)]

A tombstone found about 1849 approximately 900m west of Caerleon fortress. Now in Caerleon Museum.

The German expedition cannot be identified with certainty. Ritterling suggested the German campaign of Caracalla. In the gable, in between the letters D and M, are a crescent and two rosettes. The lettering has traces of its original red paint. Vallaunius is a Celtic feminine.

SECTION H

CIVILIAN LIFE AND ECONOMIC ACTIVITY

INTRODUCTION

This section includes a range of inscriptions which illustrate civilian activity in Roman Britain, which was largely overlooked in the traditional histories of Roman Britain particularly in the early twentieth century, but which has in recent years attracted a great deal of attention, to the point where exploration of rural sites has now become a primary focus of archaeological work on Roman Britain. When one considers that the army is unlikely to have exceeded 40,000 personnel in total, compared to a population of Roman Britain of anywhere between 2,000,000 and 5,000,000 (current estimates seem to be moving back to a higher end of this spectrum), it is obvious that soldiers and military activity are over-represented in the surviving evidence, particularly in the Hadrian's Wall area. Since the 'epigraphic habit' was primarily part of military culture, this skewing of the surviving evidence is only to be expected. Moreover, as will be seen from the examples listed below, the surviving inscriptional evidence inevitably provides information about those from levels of society where literacy was prevalent in some way and who owned precious objects. It might be argued that the presence of graffiti indicates some ability in literacy at a fairly low level, especially the examples of casual writing in tileries (**H59, H60** for example). This may also be indicated by the survival of curse-tablets, which due to their religious nature are listed in **Section J** below but whose banality seems to points to some awareness of writing among what we might call 'ordinary members of Romano-British Society' for whom the loss of a cloak was a major issue (see also the introductory comments about curse-tablets in **Section J** on 'Religion'). On the other hand the find-spots indicate that most evidence for literacy comes from industrial or urban contexts, and it must always be recalled that in Roman Britain some 90% of the population was engaged in agriculture, and the vast majority of these people lived outside the urban areas which are often considered the hallmark of the 'Roman way of life'.

As has been noted above, inscriptions on stone largely reflect the 'epigraphic habit' of the military; those included in this section are from a much wider range of locations, many of them urban or rural, and many provide evidence for low-level literacy, particularly the graffiti scratched on dishes, pots and other possessions, usually the name of the owner (using the Latin genitive case as a rule), and on bricks and tiles. They represent a very small percentage of the enormous volume of tiny fragments, often of a single letter, not recorded in this collection but which indicate the wealth of epigraphic material which was created in the occupation period and which is now largely lost but can be glimpsed from the excavations at the Bloomberg site in London from 2010 to 2014. A number of these are included here, (**H15 – H20**), and they illustrate the possibilities that still more evidence may come to light in the future (see Roger S. O. Tomlin, *Roman London's first voices: writing tablets from the London* (Londinium). *Bloomberg Excavations, 2010–14* (Museum of London Archaeology Monograph 72, London, 2016). The finds of this site are of the utmost importance, not just because of the information which the writing tablets themselves contain, but because in the archaeological excavation it was possible to identify successive occurrences of raising up the ground level and constructing buildings, then levelling the site once again, leading to a very well-defined stratification into four periods, themselves sub-divided into two or three phases, and even tablets which did not carry a year-date could therefore be allocated to a very closely-defined time-frame (see Jessica Bryan, Julian Hill and Sadie Watson, 'The archaeological provenance and social and historical context of the tablets', in *Roman London's first voices*, pp. 31–58). In addition, they provide a wealth of evidence for trade and commercial practice in London's earliest years, and have enabled this section on civilian life to be expanded considerably over previous editions of this volume.

(a) PERSONAL (including marks of ownership)

There are numerous short inscriptions indicating ownership or some token of good wishes which can be seen on rings in *RIB* 2422 and on gemstones in *RIB* 2423. The presence of writing on such items indicates some pride in or demonstration of literacy among people wealthy enough to own them. More obvious signs of ownership are indicated on military equipment by graffiti or writing stamped and punched on to various items listed in *RIB* 2427 (weapons and other military equipment), 2428 (iron tools), 2429 (baldric and belt-fittings), and roundels in stone, pottery and bone (*RIB* 2438, 2439, 2440). Of the items below, **H3**, **H7**, **H13**, **H14** mark ownership.

H1 Addressees from the Bloomberg site London AD 65/70–80

(i) In London, to Mogontius

[*Bloomberg WT* 6 = EDCS-69100046. London (Londinium)]

Fragment of a silver fir writing-tablet

The address is not necessarily complete.The addressee's details are written on the outer face; the inner side is illegible, having been re-used many times.

(ii) You will give (this) to Junius the cooper, opposite (the house of) Catullus.

[*Bloomberg WT* 14 = EDCS-69100054. London (Londinium)]

A silver fir writing-tablet.

This address is probably complete; 'opposite' (Latin *contra*) would imply that Catullus is a better-known individual than Junius. The interior face was probably subjected to multiple re-use and has left no legible traces.

H2 An inscribed ring Pre-Flavian

(The seal) of Tiberius Claudius Catuarus

[*Britannia* 27 (1996), 455–56 no 48. Fishbourne, near Chichester, Sussex]

Gold ring found in excavations 200 m east of Fishbourne palace. The original is in the possession of the site developer; a copy is on display at Fishbourne Museum.

The inscription is incised retrograde. The name 'Catuarus' is Celtic, the *Catu*-element meaning 'battle'. Catuarus acquired Roman citizenship from the emperor Claudius or Nero. His possession of a gold ring, the badge of the aristocrat (Pliny, *Nat. Hist.* 33.32), suggests his elevation to the equestrian aristocracy, a reward, perhaps, for collaboration at the time of the Roman invasion. A parallel may be drawn with Ti. Claudius [To]gidubnus (**F16**), from the same area, perhaps a kinsman or ally, who also owed his citizenship and advance to Claudius or Nero.

H3 A boxwood comb AD 95–105

"Capictinus son of Carantius."

[*Britannia* 42 (2011), 451 = EDCS-64100329. Chesterholm (Vindolanda)]

A complete boxwood comb 96 x 59mm, 10mm thick, found in a Period II or III context (AD 95–105), scratched in cursive letters along the spine.

H4 Aufidius Olussa from Athens 1st or early 2nd century AD

Aulus Aufidius Olussa, of the voting tribe Pomptina, set up by his heir in accordance with his will, aged 70, born in Athens, here he lies.

[*RIB* 9 = BM 1852,0806.3. London (Londinium)]

Tombstone found in 1852 on Tower Hill. Now in the British Museum.

The phrase 'born in Athens' appears to be an addition, but is probably contemporary – an inadvertent omission by the stone-cutter?

H5 A woman of the Mediomatrici 1st or 2nd century AD

[...] To Rusonia Aventina, a citizen of the Mediomatrici, aged 58 years, here she lies: Lucius Ulpius Sestius, her heir, had this set up.

[*RIB* 163. Bath (Aquae Sulis)]

Tombstone found in 1803 in the borough walls. Now in the Roman Baths Museum.

The top of this tombstone is broken, though only decoration rather than words may be lost. The Mediomatrici were centred on Metz in northern France, in the province of Gallia Belgica.

H6 Tombstone of Philus 1st or 2nd century AD

Philus, son of Cassavus, a Sequanian, aged 45 years, here he lies.

[*RIB* 110. Cirencester (Corinium Dobunnorum)]

Tombstone found in 1836 at Watermoor. Now in Gloucester City Museum.

A hooded and cloaked man stands in a niche formed by two fluted pilasters and a pediment with leaf rosettes flanking the gable (photo in *RIB* online). Haverfield (1918) suggested that Philus might be a merchant as he has died so far from his native land. The Sequani were centred on Besançon *(Vesontio)* in the upper Saône valley, eastern France. The slender letters of the inscription and the formula 'here he lies' (HSE) may suggest a relatively early date; military tombstones found near to this one belong to the first century.

H7 A Samian bowl before *c.* AD 155

(property) of Materna.

[*Britannia* 31 (2000), 445.49 = EDCS-20500225 Mumrills, Stirlingshire]

Two conjoining sherds of a Samian bowl, found in the outer ditch of the fort, backfilled by the Romans in c. AD 155: scratched after firing above the foot ring,

H8 The Tammonii family ?2nd century AD

(i) To the god Hercules Saegon[...], Titus Tammonius Vitalis, son of Saenius Tammonius *(set this up)* in honour of [...]

[*RIB* 67 add. Silchester (Calleva Atrebatum)]

Dedication slab found in 1744 in the forum at Silchester. Now lost.

(ii) In memory of Flavia Victorina. Titus Tammonius Victor, her husband, set this up.

[*RIB* 87 add. Silchester (Calleva Atrebatum)]

Tombstone found in or before 1577 at Silchester. Now at the Museum of Archaeology and Ethnography, Cambridge.

The stone of which (i) was made is described as 'black marble' and the letters are well-cut. Boon (*Britannia* 4 (1973), 113) suggests the name of the god should be *Saegon[tio]*. The Tammoni(i) appear to have been a family of local worthies. Titus Tammonius Vitalis is a Roman citizen who, instead of adopting the *nomen* of the emperor under whom he was enfranchised, has adopted a Romanised form of his Celtic family name.

H9 Lossio Veda the Caledonian *c.* AD 222–235

To the god Mars Medocius of the Campeses and to the Victory of our Emperor Alexander Pius Felix, Lossio Veda, descendant of Vepogenus, a Caledonian, set up this gift from his own resources.

[*RIB* 191. Colchester (Camulodunum)]

Bronze ansate plate found in 1891 on the south side of Colchester. Now in the British Museum.

The god Mars was the one most frequently associated with the Celtic deities, in this case (given the accompanying dedication to the emperor's Victory) presumably in his guise as a war god. Medocius is unparalleled, as is *Campesium*; Haverfield suggested that *Campestrium* may have been intended. The Campestres were mother goddesses particularly concerned with the exercise grounds of the cavalry (cf. *RIB* 2121). Lossio Veda and Vepogenus appear to be Celtic names. Birley (1979, 128) suggests that since Veda gives, not his filiation, but the names of the person whose *nepos* he was, he was Pictish – with matriarchal descent, Vepogenus would be his mother's brother. Veda's status and the reason for his sojourn in Colchester are open to discussion. He has been seen variously as a merchant, a mercenary in Roman service, a noble hostage and a friendly chief.

H10 Barates and his wife from Palmyra 3rd century AD

(i) To the spirits of the departed, Barates of Palmyra, *vexillarius*, lived 68 years

[*RIB* 1171 add. Corbridge (Corstopitum)]

Tombstone found in 1911 reused as a paving-stone. Now in Corbridge Museum.

The identification with Barates in **H10 (ii)** is near certain. The meaning of *vexillarius* is unclear. Barates was not a soldier; no army unit is mentioned, so he was not a military standard-bearer. He may have been the standard-bearer of a trade guild. This tombstone is of poor quality, in stark contrast to the fine memorial which he set up to his wife (**H10 (ii)**).

(ii) To the spirits of the departed (and) to Regina (his) freedwoman and wife, a Catuvellaunian, aged 30, Barates of Palmyra *(set this up)*.

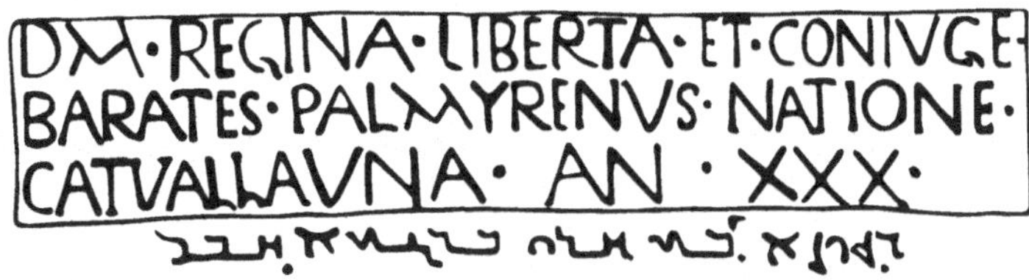

Fig. 10

Beneath the Latin text is another in Palmyrene script: "Regina, the freedwoman of Barates, alas."

[*RIB* 1065 add. South Shields (Arbeia)]

A tombstone found in 1878 south of Bath Street, to the south-west of the fort of South Shields. Now in South Shields Museum. (Fig.7).

In a gabled niche above the inscription is the seated figure of Regina wearing a long-sleeved robe over her tunic, reaching to her feet. Round her neck is a necklace of cable pattern, and on her wrists similar bracelets. On her lap she holds a distaff and spindle, while at her left side is her work-basket with balls of wool. With her right hand she holds open her unlocked jewellery box (drawings and photo in *RIB* online). Regina had been a slave; Barates freed her and married her. Note the cosmopolitan touch given by Barates' use of his native tongue in the final line.

H11 A Roman equestrian — Date unknown

[...] Macri[...]us, of equestrian rank, lived 20 years; Valeria Frontina, his wife, and Florius Cogitatus and Florius Fidelis set this up.

[*RIB* 202 add. Colchester (Camulodunum)]

Tombstone found in 1910 in grounds of Colchester Grammar School. Now in Colchester Museum.

This is the sole explicit mention of an *eques Romanus*, a member of the lesser aristocracy, apparently originating in Britain. (But note the implications of the gold rings, **H2** and that found on the skeleton of Flavius Bellator, **F22**). The name Macri[...] may suggest a connection with the two Macrinii Vindices, prominent generals of the later second century, for whom an origin at Colchester is possible (Birley 1979, 116–17). Birley further suggests that the prefect Q. Florius Modestus, a unit commander at Housesteads, may belong to the same equestrian family as the Florii attested here.

H12 Flavius Helius the Greek — Date unknown

To the spirits of the departed, Flavius Helius, a Greek, lived 40 years. Flavia Ingenua set this up to her husband.

[*RIB* 251. Lincoln (Lindum)]

Tombstone found in 1785 south of the Roman north wall, west of the north gateway. Now in Lincoln Museum.

Flavius Helius may perhaps have been a trader.

H13 Inscription on a lead brine-pan. Date unknown

(Property) of Clutamus.

[*Britannia* 36 (2005), 486. 20 = *EDCS*-37600989. Middlewich, Cheshire]

Found in 1997. A rectangular fragment of a cast-lead sheet from a brine-pan, *c.* 0.60 x .0.33 m.

The low relief cast inscription below the rim is slightly damaged, with the first letter missing, and only part of the 'L' remaining, but no other letter is likely, and Tomlin and Hassall note that 'the name *Clutamus* (a Celtic superlative meaning 'very famous') is found in Spain (*CIL* ii 2584, 2633) and as the patronymic of a cavalry officer likely to be Spanish in origin (*CIL* iii 2016).'

H14 A chalk roundel with graffito. Date unknown

(property) of Creticus. (?? or "made of chalk?")

[*Britannia* 31 (2000), 444.48 = *EDCS*-20401649. Angmering, West Sussex]

On a chalk roundel 110mm in diameter and 16mm thick, a graffito has been scratched round the side.

(b) TRADE and ECONOMY

H15 A contract for transporting goods. 21st October AD 62

In the consulship of Publius Marius Celsus and Lucius Afinius Gallus, on the 12th day before the Kalends of November [21st October AD 62], I, Marcus Rennius Venustus (certify) that I have made a contract with Gaius Valerius Proculus that he bring from ~~Londi~~ Verulamium by the Ides of November [13 November] 20 loads of provisions at a charge of one-quarter denarius for each, on condition that . . . one *as* . . . to London; but if . . . the whole . . .

[*Bloomberg WT* 45 = EDCS-69100085. London (Londinium]

An incomplete silver fir writing-tablet, in three conjoining fragments, with text preserved on the inner, recessed face.

There are a number of grammatical slips in the Latin text, noted by Tomlin in the commentary on this tablet, which may indicate that this was a copy kept by Proculus and that his transport business was based in London rather than Verulamium. The scribe also started to write 'London' rather than Verulamium: the stylus marked the wood, while the resmoothing of the wax left no trace, as he left a space before starting to write Verulamium on the next line. Like **H43** and **49**, its date matches the archaeological context (period 2 phase 3 (early) – AD 60/1–62 – very closely, and it indicates how quickly economic activity was re-established between two locations which were the focus in part at least of the destruction wrought during the Boudiccan rebellion. The quantities involved do not seem great, as 22 days are allowed for the 20 loads – Tomlin suggests that this 'might imply one load per day,' – but even by the old Roman road system the distance is just over 23 miles, which would probably be as far as a mule-train or ox-cart could be expected to travel in a day, and return journeys would have to factored in. The term used for 'one quarter denarius' is a *quadrans*, used strictly to denote a quarter-*as*, but a quarter-denarius seems to be implied here (as Tomlin points out, according to Tacitus, *Annals* 1.17, a soldier earned 10 *asses* a day, and a quarter-*as* seems far too small a sum); the fragmentary end of the text would indicate that as was usual in contracts of this type, part of the sum agreed was retained until the job was complete; three *asses* were paid per load in advance, and the balance of 20 *asses* kept back until the work was finished by the stipulated date.

H16 A merchant *c.* AD 65/70–80

To Optatus, merchant in [...]

[*Bloomberg WT* 7 = EDCS-69100047. London (Londinium)]

Fragment of a silver fir writing-tablet.

The cognomen *Optatus* is common, so this is not necessarily the same man identified as a *bracearius* or 'brewer' in the next example below. There are traces of letters on a second line which probably gave more precise details of the address to which the tablet was sent.

H17 A brewer *c.* AD 65/70–80

To Tertius, the brewer.

[*Bloomberg WT* 12 = EDCS-69100052. London (Londinium)]

Part of a re-used silver fir writing tablet.

A *braciiarius* or 'brewer' called Optatus is the addressee of one of the Vindolanda tablets, *Tab. Vind.* 3. 646. *bracae* was a type of grain – possibly de-hulled – and a *bracearius* (the spelling here) might have been responsible for malting wheat or barley, though in medieval Latin the word is explained generally as 'brewer.' See also the next entries for a trade linked to this, and **H18** below for evidence for a burgeoning beer-trade in London.

H18 Accounts for the supply of beer *c.* AD 65/70–80

Account of Crispus, beer: 5 (*denarii*).
[...] 105? [*units*]: 7 (*denarii*)
(and) 3 (*asses*). Beer, through Butus: ½ (a *denarius*).
[...] 2 (*asses*) [...]
Beer: 2 (*asses*). Beer: ½ (a denarius and) [...].
Through Januarius, beer: 1½ (*denarii*).
From this [...]

[*Bloomberg WT* 72 = EDCS-69100112. London (Londinium)]

Two conjoining fragments of a silver fir writing-tablet, making an incomplete piece with faint traces and some 'firmly incised and quite legible text' on the inner, recessed, face.

This type of *ratio* or statement of accounts is familiar from similar documents from Vindolanda such as *Tab. Vind.* 3.686). The person named is probably the supplier; thus this document would indicate sums owed to Crispus for beer supplied through the agency of others named in the document, probably in units of *modii* (16 *heminae* or Roman pints). Tomlin ad loc. notes the variations in spelling and use of abbreviations using the denarius symbol 'in no more than six, somewhat repetitive, lines . . . (which) all suggests that the account was not drawn up at one time, but that entries were made progressively probably by more than one hand, when each delivery was made'.

H19 A statement of accounts *c.* AD 65/70–80

Cat[ullus? ...]
?total [...]
[*name*], slave [*of name*], 500 (items): 16¼ denarii.
Catullus, the slave of Romanius Faustinus, 2000 (items): 65 denarii.
[*name*], the slave of Senecio [*numeral*], 6 denarii.

[*Bloomberg WT* 70 = EDCS-69100110. London (Londinium)]

An incomplete fragment of a silver fir writing-tablet, with faint traces of five lines of writing preserved on the ungrooved face.

This appears to be a record of accounts, transactions being carried out for their masters by slaves. The Catullus in this tablet is a slave, and so is unlikely to be the Catullus in *WT* 14 (**H1(ii)**), whose residence was well-known enough to form part of the address. What was being traded is not known, but, whatever the items were, from the identifiable figures they were 32½ denarii per 1,000. One denarius buys twice as many of these as it does in the beer account (see **H18**); the last line, which is very defective, would better be read as 6½, as this would equate to 200 items (whatever they were: 6 denarii would have bought 184 and 8/13 items!). The third line of the original, involving the 500 items at 16¼ denarii, has been crossed through, and there are two diagonal lines through line 4, involving Catullus, suggesting that these accounts had been paid.

H20 Trouble over beasts of burden — AD 80 – 90/95

~~Taurnius~~ Taurus to Macrinus his dearest lord, greetings [...] in good health [...] when Catarrius had come and had taken the beasts of burden away, investments which I cannot replace in three months. ?Yesterday I was at (the house of) Diadumenus, but he (Catarrius) arrived unexpectedly for a single day [...]

[*Bloomberg WT* 29 = EDCS-69100069. London (Londinium)]

A silver fir writing-tablet, complete in two conjoining pieces. There is no addressee, but the first page of a letter is on the inner (recessed) face of the outer tablet:

The writing is made more difficult to decipher because the tablet may have used for an earlier letter (see detailed discussion by Tomlin, *Roman London's first voices*, pp. 118–19), with a whole line of a previous letter intruding. The correction to 'Taurus', sender of the letter, indicates that someone else was doing the actual writing; 'Macrinus' is found frequently as a cognomen, but as Tomlin suggests it is possible that he is the same man as the Julius Macrinus to whom a writing-tablet was addressed at Carlisle (*RIB* 2(4). 2443.3). 'Catarrius' is not found elsewhere, but is probably derived from the Celtic, *catu-* or 'battle'. The writer's dilemma stems from the removal of his *iumenta* or 'animals used for pulling or carrying' which he does not have the funds to replace in the immediate future. The letter is full of 'vulgarisms', many deriving from frequently-found aural confusions in writing words down. The document is interesting not least because it seems to indicate the carriage of goods from London to other areas, and its involvement of recently-Romanized personnel.

H21 Copper-alloy ladle with maker's name — Probably after AD 70

Bodukus made (this).

[*Britannia* 33 (2002), 359 = *EDCS*-28500391. Edgbaston, Birmingham]

Found in 2001 in the top backfill of a ditch containing Samian ware dated to AD 40–70, AD 55–70 and AD 60–70.

'Oar-shaped' knobbed terminal of a copper-alloy ladle (*cyathus*) now 58 mm in length, bearing an impressed rectangular stamp. The name *Bodukus* has not been found in Britain before and is not attested elsewhere. The name is presumably Gallic, deriving from the name-element *boduo.*

H22 Descriptions of fish-products on amphorae. Flavian

(i) Finest Antibes *liquamen* (fish sauce) from Lucius Tettius Africanus.

[*RIB* 2.6.2492.24 = EDCS-51100300 London (Londinium)]

Found on the foreshore of the Thames at Winchester Palace, Southwark. A Dressel 16 fish-sauce amphora manufactured at Fréjus (Forum Iulii) and inscribed in ink on the neck, at the point of usage, in Antibes, not in Britain. Now in the Museum of London.

This 'marketing' may have been intended for the wholesaler or retailer who imported the fish sauce, as much as for the final user, as the product is now thought to have been decanted. *Liquamen,* like *garum* was a fish sauce used by all groups in Roman society, and could be relatively cheap when made from small sardine and anchovy, and more expensive when made from larger fish such as mackerel (see Pliny, *NH* 31.93–94). Many contemporary examples of labelling of fish-sauce are known from Pompeii which was famous for its *garum* (see Cooley[2] 2014, 247 and 250–252). There is a fine image and description of this amphora on the Museum of London's website, where it is however mistakenly identified as a Dressel 2.4 type.

(ii) Finest aged salted young tuna (*cordyla*), to be stored (?) (*penuaria*).

[*Britannia* 33 (2002), p. 361 = EDCS-28500402. Carlisle (Luguvalium)]

White slip panels from the neck of a Beltrán 2A amphora, found in 2000 in the praetentura of the Roman fort at Carlisle (Luguvalium), in the context of the demolition of the first fort, c. AD *103/105. Written in ink in cursive letters.*

Again, the inscription comes from the point of shipping but was evidently thought to be useful in Britain, its destination. *Cordyla* are very small tuna (Pliny, *NH* 32.146) probably shipped whole. By aging the product, both the fish and the brine (*muria*) produced as a result would have been regarded as a valuable product.

H23 The sale of a slave-girl before *c.* AD 155

(i) *on the plain (outside) face in large cursive letters apparently scoured with a metal nib:*

'At London. To . . . '

(ii) *on the recessed (inner) face:*

Rufus, son of Callisunus, greetings to Epicillus and all his fellows. I believe you know that I am very well. If you have made the list, please send it. See that you do everything carefully so as to extract the last coin from that girl . . .

[*RIB* 2.4.2443.7 = EDCS-13800058 = BM 1953, 1002.1. London (Londinium)]

Part of a stilus-tablet of fir-wood, 146 by 43 mm, recessed on one face and with a nick at the top edge for the binding cord, Richmond *AJ* 33, 1953, 206–8. Now in the British Museum.

The tablet is dated on the basis of other deposits in the Walbrook being pre-*c.* AD 155, and on the style of the handwriting, which suggests a similar date. The inner face is written in cursive script without word-division: The names *Callisunus* and *Epicillus* are unparalleled.

H24 A *moritix* in London later 2nd century AD

To the Divine Powers of the Emperors (and) to the god Mars Camulus. Tiberinius Celerianus, a citizen of the Bellovaci, sea-trader (*moritix*), of Londoners the first [...]

[*Britannia* 34 (2003), 364–65, no 5 = *RIB* 3.3014 = EDCS-28500378* London (Londinium)]

Slab of white marble, found in 2002 during excavations in Southwark. Now in the Museum of London.

The dedication, referring to two living emperors, belongs no earlier than Marcus Aurelius and colleagues. This, combined with the good quality of the lettering, suggests a date in the later 2nd century (AD 161–169 or AD 176–180). Mars Camulus is attested elsewhere in Britain only at Bar Hill (*RIB* 2166); he is particularly associated with the Remi (the area of Rheims) in northern Gaul. The dedicator is otherwise unknown, but the Bellovaci were a *civitas* 'somewhat to the west of the Remi' – in the area of modern Normandy, centred on Beauvais *(Caesaromagnus Bellovacorum)*. Tomlin and Hassall note that 'this Gallic citizen evidently called himself a 'Londoner' in the same way that Verecundius Diogenes, citizen of the Bituriges Cubi, was also a *sevir Augustalis* of the *colonia Eboracensis* at York (*RIB* 678 (**F24(i)**).' Another example relevant to Britain is **H27,** from Cologne.

H25 A trader at York AD 221

[To ...] and the Spirit of the place and [the Divine Powers of the Empe]rors, Lucius Viducius Pla[cidus, the son of Viducius], from the Veliocasses [...], trader [with Britain, pre]se[nted] the arch and gate [in the consulship] of Gratus [and Seleucus].

[*RIB* 3.3195 = EDCS-09301079. York (nEboracum)]

Upper three-quarters of the right-hand portion of a gritstone dedication slab found in 1976 at Clementhorpe, reused in a medieval limekiln. Now in the Yorkshire Museum.

The entire left half of the text is missing. Detail is restored with the help of another dedication made by Placidus to the goddess Nehalennia, at Colijnsplaat (Holland), "To the goddess Nehalennia, Placidus, son of Viducius, a citizen of the Veliocasses, trader with Britain, fulfilled his vow willingly and deservedly." (EDCS-09400569*, compare **H26**). The Veliocasses lived in the area around Rouen, northern France.

H26 A trader in pottery later 2nd – 3rd century AD

To the goddess Nehalennia, on account of goods duly kept safe, Marcus Secund(inius?) Silvanus, trader in pottery with Britain, fulfilled his vow willingly and deservedly.

[*ILS* 4751 = EDCS-09401495. Domburg, Holland]

Altar found in 1647 near the mouth of the East Scheldt estuary. Now in the Rijksmuseum van Oudheden, Leiden.

Example from one of two remarkable collections of altars, the vast majority dedicated to the goddess Nehalennia, set up by traders at shrines at Domburg (as this) and Colijnsplaat, which lay, in Roman times, on either side of the Scheldt estuary, presumably at or near harbour sites. 32 dedications are known from Domburg, 125 from Colijnsplaat. Silvanus made a second dedication to Nehalennia at Colijnsplaat (*AE* 1973, 370).

H27 A trader with Britain — later 2nd – 3rd century AD

To Apollo, Gaius Aurelius Verus, freedman of Gaius, trader with Britain, seafarer (*moritex*), gave as a gift, the site being given by decree of the decurions.

[*ILS* 7522 = EDCS-01200002*. Cologne, Germany (Colonia Claudia Ara Agrippinensium)]

Dedication slab of black marble found at St Pantaleon. Now in the Römisch- Germanisches Museum, Köln.
This inscription provides a parallel for the restoration of the term *moritex* in **F24(i)**. The term *moritix* (or *moritex*) derives from the Celtic for 'seafarer'; it implies someone involved in seaborne trade. Verus may have been trading in fine pottery or glass or perhaps salt, as was the case with two other traders from Cologne (see Hassall 1978, 43).

H28 A stonemason — Date unknown

Priscus, son of Tout(i)us, stonemason, a Carnutenian, to the goddess Sulis willingly and deservedly fulfilled his vow.

[*RIB* 149. Bath (Aquae Sulis)]

Dedication stone found about 1880 near the Great Bath. Now in the Roman Baths Museum.

The *civitas* of the Carnutes was centred on *Autricum*, modern-day Chartres. Priscus is one of two stone-workers attested at Bath. The other, Sulinus (**J35**), origin unstated but, on the evidence of his name possibly local, is a sculptor.

H29 A coppersmith — Date unknown

To the god Silvanus Callirius, Cintusmus the coppersmith willingly and deservedly fulfilled as a gift his vow.

[*RIB* 194. Colchester (Camulodunum)]

Bronze plate, with letters made with a blunt punch. Found in 1946 outside the walled area of the city, in the playing fields of Colchester Grammar School, near the remains of a Roman building.

The plaque was found in a temple precinct, which strongly suggests that the temple was dedicated to Silvanus. An alternative reading of the text is 'To the god Silvanus Calliriodacus, Cintusmus the coppersmith willingly and deservedly fulfilled his vow.' Close by, in a votive pit, was found a second dedication to Silvanus by Hermes (*RIB* 195; Hull 1958, 239–39). Most of the two dozen dedications to Silvanus are by soldiers, but these two are by civilians. Another coppersmith, Celatus, is attested as the maker of the Foss Dyke Mars (*RIB* 274: **J9**).

H30 A goldsmith's servant — Date unknown

Good luck to the Spirit of this place. Young slave, may fortune be yours in using this goldsmith's shop.

[*RIB* 712. Malton (Derventio), Yorkshire]

Building stone found in 1814 at Norton, the civil settlement south of Malton, near New Malton. Now in the Yorkshire Museum, York.

One other inscription attests gold working in Britain (*RIB* II.2, 2413, a gold handle from Ecclefechan, near Birrens). Smiths were at work in Cirencester, Southwark and Verulamium, and evidence for refining has been found on the site of the later Flavian governor's palace in London (Marsden 1980, 96–97).

H31 Oculists' stamps

(i) Junius Alexander's (salve) made from misy for granulations (of the eye-lids).

[*RIB* 2.4.2446.1 = EDCS-13600409. York (Eboracum)]

Green soapstone, 36.5 by 20 by 9.5 mm. Engraved only on one edge. Now in the Yorkshire Museum

Misy is mentioned by Pliny *NH* 33.84 and the medical writer, Celsus. It seems to have been some sort of mineral. One doubts whether many Romans or Britons would have known exactly what misy was any more than most people nowadays would understand all the ingredients of cough mixture.

(ii) *On the edges:*

(a) Gaius Valerius Amandus' vinegar (salve) for running eyes
(b) Gaius Valerius Amandus' drops for dim sight
(c) Gaius Valerius Valentinus' poppy (salve) after the onset of eye-inflammation
(d) Gaius Valerius Valentinus' mixture for clear sight

On the upper face:

(e) near (a) 'vineg(ar)'
(f) near (b) 'dro(ps)'
(g) near (c) 'poppy'
(h) near (d) 'mixt(ure)'

[*RIB* 2.4.2446.2 = BM 1882,0819. Biggleswade, Bedfordshire]

Green schist, 51mm by 41mm by 9.5 mm. Found in a ballast-pit in 1873. Now in the British Museum.

This single stamp has the name of four products, one on each edge in negative text. In each case a graffito, scratched in large, normal letters on the upper side, gives an abbreviated version to help identify the relevant text on the stamp, since the stamp necessarily has the letters back to front and left to right. The four products are by two practitioners who share the same *praenomen* and nomen and who therefore can be assumed to be relations or freedmen with the same former master. In each stamp, the name of the practitioner appears on the top line with interpuncts where space allows. The name of the medicine appears as a compound word with condition and product content abbreviated and run together. For example the first product is 'DIOXVMADREVMATIC' or 'of-vinegar-for-runniness' with all the key words being Greek (like modern medical terms). The third one is 'DIAGLAVCPOSTIMPLIC' – dia-glauc(ium) post imp(etum) lip(pitudinis), or 'of-poppy-post-onset-of-eye-inflammation', with Latin words abbreviated and compounded.

(iii)

(a) Titus Vindacius Ariovistus' nard-oil (salve).
(b) Titus Vindacius Ariovistus' green (salve).
(c) Titus Vindacius Ariovistus' unbeatable (salve).
(d) Titus Vindacius Ariovistus' frankincense (salve).

[*RIB.* 2.4. 2446.3 = BM 1931,0211.1. Kenchester (Magnis)]

'Green stone', 37 by 37 by 10 mm. Found in 1842, currently on display in British Museum (Room G49).

(iv)

(a) Atticus' salve of frankincense (to be made up with) with egg does (good) for all pains.
(b) Atticus' mild (salve) for all pains after the onset of ophthalmia.
(c) Atticus' poppy (salve) does good for all pains.
(d) Atticus' salve of quince does (good) for granulations (of the eye-lids).

[*RIB* 2.4.2446.4. Cirencester (Corinum) Gloucestershire]

Green schist, 44.5 by 44.5 by 6mm. Found in 1900. Now in Corinium Museum.

32 genuine articles in this category are listed in RIB II as numbers 2446.1 – 2446.32. This compares with some 300 stamps known in the Roman Empire as a whole, most coming from the North-western provinces. The stamps are cut with a negative text so that when pressed into sticks or cakes of medicament they leave a positive impression. The stamps may have been passed on to others to use, and the distribution of the stamps seems to indicate the presence of itinerant general practitioners selling a range of preparations whose names indicate Greek origin but whose products may have been made more locally. Pliny the Elder, *NH* 34.108, corroborates this view, 'for some time ready-made plasters and eye-salves have been available to buy.' Typically the stamps are square, from 54 x 54 to 31 x 31 mm with a thickness of between 3mm for the thinnest to some 10mm, and are made of a variety of stone or china clay. Green schist seems to have been popular. The 'brands' are engraved on the narrow edges. The translations from *RIB* 2.2446 give some idea of the virtues claimed for these products in Britain. It's hard to know what, if anything, they suggest about literacy, with names compounded of abbreviated and complex (sometimes Greek) words. Presumably they at least show that a cake of medicine would appear more reliable if it had words printed on it.

H32 A lead tank — Date unknown

Malledo made (this). [?Be] happy

[*Britannia* 45 (2014), 443.16. Lincoln (Lindum)]

The upper band of two from a fragment of a lead tank.

(c) LEGAL

H33 A legal case between two Celts in London 22 October AD 76

In the consulship of the Emperor Caesar Vespasian for the seventh time (and) of Titus for the fifth time, on the 11th day before the Kalends of November (22 October AD 76). (In the case) between Litugenus and Magunus (to be heard) on the 5th day before the Ides of November (9 November). My preliminary judgement, under the emperor's authority, is [...]

[*Bloomberg WT* 51 = EDCS-69100091. London (Londinium)]

A fragment of a silver fir writing tablet, probably about 2/3 of the original, with six lines of writing preserved.

This appears to be a document confirming the appointment of a magistrate to hear a dispute between Litugenus and Magunus. Both names are Celtic, making them likely not to have been Roman citizens. The appointment is said to have been 'under the emperor's authority' but it was probably the decision of his *legatus pro praetore*, the provincial governor who acted in the emperor's name. Sextus Julius Frontinus was governor at this date. Alternatively the *iuridicus* might have appointed the judge (Salvius Liberalis was in post by AD 78 – see **F6** for *iuridicus*). At any event, this document seems to indicate that at this date in its history London did not yet have *duumviri iuri dicundo*, the two annually-elected magistrates or *duumvirs* who were empowered to make such appointments under the Roman legal system.

The tablet's contents are reported to be 'only just' residual in its archaeological context of *c.* AD 80–90/95; perhaps it lay in an archive for many years before being discarded. The layout of the Latin text is interesting in this tablet: new lines are started with large letters, new sentences are indented.

H34 An affidavit AD 84–96

(i) *on the plain (outside) face in scratched capitals*

'To [... . . . Pos]tumus at Lo[ndon]'.

(ii) *on the recessed (inner) face scratched in cursive script with word-division:*

[I swear by] Jupiter Optimus Maximus and by the *genius* of the emperor Domitian Caesar Augustus Germanicus and by (my) native gods [...] . . . and . . .[...]

[*RIB* 2.4.2443.11 = EDCS-49602568. London (Londinium)]

Part of a wooden stilus-tablet 133 by 25 mm., recessed on one face, found in 1927 in or near the Walbrook at Lothbury. Now in the Museum of London.

H35 A slave girl Late 1st or early 2nd century AD

Vegetus, assistant slave of Montanus the slave of the August Emperor and sometime assistant slave of Jucundus, has bought and received by *mancipium* the girl Fortunata, or by whatever name she is known, by nationality a Diablintian, from Albicianus [...] for six hundred denarii. And that the girl in question is transferred in good health, that she is warranted not to be liable to wander or run away, but that if anyone lays claim to the girl in question or to any share in her, [...] in the wax tablet which he has written and sworn by the *genius* of the Emperor Caesar [...].

[*Tomlin* 2003 = EDCS-36400173. London (Londinium)]

See fig. 3, page 25. A stilus tablet found in 1994 in debris above a burnt-down Flavian building, north of the main east-west route through the Roman city, just west of the Walbrook. Now in the Museum of London.

For full discussion in R. S. O. Tomlin, "The Girl in Question": a New Text from Roman London', *Britannia* XXXIV (2003), pp. 41–51. Most of the wax of the tablet has been lost, but it has not been overwritten, so that deciphering the letters scratched into the wood was easier than is often the case.

The first of (originally) three tablets tied together as a triptych, containing the first eleven lines of a contract for the sale of a slave girl. This is a legal document using conventional legal terminology. Vegetus and Montanus are the first imperial slaves to be named in Britain. Imperial slaves helped administer the emperor's property in the provinces. Their financial status is indicated by the fact that Vegetus (himself the slave of a slave), could afford to pay 600 denarii, the equivalent of two years' salary for a legionary soldier. A tentative identification may be suggested with M. Cocceius Vegetus, the addressee of one of the Vindolanda Tablets *(Tab. Vindol. II.* 352 + *Tab. Vindol. III, Appendix)*, if he is not a discharged auxiliary but an ex-slave, manumitted and enfranchised by Nerva. If the identification is correct, this tablet, which pre-dates his manumission, will be Domitianic in date. *Mancipium* 'mancipation' was the formal process by which ownership of real property was conveyed. The *Diablintes* were a Gallic tribe located in north-western Gaul, in the area of modern Jublains.

H36 More evidence for wills. Undated/ late 1st/ early 2nd century AD?

(i) ... left instructions in his will for this to be set up.

[*Britannia* 37 (2006), 467 no. 2 = EDCS-44100155. Colchester (Camulodunum)]

Fragment of a Purbeck marble plaque 20mm thick, found in 2005 in the boundary ditch of the extramural cemetery at the Garrison Urban Village, Colchester, Essex.

The fragment consists of only three letters in Latin, TPI *t(estamento) p(oneri) i(ussit)*, a reasonably common formula on tombstones.

(ii) To the shades of the dead. Insus son of Vodullus, citizen of the Treveri, cavalryman of the *ala Augusta*, troop of Victor, *curator*. Domitia his heir had this set up.

[*Britannia* 37 (2006), 468–9, no. 3 = EDCS-44500091* = *RIB* 3.3185 Lancaster]

A fragmented tombstone of buff sandstone, 0.91 x c. 2.5m overall, 0.17 m thick, found in 2005 lying down in two pieces, c. 8m from the Roman road leading south from the fort at Lancaster.

There is a full description of the tombstone, with photograph and drawing, in *Britannia* 37 (2006), p. 469–71 and also a good photograph on the *EDCS* website. Note that 'Domitia his heir' might indicate the deceased's sister, but is more likely his informal 'wife'.

H37 Ownership of a wood 14 March AD 118

In the consulship of the Emperor Trajan Hadrian Caesar Augustus for the second time, and Gnaeus Fuscus Salinator on the day before the Ides of March [14 March 118]. Whereas, on arriving at the property in question, the wood *Verlucionium*, fifteen *arepennia*, more or less, which is in the canton of the Cantiaci in Dibussu[…] parish […], neighboured by the heirs [of …] and the heirs of Caesennius Vitalis and the vicinal road, Lucius Julius Bellicus said that he had bought it from Titus Valerius Silvinus for forty *denarii*, as is contained in the deed of purchase. Lucius Julius Bellicus attested that he …

[Britannia 25 (1994), 302–4 no. 34 = RIB 2.8.2504, 29 = EDCS-00380552. London (Londinium)]

A stilus writing tablet found in 1986 in the second-century embankment of the Walbrook. Now in the Museum of London.

This tablet (the first 'page' of a longer document) appears to record a formal enquiry into the ownership of a wood in Kent. It is of interest in that it shows Roman land law operating in Britain. The term *arepennia* was current in Gaul and Spain as a unit of surface measurement equivalent to half of one *iugerum* (the area that a single plough-team can plough in one day). The wood in question thus covered 4.6 acres (1.85 hectares). The boundaries of the wood in dispute are established by reference to the neighbouring properties and to a *via vicinalis* – a minor road leading off a major road and often used as a land boundary. This may imply that the territory of the *civitas* had been professionally surveyed, as would be necessary for the census. A 'parish' (*pagus*) is a sub-division of the *civitas*. This is the first named example in Britain. The name of the wood, Verlucionium (a variant of the place name Verlucio) is discussed by Tomlin (1996). He suggests that it may have been a pre-Roman sacred grove. Tomlin points out (1994, 303 note) that the names of the landowners mentioned in the document suggest that none was of British origin. He notes that the names Julius and Valerius are common among legionaries. We are perhaps dealing with retired soldiers.

H38 A loan agreement — 3 December AD 158

...Tittius takes away ... and he affirms that he has received and owes (coins) which he asked for and counted out. It is agreed that the above money be returned to Aprilis (?) henceforth (?) with interest from the present day, without any counter-plea. [Deed] executed at Lara (?) three days before the nones of December in the consulship of Tertullus and Sacerdos [3 December 158].

[*Britannia* 42 (2011), 446, no. 9 = *EDCS*-64100292 London]

Two joining fragments of a wooden stilus writing-tablet, 168 x 70 mm, found in 2006 in Drapers' Gardens, 12 Throgmorton Avenue in the City of London.

The recessed face is too damaged to be reconstructed, and the translation above is taken from the text on the un-recessed face. Tomlin notes that contemporary parallels from Dacia indicate that we are dealing with a dated loan-note or *mutuum*. The inscription indicates the prevalence of normal Roman financial practice in Britain as elsewhere in the Roman Empire.

H39 A surety against possible legal claim on a property — late 2nd or 3rd century AD

[…] so that […] may be allowed rightfully to have (the house) free of all burdens but if anyone else the house […] aforementioned or part of it has lawfully recovered the property, so that (the above-mentioned purchaser or the person to whom the matter shall pertain) is unable to possess and enjoy it rightfully, then whatever the amount of loss shall be through the recovery of property having thus occurred, (so much) […] demanded and […] promised should be made good.

[*RIB* 2.4.2443.13 = EDCS-49600595. Chew Stoke, Avon, Somerset]

Part of a stilus-tablet of larch, 162.5 by 47 mm., recessed on one face, found in 1954 at a depth of 7.6m in a well at a Roman villa. Now in Bristol City Museum.

The translation is based on that provided for *RIB* by Professor A. M. Honoré. The text is very badly damaged. The phrasing is awkward but specific – one might say typical of legal documentation – and is very similar to a formula used in a triptych from Transylvania from AD 159 (*CIL* 3, p. 944 no.VIII, *IDR* i p. 226 no. IX). The purpose of the document is to protect anyone who purchases the property against loss in the event that there is an unknown claim or mortgage held on it.

H40 A Roman will Date unknown

Five lines missing at the start.

[*The name and status of the testator*] ... before I die, I order that [*name*] be my sole heir ...

Let all others for me be disinherited [...] on no other terms than that as much as I shall give, have given, shall have ordered to be given [...] and you [...] enter upon, accept my estate [... within] the next hundred [days] after my death in which you know or can know that you are my legitimate heir, in the presence of witnesses [...] let the heirs be those who know that they are [...] of this property.

But if you do not thus accept my estate, if you refuse to enter upon it, be you disinherited [...] whom I have instituted as my sole heir.

[*Britannia* 35 (2004), 347 no. 27 = EDCS-33800072. Trawsfynydd]

A stilus-writing tablet 147 x 99mm, 6mm thick, found in North Wales on Bodyffudau Farm, Trawsfynydd, c. 1840, during peat-cutting. When found, it was the outer leaf of a block (codex) consisting of 'some 10 or 12 leaves' secured with wire, but the others were soon lost.

Tomlin and Hassall note (n. 55, p. 347) note that details of the person who made the will, and the heir, would have been in the missing five lines at the start; but the Latin indicates that the heir was a woman. The testator was a Roman citizen, possibly an auxiliary soldier of the unit at Tomen-y-Mur (OS reference SH 706 386) who settled on retirement from the army at a settlement at Ffridd Bod y Fuddau (OS reference SH 731 343). Both sites are in one of the remotest parts of north Wales. The wording matches testamentary formulas in the *Institutes* of Gaius, a standard legal text, and surviving Roman wills, but this is the only will to have survived outside Egypt and is therefore worthy of inclusion, when one considers how many wills must have been made! See **G31**: a possible will made in the 1st century AD by a soldier of the First Cohort of Vangiones.

(d) FINANCE and NUMERACY

H41 A foolish financier *c.* AD 43–53

You will give this to Titus. Poultry-keeper.

[There are traces of an earlier message on the inner face, but the last seven lines of a second message are capable of some deciphering, as follows:]

[. . .] because they are boasting through the whole market that you have lent them money. Therefore I ask you, for your own sake, not to appear shabby [. . .] you will not thus favour your own affairs [. . .]

[*Bloomberg WT* 30 = EDCS-69100070. London (Londinium]

A silver fir writing-tablet with legible writing preserved on both the outer and inner faces. On the outer face a short but complete address is written in cursive letters:

The word *aviarius* is read after 'to Titus'; this rare word means 'poultry-keeper' and if taken with Titus should have been written in the dative case, not the nominative; and as Tomlin comments, 'Titus appears to have been a financier'. One wonders if it was part of a previous address.

Tomlin ad loc. notes that this 'is the only legible tablet from this early context (*c.* AD 43–53), and the natural implication is that London had a marketplace (that on Cornhill). However, it is possible that the phrase is abstract ('the market', rather than a physical 'marketplace'), or that the writer is referring to the forum of another town, perhaps in Gaul, to which they both belonged.' At the same time, Titus is clearly based in London; and the 'natural implication' lends support to Tacitus' statement that London before the rebellion of Boudicca 'had not yet been distinguished with the rank of colony, but was a very busy centre for businessmen and merchandise' (*Annals* 14.33, LACTOR 11 F3. 4). See also the entries following.

H42 Confirmation of a debt. — 8 January AD 57

In the consulship of Nero Claudius Caesar Augustus Germanicus for the second time and of Lucius Calpurnius Piso, on the 6th day before the Ides of January (8 January AD 57).

I, Tibullus the freedman of Venustus, have written and say that I owe Gratus the freedman of Spurius 105 (*denarii*) from the price of the merchandise which has been sold and delivered. I am due to repay this money to him or to the person whom the matter will concern . . ."

[*Bloomberg WT* 44 = EDCS-69100084. London (Londinium)]

An incomplete silver fir writing-tablet, with text preserved on a recessed face.

Tomlin ad loc. notes that 'the text is not multiple except for a few corrections and is unusually well preserved.' The date given matches the archaeological context very closely. Like **H41** above, it confirms London's early establishment as a trading centre. It is the earliest dated document yet found in London, coming a good three years before the Boudiccan destruction. The use of the name 'Tibullus' is unique, but as Tomlin comments, 'slaves often received a fanciful name which they retained as freedmen, and perhaps the master (and now patron) of Tibullus had literary tastes. Since he is identified by his cognomen, *Venustus*, not his praenomen like the master and patron of Gratus, he was probably not a Roman citizen.'

H43 Writing numbers — *c.* AD 62–65/70

(column i)		(column ii)	
. . .	. . .	. . .	. . .
I)) ∞ ∞ ∞	8,000	I)) ((I))	60,000
I)) ∞ ∞ ∞ ∞	9,000	I)) ((I)) ((I))	70,000
((I))	10,000	I)) ((I)) ((I)) ((I))	80,000
((I)) ((I))	20,000	I)) ((I)) ((I)) ((I)) ((I))	90,000
((I)) ((I)) ((I))	30,000	(((I)))	100,000
((I)) ((I)) ((I)) ((I))	40,000		

[*Bloomberg WT* 78. London (Londinium)]

A fragment of an incomplete silver fir writing-tablet, with text preserved on the inner face in two columns: the Latin symbols on the tablet are shown to the left of their modern equivalents.

Some of the symbols are not preserved completely, but the symbols for *mille*, (I) = a thousand, and its multiples are familiar from stone inscriptions. This would seem to be a writing-exercise for a clerk or book-keeper, though *arithmetica* formed part of the educational system in imperial times, and counting on fingers and using hands and arms in different positions enabled Romans to count up to 1,000,000, a system ultimately preserved by the Venerable Bede in his little treatise *De Flexibus Digitorum*.

H44 A plea for funds to be sent *c.* AD 62–65/70

"At<t>icus (sent this)."

The legible text on the inner face reads as follows:

[. . .] I ask you by bread and salt that you send as soon as possible 26 (*denarii*) in small change and the 10 (*denarii*) of Paterio [. . .]

[*Bloomberg WT* 31 = EDCS-69100071. London (Londinium)]

An incomplete silver fir writing-tablet, cut down from the original, with some legible content inside, and the remains of an address on the outer face.

The Latin name *Atticus* appears in the nominative (though with only one 't') and thus represents the sender, not the addressee, whose details have been lost. This usage is paralleled by a Gallic example, according to Tomlin.

Tomlin comments that the phrase 'by bread and salt", *per panem et salem*, 'was surely a cliché', representing as it does the minimum to sustain life and symbolizing hospitality. Tomlin concludes that 'the writer (may have) done the recipient a favour – the Roman equivalent of a free lunch at least – and is now requesting a return.' The term for 'small change' is '*victoriati*': A *victoriatus* was originally the name given to a type of silver coin worth a *quinarius* or half a *denarius* which was minted by Rome in the 2nd century BC to facilitate trade with the Greek world (as it was equivalent in weight and therefore value to a drachma). Although the coins had not been produced for some time, the name lived on (see Tomlin ad loc., and Michael Crawford, *Roman Republican Coinage*, London 1974, 628–30). Even *quinarii* had not been minted since the reign of Augustus, so either the writer wants to have a lot of small change, or is avoiding the debased silver *denarii* produced by Nero from AD 64 onwards; the latter explanation would place the letter towards the end of the period identified for its stratification.

H45 Confirmation of a financial transaction *c.* AD 65/70–80

. . . Atigniomarus came to the city on the 8th day before the Kalends of January (25 December) . . . He said that he had duly received and has from you the 300 (*denarii*). When he was asking me . . .

[*Bloomberg WT* 37 = EDCS-69100077. London (Londinium)]

An incomplete silver fir writing-tablet, with some text preserved on the inner face:

The name 'Atignomarus' is more regularly spelled 'Ategniomarus' and includes the Celtic name element *maro-* or 'great'. The syntax of the Latin in the letter is tricky, as Tomlin notes. This example, like the more fragmentary *Bloomberg WT* 35, confirms the complexity of financial transactions in the market in London at this time – the civilian equivalent of the military fussiness and attention to administrative detail exemplified by the Vindolanda tablets.

H46 Confirmation of money paid, probably as rent AD 64

In the consulship of Marcus Licinius Crassus Frugi and Gaius Laecanius Bassus [AD 64], on the [. . . day before the . . .] of [. . .]ember. I, Florentinus, the slave of Sextus Cassius [...]tus, have written at my master's orders that he has received two payments from the [...] farm [...]

[*Bloomberg WT* 50 = EDCS-69100090. London (Londinium)]

An incomplete silver fir writing-tablet with six legible lines and the end of a seventh on the inner recessed face.

The date given in the tablet matches the stratification level in which it was found of *c.* AD 80 – 90/95. From what is left of the date given, the month has to be September or later; Tomlin writes ad loc that 'slight traces suggest that it was November.' The Latin word translated as 'payments' is *pensiones*, which occurs in legal texts to indicate income received as rent.

Lines 1 and 3 are extended to the left (the opposite of modern indenting) and spaces are left between words.

H47 A loan with details of repayment c. AD 65/70–80

[…] both the sum [and the interest on it] which he owes […] to be duly managed in good (coin) whenever he requests (them) […]

To Narcissus (the slave) of Rogatus the Lingonian, Atticus […] has properly, truly, faithfully promised (it is) to be given, to Ingenuus […] or to him whom the matter concerns. And in the presence of those who have been written in (their own) hand above, Atticus has said that he owes and holds and has received prior to this day […]

[*Bloomberg WT* 55 = EDCS-69100095. London (Londinium)]

Two conjoining fragments of an almost complete silver fir writing tablet, possibly the last tablet in a three-part set, with traces of twelve lines of writing preserved.

This is the second page of a loan-note, promising to repay the principal sum (Latin *sortem*) together with any interest which accrues (Latin *ussuras*, with doubling of 's' commonly found in inscriptions to emphasize the 's' sound, as does 'promised' (*promissit*) later on; *abere* for *habere* (to 'ave) is another 'vulgarism' in the text). The tablet has traces of another text which make parts of this text difficult to decipher. Rogatus is identified as a Lingonian, and may well have been a member of a cohort of Lingones, though if this is the case, the tablet provides evidence for the presence of cohorts from this area at a much earlier date than was previously known. Four cohorts of Lingones served in Britain, and stayed for centuries: before this example, the earliest British evidence for these units are diplomas from the period of Trajan and it was assumed that they came to Britain with Cerealis in AD 71. This tablet parallels that in *WT* 33 (see **B25** in placing a cohort (that of the Nervii) in Britain at an earlier date than once thought) .

H48 Batch-numbers on ridged tiles (*imbrices*). Date unknown

200 (or more)
258

[*Britannia* 36 (2005), 485.17 = EDCS-37600981/2. Stonea, Cambridgeshire]

Two ridged tiles (*imbrices*) with Roman numerals (CC… and CCLVIII) incised before firing, presumably batch totals.

(e) LITERACY

H49 Writing practice c. AD 60/1–62

Outer face: ABCDIIFGHIKL
MNOPQRST …
Inner face: ACCDEFG . . .

[*Bloomberg WT* 79 = EDCS-69100119. London (Londinium)

Two conjoining fragments of an incomplete silver fir writing-tablet, with an alphabet in capitals written on the outer (plain) and inner (recessed) faces

This seems to be an instance of writing practice or a 'model' for someone else to follow. II was commonly used for E (compare 'braciiarius/bracearius' in **H17** the outer face of the tablet may have been largely unused as it normally carried the address.

H50 A list of names 2nd century AD

Severianus, son of Brigomalla
Patarnianus, son?
Matarnus, wife?
Catonius (son of) Potentinus
Marinianus (son of) Belcatus
Lucillius (son of) Luccianus
Aeternus (son of) Ingenuus
Bellaus (son of) Bellinus."

[Tab. Sulis *30* = EDCS-48900175; Bath (Aquae Sulis)]

A pewter plate found at Bath.

Tomlin's comment on this list (Tomlin 2002, pp. 130–1) is worth quoting in full:

> The 8 persons named are explicitly not Roman citizens: almost everyone is identified by the name of his mother or father, in peregrine fashion, like Docilianus 'son of Brucetus'. The names are almost all 'Celtic', overtly like *Brigomalia* and *Belcatus*, or covertly containing Celtic name-elements such as '*Lucillus son of* Luccianus'. Three names appear to be Roman, but in fact they are typically 'British': *Aeternus* occurs in three Welsh sub-Roman inscriptions, and *Patarnianus* and *Matarnus* show a pronunciation characteristic of Roman Britain and sub-Roman Wales. Yet the 'tablet' is a locally-made substitute for expensive Roman silverware, and its handwriting is a practised, quite beautiful cursive of 2nd- *c.* date, calligraphic in quality with its bold, exaggerated initials, unsurpassed by anything at Vindolanda. Whether or not the scribe was professional, his work might be said to illustrate 'Writing Latin, but *not* becoming Roman'.

(e) Graffiti on tiles

The brief annotations made on tiles, almost always before firing, give an indication of literacy and numeracy at even a basic level. One of the earliest finds of such graffiti was at Silchester, on which George Boon (1974, 62–64) made some thoughtful comments:

> About 150 bone, bronze or iron stili, together with part of a fir writing-tablet, indicate the widespread use of waxed tablets for accounts, memoranda and correspondence, as do little bronze seal-boxes . . . which were used to protect the soft wax impressions of signets. . . What is particularly interesting is the humble level of society which this evidence in general embraces; if a tile-maker, for example, could not only write his name and total up his production, and perhaps date it according to the Roman system, but also scribble a remark about a girl, it can certainly be concluded that literacy was prevalent. . . . Some of the graffiti display practised hands.

The interpretation can, however, be tricky: as Frere and Tomlin commented in *RIB* II.5 p. 92, 'Graffiti on tiles are often fragmentary and sometimes, particularly when written in cursive letters with a sharp point, they are difficult to read; for the coarse texture of tile is not readily receptive of fine script.' The problems are made worse in the case of some tiles which are now lost, when only a copy survives, and 'it is interesting to note that even when a graffito is reasonably complete and easily legible, at *RIB* 2491.209 (**H61** below), it may nevertheless fail to make sense.'

It is evident that many persons present at a tilery could read and write. Some were workers who recorded the progress of their work (*RB* 2491.1 and 3); others, it seems, were being instructed in literacy, if this is the true purpose of the alphabets (*RIB* 2491.135–145) and of other fragments thought to indicate reading- or writing-practice (*RIB* 2491.148, 152, 154, 155, 209 and 222); the best-known of these (*RIB* 2491.148, **H58** below) contains a Vergilian tag. Many of the graffiti on tiles record details of production; quantities made or a date (probably as a check on the length of time for the tiles to 'cure' before firing); numerals on the edges of tiles are probably tally-marks, while other marks have been identified as 'Signatures' and sometimes the tiler has left his name or a simple wish for good luck (*RIB* 2491.114, 153 and 155). All the graffiti were done before the bricks or tiles were fired unless specifically noted.

In passing it is worth drawing attention to the similar production practice used in the manufacture of barrels, as is shown from the evidence of a barrel from Silchester (*Calleva*) made of silver fir, height 1956 mm, maximum width of a stave 152.5 mm, diameter of the barrel 800 mm (*RIB* 2442.28); now in Reading Museum. The barrel was found in 1897 lining a well in Insula XVII, but the marks were not noted until 1960. Its eighteen staves were numbered with a blunt implement on the inside of each face between 432–889 mm from the top in anticlockwise order I – XVIII; the staves have earlier alphabetical marks on them showing that they were re-used in the manufacture of this barrel. See also *RIB* 2442.29 for a similar barrel with staves marked I – XVI from London, found in 1933 on the site of the Bank of England.

H51 A maker's mark — Date unknown

Clementinus made (this) box-flue tile.

[*RIB* 2.5.2491.1 = EDCS-50800398. Silchester (Calleva)]

Part of a brick (1/4) found in 1901 during excavations in Insula XXVII. Now in Reading Museum.

H52 A tally of production. — Date unknown

Twenty *pila*-bricks, four voussoir flue-tiles (*cuniati*), five hundred and sixty-five box flue-tiles (*tubi*).

[*RIB* 2.5.2491.2 = EDCS-50801141. *JRS* (1940), 187–8 No. 20. Wiggonholt, West Sussex]

Part of a pila-brick (1/2), found in 1939 during excavation of a bath-house at Lickfold. Parham Park. Cursive graffito.

H53 A man's pride in his work – or a mark of ownership — Date unknown

Primus has made sixty.

[*RIB* 2.5.2491.3 = EDCS-50800920. Leicester (Ratae)]

Box-flue tile found in 1882 near High Cross. Now in Leicester Museum. Graffito drawn with a comb, creating a calligraphic effect.

H54 Phew! Job done! — Date unknown

Enough!

[*RIB* 2.5.2491.159 = EDCS-50800391. Silchester (Calleva Atrebatum)]

Graffito drawn with a finger on a brick, 'satis' – implying daily task or batch completed!

H55 A batch-mark — Date unknown

By the hand of [...]. . . days before the Nones of August [2, 3 or 4 August] twenty-five (or more) tiles.

[*RIB* 2.5.2491.10. London (Londinium)]

Part of a tegula found in 1978 at Watling Court, re-used in a wall of a building destroyed in the Hadrianic fire. Now in the Museum of London. Graffiti partly overlapping a finger-drawn 'signature'.

H56 A batch-mark — Date unknown

Six days before the Kalends of October (26 September), by hand 199 (tiles).

[*RIB* 2.5.2491.14. Silchester (Calleva Atrebatum)]

Fragment of brick, now in Reading Museum. Graffito.

The number form, 'ICC' is unorthodox for 199 (CXCIX), but more plausible than part of a name.

H57 Trouble at work? — ? 4th century AD

Every day for thirteen days Austalis has been wandering by himself.

[*RIB* 2.5.2491.147; *EDCS*-50800214*. London (Londinium)]

Graffito on a brick 425 by 311 mm., found in 1886 in Warwick Lane. Now in the Museum of London.

The Latin is in a poetic couplet modelled on that popularised by the hymns of St Ambrose, thus showing a late date.

H58 A slight hint of learning? — Date unknown

Untrustworthy Pertacus, Campester, Lucilianus, Campanus, all fell silent.

[*RIB* 2.5.2491.148. Silchester (Calleva Atrebatum)]

Graffito on part of a box-flue tile found c. 1850. Now in Reading Museum.

The cursive graffito is written in three separate lines, *Pertacus perfidus / Campester Lucilianus/ Campanus conticuere omnes.* Boon (1974, 64) suggests that this was 'probably a writing-lesson which was meant to be copied. The unmanageable shape of the specimen, an unbaked flue-tile (or *tibulus*, as another Silchester graffito names it) subsequently returned to stock, fired, and sold, suggests that the lesson was given at the tilery, in order that workmen should have the necessary skill to keep their tallies and mark each batch appropriately. The circumstances which may have led learners beyond this stage are quite obscure. A similar list of names written on a thin sheet of lead was found at Leintwardine, see *JRS* LIX, 241. Frere and Tomlin (*RIB* 2.5.138) suggest that 'All fell silent' (*conticuere omnes)* is a quotation from one of the most famous lines of Virgil's *Aeneid,* the first line of book two. It is the most frequently quoted on the walls of Pompeii (Cooley 2014, appendix 2).

H59 Two examples of metrical graffiti — Date unknown

Armea has taught me to say 'No, thank you' to everyone (else).

[*RIB* 2.5.2491.146 (i) and (ii); =*EDCS*-09200330*. Binchester (Vinovia)]

Parts of a tegula (1/2 and 1/4 ¼), 170 by 180 mm, thickness 35 mm, found in two conjoining pieces in 1977 and 1978 respectively, unstratified, on the site of the praetorium of the fort. Now in the Bowes Museum Barnard Castle.

A line of hexameter poetry, but with a syllable missed out, showing that it was copied. The original source is unknown, but the idea is conventional, e.g Propertius 1.10.9 and a graffito from Pompeii (*CIL* 4.1520 = Cooley 2014, D87). The translation, 'No, thank you' is a likely guess suggested by Frere and Tomlin for the Latin '*recte tibi*', literally 'rightly for you' which seems to have had a colloquial meaning. Another broken tile had been found 100 years previously with just the first half of this line. For full details, see *RIB* 2.5, page 137.

H60 Writing practice in the tilery? probably 4th century AD

ABCDEFGHIKLMOPR [. . .]/ ABCDEF [. . .]HIKL [. . .]

[*RIB* 2.5.2491.135. Caves Inn (Tripontium), Warwickshire]

Four conjoining fragments of a tegula found in 1965 during excavation of a Roman building on the west side of Watling Street. Now in Warwick Museum.

Cursive graffito: some of the letters are in New Roman Cursive.

H61 More writing practice? Date unknown

[. . .]/ SVIG [. . .]/ INSRBISEVVI [. . .]

[*RIB* 2.5.2491.209]

Unrecorded provenance, but probably from the Roman villa at Lillyhorn, Bisley with Lipiatt, Gloucestershire. Now in Stroud Museum. Part of a tegula on which graffito has been cut with a fine point in capital letters:

'The graffito makes no sense and is probably a practice exercise in forming capitals' (so *RIB*).

SECTION J

RELIGION

The Romans made no attempt to force their religion on other peoples, or to interfere with native religions, unless the latter involved inhuman or obscene practices. Thus they suppressed the human sacrifice associated with the cult of Baal in North Africa, and with Druidism in Gaul and Britain, hence the opposition of the Druids to Rome. They did not rally popular opposition, and their political importance has been exaggerated.

The effect of the Roman presence varied. In remote rural areas Celtic religious practices undoubtedly survived little changed. (Inscriptions tell us nothing of this: their evidence is therefore partial and distorting.) Celtic religion does not seem to have advanced far beyond the merely propitiatory stage – appeasing vaguely-defined supernatural powers in advance, to avert disasters – and had only just begun to create individual deities. Roman influence, where it impinged, helped to "crystallise" Celtic deities as individual powers. Roman religion had advanced further. Relations with gods involved a sort of contract. The dedicant vowed (in advance) to do something afterwards – usually to dedicate an altar – if the god would act for him (e.g. give him a safe journey home, **J7**). After the desired end was achieved, the dedicant "paid his vow". The commonest formula is *VSLM* (*uotum soluit libens merito,* 'fulfilled his vow willingly and deservedly', found very frequently in the examples which follow). Romans and Britons alike saw no real difference between Roman and Celtic deities, or deities originating elsewhere. Thus the Roman Mars and the Celtic Lenus (**F44**) appeared to be the same war-god. (The Celts might have different names for the same god in different areas, cf. **J25–J27, J29**). So we find Romans worshipping British gods (**C42, G14**, **J24**, **J17, J19**, **J44 (ii)**, **J46**) and Britons worshipping Roman gods (**F16**, **H29**, **J7**, **J10**, cf. **F40**), and Roman and native gods are often fused together (**D9**, **F36**, **F44**, **H8**, **H9**, **J14**, **J22**, **J25–J27**, **J29**, **J37**, **J41**).

The Romans made political use of religion in only two ways:

(a) By instituting the "Provincial Cult" honouring deified (former) emperors, the cult maintained by a council of delegates from the cities (which contributed according to wealth), which met probably at or near London (**F18**, **J4**). This provided an outlet for the loyalty, and ambition, of leading provincials (the Council chose annually a "High Priest of the Province"), but its most important function was not religious: it formed a means of direct communication with the emperor – for petitions, complaints, etc., bypassing the governor.

(b) By instituting a very full military religious calendar of festivals, to promote the loyalty of troops to their unit, to the empire and especially to the emperor. The "official" deities cultivated – on fixed days – by units included both traditional Roman gods like Jupiter, Juno, Minerva and Mars, and even Hercules, and also military aspects like Victoria (**D14**, **H9**), Disciplina (e.g. *RIB* 1127) and the standards of the unit (**D36** cf. **J2**). The calendar included annual vows to Jupiter on 3 January (**C17**, **C18**, **G43**, **J5–J6**), and ceremonies on the birthday and accession-day of the emperor, or previous emperors (**J3**), and the 'birthday' of the unit. In private life, while soldiers (and provincials) might thus be influenced to cultivate "official", or other Roman deities (**C31**, **J7**, **J9**, **J12**, **J59**) they often preferred non-Roman gods, both British, like Belatucadrus (**J24**) or Veteris **J44 (i)**), and others from elsewhere, like Jupiter Dolichenus from Syria (**J51**, **J52** or Serapis from Egypt (**G15**). The official military religious policy probably had little effect.

A widespread and spontaneous development was the cult of the *numen* of the emperor. As defined by Varro and Festus, *numen* implies power – the god-like power of the emperor. Some of the first emperors were reluctant to allow direct worship of themselves. Instead a deity was created out of his enormous power. Dedications, whether to "official" gods (**D9**, **F9**, **F41**, **J5 (i)**, **J2**, **J9**) or others (**F44**, **F46**, **J28**, **J21**), whether public dedications, e.g. by units (**F41**, **J5 (i)**, **J28**, **J21**, cf. **F18**) or by private individuals (**F9**, **F38**, **F44**, **J9**) are often accompanied, and reinforced, by a dedication to the *numen Augusti*. This development is a natural growth: it has nothing to do with the Provincial Cult.

But as imperial bureaucracy expanded, and government became more and more impersonal and crushing, so the ordinary provincial felt less and less direct personal involvement in the empire's fate. The old, mechanical paganism, in spite of some vague belief in a shadowy after-life (cf. the formula *Dis Manibus* and note **J8**), ceased to seem meaningful, and more and more people turned to systems of belief which did offer a place, and a commitment, to the individual – the "mystery religions", particularly Mithraism (**J54**) and Christianity (**J57** note; **J64**, note; **J81**). These have much in common – involving man in the struggle of good with evil, in which man is championed by a saviour who appears as divine. Mithraism taught bravery and honesty, and thus was popular with military officers and merchants, but it was expensive for its adherents, and excluded women. Christianity had more to offer, to all ranks, and to both men and women. It spread slowly, in the cities at first, only beginning to win over the countryside after the middle of the fourth century. But when Roman rule came to an end the Britons were essentially a Christian people.

Durham 1971; Milton Keynes 1994 J. C. Mann

(a) THE ROMAN DEITIES

Gods of Rome mentioned in earlier sections are Apollo, **F36**, **F45**, **H27**; Diana Regina, **C31**; Fortuna, **C21**, **D4**, **G20**, **G42**; Hercules **H8**; Jupiter **C17, C18, D37, F3, F9, F40, G43**; Mars (identified with Celtic gods), **F44**, **H9**, **H24**; Mercury, **C46**, **F45**; Minerva, **F16**; Neptune, **F16**, **G44**, **H25?**; Neptune and Ocean, **C6**; Ocean and Tethys, **F2**; Parcae (Fates), **F46**; Silvanus, **G36**, **H29**; Victoria, **D14**, **H9** (and see index for her representation on coins and monuments); Vulcan **F40, F41** Note also the cult of the *Genius*, *Genius Domini et Signorum*, **D36**; *Genius Loci*, **H30** and **J18**.

J1 An altar to Apollo — Date unknown

To the god Apollo, Aprilis has paid his vow, willingly, deservedly.

[*Britannia* 45 (2014) 436.5. Chesterholm (Vindolanda)]

A buff sandstone altar, 0.18 x 0.265m, 0.165 m deep. Found in a barrack-block south of the praetorium at Vindolanda in the 2013 excavations.

See also **J14** below, where Apollo is identified with the Celtic god Maponus.

J2 The birthday of Augustus — 23 September AD 244

To the Divine Powers of the Emperor and the Genius of the Second Legion Augusta, in honour of the [Eagle? ... *(four lines lost)*...], the senior centurion gave this gift; dedicated on 23 September in the consulship of Peregrinus and Aemilianus, under the charge of Ursus, *actarius* of the same le[gion ...]

[*RIB* 327 add. Caerleon (Isca)]

Fragments from an inscribed pilaster or door jamb, found in 1800 on the site of the offices of the headquarters building in the fortress. All are now lost except for one fragment which is in the Caerleon Museum.

23 September was the birthday of Augustus, which the legion celebrated as its own 'birthday'. On 'Divine Powers' (*numina Augustorum*), and the various ways in which honouring the emperors was included in official and non-official worship of the gods, see the introduction on Religion. 'Eagle' (*Aquila*) is restored in line 7 because of the well-known association between the *primus pilus* and the eagle (Keppie 1984, 67).

J3 Personal payment of a vow in London — Date unknown

To [...] goddess and [the Diviniti]es of the Emperors ... [...]bogius, [by nationality] a Pannonian, (paid his) vow.

[*Britannia* 44 (2013), 381 = EDCS-69200366. London (Londinium)]

A copper-alloy plaque found in 2012 on the Thames foreshore at Wandsworth Reach, London.

J4 Anencletus *provincialis* Late 1st–early 2nd century AD

To the spirits of the departed (and) to Claudia Martina, aged 19; Anencletus, slave of the province, *(set this up)* to his most devoted wife; here she lies.

[*RIB* 21. London (Londinium)]

A statue-base found in 1806 near the London Coffee House, Ludgate Hill. Now in the Museum of London.

The "provincial cult" honoured past emperors who had been deified. It was maintained by the provincial council, which, on the strength of this inscription and **F18** is thought to have met at or near London. It had its own staff, including slaves, who were termed "slaves of the province".

J5 Maryport altars

Iuppiter Optimus Maximus, Jupiter Best and Greatest, normally abbreviated to IOM, was the most important and by far the most invoked of the official gods of Rome. Auxiliary units appear to have set up annual dedications to him. The clearest evidence comes from Maryport, where seventeen altars dedicated to 'Jupiter, Best and Greatest' (*IOM*) were discovered in excavations carried out in 1870 on a site about 300m north-east of the Roman fort. Together these altars appear to be part of a sequence of altars, perhaps dedicated annually on 3 January, when vows were taken and paid for the safety and welfare of the emperor, two days after the renewal of the military oath of loyalty. As these examples here show, the dedications are extremely formulaic; altars **(ii)** and **(iii)** below are almost identical in their wording, and perhaps illustrate the military 'epigraphic habit' more than any other examples in this volume. See also **C17** and **C18** for two more examples. In **J5 i** the cult of the *Numen Augusti* is linked with him: see the Introduction on Religion.

(i) To *IOM* by the First Cohort of Spaniards Hadrianic

To Jupiter, Best and Greatest, and to the Divine Power of the Emperor, the First Cohort of Spaniards set this up.

[*RIB* 815. Maryport, Cumbria (Alauna)]

Altar found in 1870 outside the fort at Maryport. Now in the Senhouse Museum, Maryport.

(ii) To *IOM* by the First Cohort of Baetasians 2nd half of 2nd century AD

To Jupiter, Best and Greatest, the First Cohort of Baetasians, Roman citizens, which is commanded by Titus Attius Tutor, prefect, willingly, gladly and deservedly fulfilled its vow.

[*RIB* 830 add. = EDCS-07801121. Maryport, Cumbria (Alauna)]

Altar found in 1870 near the fort. Now in the Senhouse Museum, Maryport.

For Tutor's later career see *CIL* 3.5331 (*ILS* 2734).

(iii) To *IOM* by the First Cohort of Baetasians 2nd half of 2nd century AD

To Jupiter Best and Greatest, the First Cohort of Baetasians, Roman Citizens, which is commanded by Attius Tutor, prefect, willingly, gladly and deservedly fulfilled its vow.

[EDCS-69200370. Maryport, Cumbria (Alauna)]

A red sandstone altar found in 2012 at Camp Farm, Maryport. See Britannia *44 (2013), pp. 382–3.*

Apart from the omission of Attius Tutor's praenomen the altar is almost identical to **(ii)** above. Similarities of letter-shape and layout suggest that these two altars, together with two others, (*RIB* 837 and 842), which Attius Tutor dedicated to Mars Militaris and Victoria Augusta, while he was prefect were carved by the same person.

J6 To *IOM* at Moresby — Date unknown

To Jupiter, Best and Greatest, the Second Cohort of Thracians, *equitata* under the command of its prefect Mamius Nepos, *(set this up).*

[*RIB* 797 add. Moresby, Cumbria (Gabrosentum?)]

A base found about 1878 outside the fort. Now in Carlisle Museum.

For other dedications to IOM by units or commanding officers see **D37** and **G43**; **F9** and **J31** are by *beneficiarii consulares;* **F3** by a governor; **F40** by *vicani;* **J18** by legionaries. Birley reads the prefect's name as Mani[li]us Nepos.

J7 A promise to Jupiter and Vulcan — Date unknown

To the god Jupiter and Volcanus, I, Vassinus, promised six denarii when they might be pleased to bring me, their votary, safe home; and on the fulfilment of my vow I have paid the money.

[*RIB* 215 = BM OA.252.6. Stony Stratford, Buckinghamshire]

A piece of silver plate, found in 1789 with other silver articles in an urn on the line of Watling Street. Now in the British Museum.

The letters are small, since the plate is less than 8 centimetres square, but neatly executed. Jupiter and Vulcan are worshipped together by an individual. They appear together also on **F40**; Vulcan appears alone on **F41**; both are by *vicani.*

J8 Manes — Date unknown

To the spirits of the departed: Corellia Optata, aged 13.

> You mysterious spirits of the departed, who dwell
> in Pluto's Acherusian realms, who are sought by
> the paltry ashes and by the shade the phantom
> of the body, after the brief light of life. I, the
> father of an innocent daughter, a pitiable victim
> of unfair hope, lament this, her final end.

Quintus Corellius Fortis, her father, had this set up.

[*RIB* 684 add. York (Eboracum)]

Part of a tombstone, found in 1861 at The Mount, York. Now in the Yorkshire Museum,

Drawing in *RIB* online. A large glass vessel, sealed with lead and containing the ashes of the girl, was found near the tombstone. This is of interest because it reflects Roman philosophy about death, although it does not name a god. Lines 3–11 of the Latin, indented in the translation above, are hexameter verses. **G12** also included verses as part of the epitaph.

J9 The Foss Dyke Mars — Late 2nd or 3rd century AD

To the god Mars and the Divine Powers of the Emperors; the Colasuni, Bruccius and Caratius, presented this at their own expense at a cost of 100 sesterces; Celatus the coppersmith fashioned it and gave a pound of bronze made at the cost of 3 denarii.

[*RIB* 274 = BM OA.248. The Foss Dyke, Lincolnshire]

Two panels of a bronze statuette of Mars, found about 1774 on the Foss Dyke (the canal which connects Lincoln with the Trent). Now in the British Museum.

The engraving, which is on two panels of the base of the statuette (standing 27 centimetres high) is well executed. Mars was popular in his own right, not only in his military but his agricultural aspects; he is frequently identified with other gods – see below, **J22–J29**, **J58** also **F44**, **H9**, **H24**.

J10 To the god Romulus — Date unknown

To the god Romulus: Gulioepius presented this, Juventinus made it.

[*RIB* 132. Custom Scrubs, Bisley, Gloucestershire]

A gabled relief found in 1799 built into a summer-house at Watercombe House. Now in the Gloucester City Museum.

The inscription is above the figure of the war-clad Romulus, who has a crested helmet with side-plumes and cheek-pieces, and also a large protective apron. He holds spear and shield, rather clumsily carved, and on his right is an altar with offerings (drawing in *RIB* online). It was found with *RIB* 131 which is a similar relief, dedicated to Mars Olludius (drawing in *RIB* online).

J11 An altar to Silvanus — Date unknown

Sacred to Silvanus […] Publius Fabius [..., freedman of Publius], (and) Publius Fabius [..., freedman of Publius], in accordance with their vow […]

[*Britannia* 43 (2012). 395 = EDCS-67400307. London (Londinium)]

Fragment of a limestone columnar statue-base originally c. 0.37m in diameter, found in 2011 at 25 London Bridge Street, London SE1, in the borough of Southwark.

The Latin remaining gives only *P. FAB*. . . in both lines 2 and three of the fragment; these might have been father and son, but as Roger Tomlin notes in *Britannia*, p. 396 n.3, 'they are much more likely to have been freedmen of a Publius Fabius [...], with *Publii l(ibertus)* forming the middle part of their nomenclature; they would have been distinguished by their cognomina, now lost.'

J12 To the god Silvanus — Date unknown

To the god Silvanus, Marcus Didius Provincialis, *beneficiarius* (on the staff) of the governor, willingly and deservedly fulfilled his vow.

[*RIB* 1085. Lanchester, Co. Durham (Longovicium)]

A pedestal found before 1807 at Lanchester. Now in the Great North Museum, Hancock.

For *beneficiarii* see **F8–F10, F47, G19, J31**. For other dedications to Silvanus, see **G36, H29** and **J41**.

(b) CELTIC AND GERMANIC DEITIES

Celtic gods from earlier sections include Anociticus (**C42**), Boudiga (**F23**), Camulus (**H24**), Gallic (and other) Mother Goddesses (**F10**, **G16**), Nehalennia (**H27**), (Hercules) Saegon (**H8 (i)**), Sattada (**F42**), Sulis (**H28**). And see also curses addressed to Celtic deities, **J57, J60, J64.**

J13 The goddess Ahuarda — Early Hadrianic (*c*. AD 120 – 130)

To the goddess Ahuarda, the First Cohort of Tungrians [. . .]

[*Britannia* 44 (2013) 384.5 = EDCS-58700044*. Chesterholm (Vindolanda)]

A fragmentary sandstone dedication slab found in 2012 at Vindolanda on the edge of a filled-in ditch of the Period 4 fort, 12m south of a second-century temple where it have may originally been sited. Neatly written within a carved wreath pattern.

J14 To Apollo Maponus — 2nd–early 3rd century AD

To Apollo Maponus, Quintus Terentius Firmus, son of Quintus, of the Oufentine voting-tribe, from Saena, prefect of the camp of the Sixth Legion Victrix Pia Fidelis, gave and dedicated this.

[*RIB* 1120. Corbridge (Coria?)]

Altar found c. 1866 beside Hexham Abbey. Now in the south transept, Hexham Abbey.

Saena is Sena Julia, in Etruria, N. Italy. For Apollo Maponus cf. **F36**. The title *praefectus castrorum legionis* is gradually replaced by *praefectus legionis,* and the last known example of the fuller title is early third century *(CIL* 13.8014, AD 201; *RIB* 490 should be later, but cannot be precisely dated). For an inscription to Apollo alone, see **J1**.

J15 To the goddess Brigantia — Date unknown

Sacred to the goddess Brigantia; Congenniccus willingly and deservedly fulfilled his vow.

[*RIB* 1053. South Shields (Arbeia)]

Altar found in 1895 near the fort at South Shields. Now in Arbeia Fort Museum, South Shields.

On the back is carved a bird; on the right side a *patera,* on the left a jug (*CSIR* I.1, no. 233). Brigantia is presumably the goddess of the Brigantes, and is identified with Victory (**D9**), Minerva Victrix (**G14**) and with Juno Caelestis, the consort of Jupiter Dolichenus (**J51**). The dedications all come from the territory ascribed to the Brigantes, if **G14** is evidence for Birrens being in Brigantian territory.

J16 An altar to the goddess Britania ?before AD 208

To the goddess Britania (*sic*).

[*Britannia* 43 (2012) 396 = EDCS-67400303. Dover (Dubris)]

The capital and upper part of a limestone altar, 0.29 x 0.26m, 0.222m deep. Found in 1976 in a late Roman context in the Saxon Shore fort at Dover (Dubris), but probably from the fort of the classis Britannica, which was abandoned in c. AD 208.

This is the first example from Britain of a dedication to this goddess, though cf. *RIB* 643, *Britanniae sanctae,* 2175, *genio terrae Britannicae*, and 2195, *campestribus et Britanni(ae)*. Roger Tomlin comments in *Britannia* ad loc. n. 5 that 'the mis-spelling . . is trivial and well-attested, but is previously unknown from Britain itself, since the Carlisle writing-tablet (*RIB* II.4, 2443.5) 'addressed to someone *IN BRITANIA'* must have originated from elsewhere. In Dover, a port of entry, the mis-spelling might suggest that the dedicator had just arrived from another province . . .'

J17 Altars to Cocidius 3rd or early 4th century AD

(i) To holy Cocidius, Aurunceius Felicessemus, tribune, promoted from *evocatus,* willingly and deservedly fulfilled his vow.

[*RIB* 988. Bewcastle, Cumbria (Fanum Cocidi)]

Altar found c. 1792 in the bed of the Kirk Beck at Bewcastle. Now in Carlisle Museum.

Fanum Cocidi means "the shrine of Cocidius". For the identification of Bewcastle as *Fanum Cocidi* see Rivet and Smith 1979, 363. An *evocatus* was a soldier of the Praetorian Guard who had been retained in the army after completion of his sixteen years' service. Some *evocati* were promoted to a higher rank: 'from' does not necessarily imply that the promotion here was directly from *evocatus* to tribune.

(ii) To the holy god Cocidius, Quintus Peltrasius Maximus, tribune, promoted from *cornicularius* to their Eminences, the Praetorian Prefects, willingly and deservedly fulfilled his vow.

[*RIB* 989. Bewcastle, Cumbria (Fanum Cocidi)]

Altar found in 1898 built into the foundations of Bewcastle church. Now in Carlisle Museum.

For the identification of Bewcastle as *Fanum Cocidi* see **J17(i)**. As in **J17(i)**, 'from' does not necessarily imply a direct promotion to tribune. A *cornicularius* was a senior soldier, ranking just below centurion, in charge of the clerical office of a senior officer, in this case the commanders of the Praetorian Guard.

J18 To *IOM*, Cocidius and the *Genius Loci* Date unknown

To Jupiter, Best and Greatest, and to the god Cocidius, and to the Spirit of This Place (*Genius Huius Loci*), the soldiers of the Second Legion Augusta on garrison-duty willingly and deservedly fulfilled their vow.

[*RIB* 1583. Housesteads (Vercovicium)]

Altar found in 1898 in the Mithraeum, south of Housesteads fort. Now in Chesters Museum.

For Cocidius, a local god of the north-west of England, with worship centred on Bewcastle *(Fanum Cocidi)*, see also **J17**. For worship of the *Genius Loci*, the tutelary deity of a place, cf. **H30.** *CSIR* I.6, no. 39.

J19 Dedication to Coventina — Probably 3rd century AD

To the goddess Covventina, Titus D[...] Cosconianus, prefect of the First Cohort of Batavians, willingly and deservedly *(fulfilled his vow).*

[*RIB* 1534. Carrawburgh (Brocolitia)]

Dedication found in 1876 in Coventina's Well, west of Carrawburgh fort. Now in Chesters Museum.

The inscription is set beneath a relief of the goddess reclining with a branch in her right hand. The First Cohort of Batavians is well attested at Carrawburgh in the third century AD (the earliest instance, *RIB* 1544, being dated AD 213–217) and is still there in the *Notitia Dignitatum* (LACTOR 11, Z2.1, line 39). For the sculpture see (drawing in *RIB* online).

J20 The Goddess *Gallia* at Vindolanda — 3rd century AD

The citizens of Gaul to the goddess *Gallia*, and the (citizens of) Britain in harmony (dedicated this).

[Britannia 38 (2007) 346.2 = EDCS-46600262. Chesterholm (Vindolanda)]

A quadrangular base of buff sandstone, 0.56 x 0.30m, 0.39m deep, re-used in a Roman drainage channel at the SW corner of the stone fort. Full detail in A. Birley and J. Blake, Vindolanda Excavations *2005–2006 (2007), 104–12, with fig. 130.*

The *cives Galli* were almost certainly citizens of Gallia Lugdunensis recruited to serve in the *cohors IIII Gallorum*, based at Vindolanda in the third century; the context in which the stone was found is probably early fourth century. This inscription is evidence that the army in Britain was not altogether recruited locally.

J21 To the goddess Garmanagabis — AD 238–244

To the goddess Garmangabis and to the Divine Power of our Emperor Gordian for the welfare of the detachment of Suebians of Longovicium, *Gordiana,* the soldiers deservedly fulfilled their vow.

[*RIB* 1074. Lanchester (Longovicium)]

Altar found in 1893 near Lanchester fort. Now in the south porch, Lanchester church.

On the left side is carved a knife and a jug; on the right a *patera* and a disk. Cf. **D34–D35**, inscriptions from Lanchester also set up under Gordian III. For irregular units in forts in the third century cf. **D36**, **G42–G43**, **J28**.

J22 Barkway Mars Alator

Date unknown

To the god Mars Alator Dum[...], Censorinus, son of Gemellus, willingly and deservedly fulfilled his vow.

[*RIB* 218 = BM 1817,0308.3. Barkway, Herts]

A fine gold plaque, found in 1744 during the digging of a chalk pit in Rookery Wood near Barkway. Now in the British Museum.

This and **J29** formed part of a small but valuable cache. They had probably been looted from a shrine on the line of Ermine Street. This one is a votive plaque 10 cm x 18 cm high, with the inscription surmounted by Mars, standing in his shrine and looking to his right. The whole is surrounded by a leaf-pattern. It was probably attached to wood. Celtic gods and goddesses are diverse and elusive; where it suits the worshipper, he may identify them with Roman counterparts. Mars appealed most strongly to the Celts, and he appears conjoined with a wide range of local deities: note **F44** and **H9** in addition to those in this section, **J23**, **J25–29**.

J23 To Mars Belatucadrus

Late 2nd or 3rd century AD

To Mars Belatucadrus and to the Divine Powers of the Emperors, Julius Augustalis, agent of Julius Lupus, the prefect, *(set this up)*.

[*RIB* 918 = BM 1868,1004.1. Old Penrith, Cumbria (Voreda)]

Altar found about 1783 apparently within the fort at Old Penrith, Now in the British Museum.

Belatucadrus appears also in a number of inscriptions from Brougham, Cumbria, without reference to Mars, *RIB* 772–777.

J24 To Belatucadrus at Old Carlisle

Late 2nd or 3rd century AD

To the holy god Belatucadrus, Aurelius Tasulus, veteran, willingly and deservedly fulfilled his vow.

[*RIB* 887 add. Old Carlisle, Cumbria (Maglona?)]

Altar found c. 1868 at Greenhill, about 1600 metres south-west of the fort at Old Carlisle. Now in Carlisle Museum.

The veteran, like that in **G46**, does not mention his unit. For the suggestion that the Roman name of Old Carlisle was Maglona, see Rivet and Smith 1979, 407; the key inscription is **F40**.

J25 To Mars Corotiacus

Date unknown

To Mars Corotiacus, Simplicia for herself willingly [and deservedly] set up this offering. Glaucus made it.

[*RIB* 213 = BM 1858,0113.1. Martlesham, Suffolk]

Bronze shield-shaped base of a statuette with rounded recesses; inscribed round rim. Now in the British Museum.

All that remains of the statuette is a headless foeman and traces of hooves.

J26 To Mars Loucetius and Nemetona

Date unknown

Peregrinus, son of Secundus, a Trever, to Loucetius Mars and Nemetona willingly and deservedly fulfilled his vow.

[*RIB* 140. Bath (Aquae Sulis)]

An altar found in Stall Street, Bath, in 1753. Now in the Roman Baths Museum.

The height of lettering and the spacing are both uneven, suggesting inferior workmanship, and there is a grammatical mistake. Mars Loucetius and Nemetona were Celtic deities sometimes worshipped together: an example occurs on the west bank of the Rhine (*CIL* 13.6131 = *ILS* 4586).

J27 To Mars Rigisamus

Date unknown

To Mars Rigisamus, Iventius Sabinus gladly, willingly and deservedly fulfilled his vow.

[*RIB* 187. West Coker, Somerset]

A bronze plate found on the site of the villa at West Coker in 1862. Yeovil Museum/Museum of South Somerset: from 2011 in the Community Heritage Access Centre.

This plate, which has punched letters and a central hole for attaching it to a wooden base, may well be associated with a bronze statuette of Mars found elsewhere on the site. Mars Rigisamus comes from Aquitania.

J28 To Mars Thincsus and Alaisiagae

(i)

Probably third century AD

To the god Mars Thincsus and the two Alaisiagae, Beda and Fimmilena, and to the Divine Power of the Emperor, the Germans, being citizens of the Tuihanti, willingly and deservedly fulfilled their vow.

[*RIB* 1593. Housesteads (Vercovicium)]

Tall square pillar, probably the left-hand jamb of the doorway to the shrine. Found in 1883 at the foot of the north slope of Chapel Hill, Housesteads. Now in Chesters Museum.

The Tuihanti may have come from the district of Twenthe, which is in the province of Overijssel, Holland. The pillar has a female figure, presumably a goddess, carved on its right side, and nothing on its left. With it was found **J28(iii)** and a sculptured arcuate lintel, having in its central panel a figure of Mars with sword, shield, and spear, and at his right hand a goose. The Alaisiagae, portrayed naked, cross-legged and as male, each extend towards Mars what appears to be a palm branch, and carry a wreath in their other hand *(CSIR* 1.6, no. 159, plate 44). These German deities are brought from the lower Rhine area. Note the linkage of this and **J28(ii)** and **(iii)** with the *Numen Augusti,* on which see the Introduction, 'Religion'.

(ii) *c.* AD 222–235

To the god Mars and the two Alaisiagae and to the Divine Power of the Emperor, the Germans being citizens of the Tuihanti of the block of Frisians of Vercovicium, *Severiana Alexandriana,* willingly and deservedly fulfilled their vow.

[*RIB* 1594. Housesteads (Vercovicium)]

Altar found in 1883 with **J28(i)** *and a sculptured arcuate lintel. Now in Chesters Museum.*

On the left side are carved a knife and an axe, on the right a *patera* and a jug (*CSIR* I.6, no. 160). For the Tuihanti see **J28(i)**.

(iii) 3rd century AD

To the goddesses the Alaisiagae, Baudihillia and Friagabis, and to the Divine Power of the Emperor, the unit of Hnaudifridus gladly and deservedly fulfilled its vow.

[*RIB* 1576. Housesteads (Vercovicium)]

Altar found in 1920 on the Chapel Hill, Housesteads. Now in Housesteads Museum.

J29 Barkway Mars Toutatis — Date unknown

To Mars Toutatis, Tiberius Claudius Primus, freedman of Attius, willingly and deservedly fulfilled his vow.

[*RIB* 219 = BM 1817,0308.2. Barkway, Herts]

A silver votive plaque found with ***J22****. Now in the British Museum.*

Silver plaque, 53 x 26 cm. Part of the same find as **J22**, this plaque is much bigger, again in a leaf shape, but less elaborate than **J22.** This plaque has no nail-holes. The inscription is punched in dots in an ansate panel.Toutatis (or -es) is well-known in north-east Gaul.

J30 To Toutatis — Date unknown

To the god Toutatis.
[Use and] be happy.

[*Britannia* 41 (2010) 448 = EDCS-59500227*. Hockliffe, Bedfordshire]

Fragment of a silver finger-ring found in 2005, and incised on the bezel and the shoulders.

J31 To Jupiter and the Matres Ollototae Date unknown

To Jupiter, Best and Greatest, and to the Mother Goddesses Ollototae, or Overseas, Pomponius Donatus, *beneficiarius* of the governor, for the welfare of himself and his household willingly fulfilled his vow.

[*RIB* 1030. Binchester (Vinovia)]

Altar found in 1891 about 70 metres south of Binchester fort. Now in the Great North Museum, Hancock.

For *beneficiarius consularis* cf. **F8–F10**, **J12**. For other dedications to Mother Goddesses cf. **F10**, **G16**, **J32–J36**.

J32 A promise to the Mother Goddesses Date unknown

[To the Mother Goddesses] I, [Ant]onianus, dedicate this shrine. But grant that the increase of my venture may confirm my prayers, and soon I will hallow this poem with golden letters one by one.

[*RIB* 2059. Bowness-on-Solway (Maia)]

A dedication slab found c. 1790 at Bowness. Now in Carlisle Museum.

The Mother Goddess triad is frequently found in Britain and the Rhineland – cf. **F10**, and **G16**. Lines 3–4 and 5–6 in the original are in verse, and the probable inspiration of the verses was Virgil, *Eclogues* 7.35–36 (to Priapus).

J33 The Mother Goddesses Hananeftae and Ollolotae Date unknown

To the Mother Goddesses Hananeftae and Ollolotae. Aelius Victor gladly, willingly, and deservedly fulfilled his vow.

[*Britannia* 42 (2011) 463–4 = EDCS-55701802. Manchester]

A pale buff sandstone altar, 0.37 x 0.97 m, 0.29 m deep, found in 2008, in Chester Road/ Great Jackson Street.

This is the first British instance of the *matres Hananeftae*, who are attested in Lower Germany at Cologne and Wissen. The *Matres Ollolotae* were attested only in Britain, at Heronbridge near Chester (*RIB* 574) and at Binchester (**J31**).

J34 To the Matres Suleviae at Colchester Date unknown

To the Mother Goddesses Suleviae, Similis, son of Attius, a citizen of the Cantiaci, willingly fulfilled his vow.

[*RIB* 192 Colchester (Camulodunum)]

Dedication stone found in 1881 just west of the west wall. Now in Colchester Museum.

The *civitas* of the Cantiaci was centred around Canterbury. The Suleviae seem to have originated in Gaul.

J35 To the Suleviae at Bath ?2nd century AD

To the Suleviae, Sulinus, a sculptor, son of Brucetus, gladly and deservedly made this offering.

[*RIB* 151. Bath (Aquae Suits).]

Statue-base found in 1753 in Stall Street. Now in the Roman Baths Museum.

Cf. **H28**, made by a *lapidarius* at Bath.

J36 To the Suleviae at Cirencester ?2nd century AD

To the Suleviae, Sulinus, son of Brucetus, willingly and deservedly fulfilled his vow.

[*RIB* 105. Cirencester (Corinium)]

Altar found in 1899 in the north-west part of the town. Now in the Corinium Museum.

Two reliefs of the three *matres* and other sculptures were found with this altar (*CSIR* I.7, nos 116–7). The site may possibly have been the workshop of Sulinus, who was a sculptor, **J35** but is more likely to have been a local shrine of the Matres Suleviae, as Haverfield proposed.

J37 To Sulis Minerva Late 2nd or 3rd century AD

To the goddess Sulis Minerva and to the Divine Powers of the Emperors, Gaius Curiatius Saturninus, centurion of the Second Legion Augusta, willingly and deservedly fulfilled his vow for himself and his kindred.

[*RIB* 146. Bath (Aquae Sulis)]

An altar found in 1809 in the cistern of the Cross Bath. Now in the Roman Baths Museum.

The altar is plain, but stylishly engraved.

J38 To the goddess Sulis 2nd or 3rd century AD

To the goddess Sulis for the welfare and safety of Marcus Aufidius Maximus, centurion of the Sixth Legion Victrix, Aufidius Eutuches, his freedman, willingly and deservedly fulfilled his vow.

[*RIB* 143. Bath (Aquae Sulis)]

An altar found in 1790 on the site of the Pump Room. Now in the Roman Baths Museum.

The Sixth Legion was transferred to Britain in or about AD 122. For Sulis cf. **H28**. The word 'freeman' (*libertus*) is here written 'LEB(ERTVS'). The important temple and sacred spring complex at Bath has produced a number of notable inscriptions and sculpture, the majority of which are made from the high quality local stone, Bath oolite.

J39 A priest of the goddess Sulis 2nd or 3rd century AD

To the spirits of the departed: Gaius Calpurnius Receptus, priest of the goddess Sulis, lived 75 years; Calpurnia Trifosa his freedwoman and wife had this set up.

[*RIB* 155. Bath (Aquae Sulis)]

Altar-shaped tombstone found near the Baths. Now in Roman Baths Museum.

J40 A *haruspex* of the goddess Sulis Date unknown

To the goddess Sulis, Lucius Marcius Memor, *haruspex*, dedicated (*this*).

[*JRS* 56 (1966), 217 no. 1 = *RIB* 3.3049 = EDCS-10701776. Bath (Aquae Sulis)]

Base found below a cellar floor beneath the Pump Room. Now in Roman Baths Museum.

HAR was carved originally, and centred on the line. VSP was added later. This is the first mention of HARVSPEX ("soothsayer") in Britain. This official, often of high standing in the town, interpreted omens and inspected sacrificial victims. Illustrated in *Cambridge Latin Course* III, page 8.

J41 Altar to Vinotonus Silvanus ?Early 3rd century AD

[To the god] Vinotonus Silvanus, Julius Secundus, centurion of the First Cohort of Thracians, gladly, willingly and deservedly fulfilled his vow.

[*RIB* 732 add. Bowes, Yorkshire (Lavatrae)]

Altar of millstone grit, found in 1936 in a rectangular shrine near the Eller Beck. Now in the Bowes Museum, Barnard Castle.

This and the next inscription were found in separate shrines on the Pennine moors. They commemorate successful hunting expeditions. Silvanus was the god of the country wilds and of hunting (see also **G36** and **H29**). Vinotonus was a stream-god whom the centurion identified with Silvanus. The First Cohort of Thracians was stationed at Bowes under Severus.

J42 Altar to Vinotonus ?Early 3rd century AD

To the god Vinotonus, Lucius Caesius Frontinus, prefect of the First Cohort of Thracians, from Parma, gladly, willingly, and deservedly fulfilled his vow.

[*RIB* 733. Bowes (Lavatrae)]

An altar of sandstone, found in 1946 in a circular shrine near the Eller Beck. Now on loan in the Bowes Museum, Barnard Castle.

Parma is in North Italy. The careful and elegant lettering of this altar contrasts with the firm, unadorned style of the previous one (drawings of both in *RIB* online). The First Cohort of Thracians was stationed at Bowes under Severus.

J43 Dedications to Viridius ?fourth century AD

(i) To the god Viridius; Trenico made (this) arch and gave it from his own resources.

[*RIB* 3.3170 = EDCS-44500083*. Ancaster, Lincolnshire (Causenna)]

A stone plaque found at Ancaster, Lincolnshire (Causenna) in 1961 in a modern cemetery which lies over a Roman one.

(ii) To the holy god Viridius.

[*RIB* 3.3171 = EDCS-28500397 =. Ancaster, Lincolnshire (Causenna)]

A fragment of a limestone slab, 0.52 x 0.34m, 0.13m thick, found in 2001 at Ancaster, re-used as the lining of a late Roman inhumation.

These are the only references to the god Viridius, and his cult is probably local. Tomlin, Wright and Hassall comment on *RIB* 3.3170 that 'his name derives from the first element in the Gallic names *Viridomaros* and *Viridovix*, and probably meant "vigorous," but there are no derivatives in medieval or modern Celtic languages to confirm this.'

J44 The god or goddesses 'Veteris'

The name of this god or gods appears in a number of forms, singular and plural, masculine and feminine. The following forms are known: Veteris (god – **i**); Hueteris (god – **ii**); Huitris (god – *RIB* 1603); Vitires (goddesses – **iii**); Hueteres (plural in Latin, but described as a 'god' – **iv**); Veteres (plural in Latin, but described as a god – *RIB* 1604 from Housesteads). In short, it is clear, as suggested by Birley 1979, 107 that the worshippers have difficulty in representing the god's name in the Latin alphabet. This is a poor person's deity, and the altars are small and clumsily inscribed. Of over 50 altars known, the name of the dedicator is not given or is illegible in many instances, and only two of the 30 or so named worshippers record a military rank. See further the discussion in Birley 1979, 107f.

(i) To Veteris 3rd or 4th century AD

To the holy god Veteris, Julius Pastor, *imaginifer* of the Second Cohort of Dalmatians, willingly and deservedly fulfilled his vow.

[*RIB* 1795. Carvoran (Magnis) Northumberland]

Altar found c. 1757 near Thirlwall Castle. Now in the Great North Museum, Hancock.

The *imaginifer* carried on a standard the *imago,* the portrait of the emperor.

(ii) To Hueteris Date unknown

To the god Hueteris, Superstes [and] Regulus willingly and deservedly fulfilled their vow.

[*RIB* 1602. Housesteads (Vercovicium)]

Altar found in 1910 in the north-west or northeast angle tower at Housesteads. Now in Chesters Museum.

(iii) To the Goddesses Vitires Date unknown

To the goddesses Vitires, Vitalis willingly and deservedly fulfilled his vow.

[*RIB* 1047. Chester-le-Street (Concangium)]

Altar found in 1849 on the north side of Chester-le-Street fort. Now in the Great North Museum, Hancock.

(iv) To Hueteres (Veteres) Date unknown

To the god Hueteres.

[*Britannia* 41 (2010) 447 = EDCS-59500267. Chesterholm (Vindolanda)]

A miniature buff sandstone altar found in 2009 in the intervallum road at Vindolanda, incised with shallow letters c. 12 mm high.

J45 A dedication to 'the unconquered god' ? before the second century AD

For the unconquered God, the First Cohort of Batavians made (this), (under) Aulus Maximus.

[*Britannia* 33 (2002) 358.4 = EDCS-28500408. Hadrian's Wall area]

Of unknown provenance (acquired from a dealer), an ansate votive plaque, 68 x 52 mm, cut from 'brassy' copper-alloy sheet c. 0.5 – 1mm thick. punched dots make up somewhat irregular capital letters.

Tomlin and Hassall (*Britannia* 33 (2002) 358–9, n. 11) note that 'the form of the name 'Aulus Maximus', without the *nomen gentilicum*, is an 'aristocratic affectation of the late Republic and Augustan period, not to be found in a provincial inscription of the second or third century.' They also note that the authenticity of this exemplar is 'not beyond doubt.'

(c) EASTERN DEITIES

For other mentions of Eastern deities within Roman Britain cf. Dea Syria (Carvoran), **C40**; Mars Thincsus and the Alaisiagae (Housesteads), **J28**; Serapis, **G15**, an Egyptian deity with a temple at York built by a legionary legate; and **C39**, a dedication to Sol Invictus by a detachment of the Sixth Legion.

J46 Dedications to Aesculapius and deities associated with healing

(i) To Asklepios, Hygeia and Panakeia Date unknown

The doctor Antiochos *(honours)* the saviours of men pre-eminent among the immortals, Asklepios of healing hand, Hygeia *(and)* Panakeia ...

[*JRS* 59 (1969), 235 no. 3 = *RIB* 3.3151. Chester (Deva)]

Altar, found in 1968 on the Old Market site, possibly the praetorium. *Now in the Grosvenor Museum, Chester.*

Doctors, often Greek themselves, naturally honoured the Greek gods of medicine and healing; this inscription is written in Greek, and raises the question of how the sculptor knew what to write – presumably a copy was given to him by Antiochos, and the shapes transcribed. See also the following, written in Latin.

(ii) To Aesculapius and Salus ?after the late 2nd century AD

To Aesculapius and Salus for the welfare of the Cavalry Regiment of Vettonians, Roman Citizens, (*ala Vettonium civium Romanorum*) Marcus Aurelius [...]ocomas, doctor, willingly and deservedly fulfilled his vow.

[*RIB* 1028. Binchester, Co. Durham (Vinovia)]

Part of a dedication slab 40 x 60 cm found in 1879 and now in the Museum of Archaeology, Durham.

The majority of the slab features a relief of Aesculapius holding hands with Salus. The doctor may well have received his citizenship simply as part of the edict of Caracalla in AD 212, granting universal citizenship, and resulting in millions of people taking the names of the emperor Caracalla (properly M. Aurelius Antonianus) as part of their 'citizen' names.

J47 Altars to Astarte and Heracles of Tyre

Date unknown

(i) You see me, an altar of Astarte; Pulcher set me up.

[*RIB* 1124. Corbridge (Coria?)]

Altar found c. 1754. *Now in Carlisle Museum.*

Pulcher was a *peregrinus,* lacking the *tria nomina* of a citizen. The altar (*CSIR* I.1, no. 47) probably came from the same shrine as **J47(ii).**

(ii) To Heracles of Tyre, Diodora the priestess *(set this up).*

[*RIB* 1129 = BM 1774,0715.1. Corbridge (Coria ?)]

Altar found in the 17th century reused as a stoup (vessel for holy water in a church). Now on display (Room 49) in the British Museum.

These inscriptions are similar and form a pair. Both were written in Greek. They indicate the presence at Corbridge of an exotic cult of Heracles (Hercules) and Astarte, worshipped (with Zeus) as a triad at Tyre, an early Phoenician city, now in Lebanon, from very early times.

J48 Hercules 1st century AD

For the god Hercules, Marus, tribune of the Twentieth Legion, made this.

[*Britannia* 32 (2001) 392.18. = EDCS-23900147. Benwell (Condercum)]

A copper alloy ansate plaque, 71 x 49mm, 1mm thick, said to have been found in the Benwell area, written with punched dots forming capital letters; provenance disputed (see below) but now in the Ashmolean Museum, Oxford.

Tomlin and Hassall note that the plaque is genuine, but that its origins in the Benwell area seems unlikely, on account of various anomalies in the inscription, and that it may have come from one of the Twentieth Legion's early British bases, such as Colchester or even from Cologne (it was based there from AD 9 to AD 43).

J49 Early Temple of Isis at London before *c.* AD 75

At London at (or near) the temple of Isis.

[*RIB* 2.8.2503.127 = EDCS-51600672. London (Londinium)]

Pottery flagon, probably reused in a burial in Southwark or the City of London.

The flagon type can be dated to before *c.* AD 75. Isis was an Egyptian goddess whose worship spread throughout the Roman empire. There was probably a temple to her at Pompeii from the late 2nd century BC (Cooley 2014, 119). Within Rome itself, Isis worship may have been viewed with some suspicion, but was promoted by the Flavian emperors (e.g. LACTOR 20, L22–L27).

J50 Restoration of Temple of Isis 3rd century AD

In honour of the Divine House, Marcus Martianius Pulcher, of senatorial rank, governor of the emperors, ordered the temple of Isis [... *(1 or 2 words lost)*...] which had collapsed through old age to be restored.

[*RIB* 3.3001 = EDCS-09300321. London (Londinium)]

Altar, found in 1975 in Upper Thames Street, reused in the Roman riverside wall.

J51 To Dolichenus 2nd or 3rd century AD

To eternal Jupiter of Doliche and to Caelestis Brigantia and to Salus; Gaius Julius Apolinaris, centurion of the Sixth Legion, at the command of the god (*set this up*).

[*RIB* 1131. Corbridge (Coria?)]

Altar, found in 1910 as a kerb-stone to the latest road level south of Site XI. Now in Corbridge Museum.

On the left side of the altar is a crowned Genius, with right hand held above an altar, and left hand supporting a cornucopia; on the right side a winged cupid with a sickle in its right hand and a bunch of grapes in its left; on either side of the capital is a head in a medallion (*CSIR* I.1, no. 51). Dolichenus was a sky-god whose worship centred on Doliche, in the Roman province of Syria. The cult enjoyed some popularity in the Roman army – cf. **D26**. The centurion of the Sixth links the worship of Dolichenus with that of Brigantia, identified with Dolichenus's consort Juno Caelestis (Heavenly Juno), and of the Roman God Salus (Well-Being).

J52 A late dedication to Dolichenus AD 286

Sacred to [Jupiter] Dolichenus [Best (and)] Greatest (and) to [Salus] Augusta [... *sy*] *mmacharii* [...] established [...] of the temple, in the consulship of [Maxi]mus and Aqui[linus].

[*RIB* 3.3299 = EDCS-44600138. Chesters (Cilurnum)]

Fragment of slab, from the bed of the North Tyne. Now in Chesters Museum.

There are considerable uncertainties about the restorations of this fragment. Dolichenus and Salus appear together in **J51** and in *AE* 1988, 937, an altar from Gerulata, in Pannonia Superior (modern Hungary). This is the latest consular date from Roman Britain, and the latest military evidence for the cult of Jupiter Dolichenus which was particularly popular there in the Severan period (see **D26**, **J51** and possibly **H25**). The *symmacharii*, restored here, are known from Pseudo-Hyginus, *On Camp Fortifications* 29 and *AE* 1935, 12. They seem to be irregular units. The *AE* reference is to *symmachariorum Asturum*, interesting as the unit at Chesters in the third century was the *ala II Asturum*, also originally raised from the Astures of north-west Spain, cf. **C43** and **D28**.

J53 Another dedication to Dolochenus ?3rd century AD

To Jupiter Dolochenus Best and Greatest, Sulpicius Pudens Prefect of the Fourth Cohort of Gauls, willingly and deservedly fulfilled his vow.

[*Britannia* 41 (2010) 444 = EDCS-59500264. Chesterholm (Vindolanda)]

A buff sandstone altar 0.49 x 1.05 m, 0.48m deep, found in situ in 2009 in a 3rd-century building thought to be a Dolichenium at Vindolanda.

J54 Inveresk altar to Mithras ?early 140s AD

To the unconquered god My(thras), Gaius Cas[sius?] Fla[vianus?] (dedicated this altar).

[*Britannia* 42 (2011) 441 = EDCS-56500302*. Lewisvale Park, East Lothian]

An altar of white sandstone, 0.55 x 1.26m, 0.26 m deep, found in 2010.

Decorated on its left side with carving of a griffin above a ram-headed patera, and on the right side with a lyre above a plectrum and a jug. The dedication on the front lies within a panel 0.41 x 0.44 m. Photos of all three decorated sides on EDCS website. The Latin of this dedication has some peculiarities: 'to god' is written *DAEO*, a hypercorrection for *DEO*, and *MY* is the rare abbreviation for the name of the god himself.

J55 Mithraic relief from London late 2nd – early 3rd century AD

Ulpius Silvanus, discharged from the Second Legion Augusta, initiated at Orange, has paid his vow.

[*RIB* 3. London (Londinium)]

Fine Mithraic relief, found in the Mithraeum at London in 1954. Now in the Museum of London.

The relief is 0.56m x 0.43m. The central image is of Mithras slaying the bull, with torchbearers, dog, serpent and scorpion (symbols of Mithraism) in attendance. This image is in a circular frame containing representations of signs of the zodiac. Further images of sun, moon and winds fill the corners, while the inscription is split up in the remaining space.

J56 Carrawburgh altar to Mithras 3rd century AD

Sacred to the Invincible god Mithras; Aulus Cluentius Habitus, prefect of the First Cohort of Batavians, of the Ultinian voting-tribe, from Colonia Septimia Aurelia Larinum, willingly and deservedly fulfilled his vow.

[*RIB* 1545. Carrawburgh (Brocolitia)]

Altar found in 1949 in the Carrawburgh Mithraeum. Now in the Great North Museum, Hancock.

This is one of three altars all dedicated by prefects of the First Batavian Cohort. The top is flat and roughly chiselled to carry some feature which may have been a statue or a container for fire or water; on the face of the capital is a frieze of three eggs (*CSIR* I.6, no. 123). The dedicator presumably belonged to the family of Aulus Cluentius Habitus, defended by Cicero in 66 BC, or was descended from a freed slave of that family, as the *nomen* Cluentius is rare, and Cicero's client also came from Larinum in central Italy.

(d) CURSES and CHARMS

Since the discovery of the substantial deposit of curse-tablets at Uley, at the temple to Nodens, beginning with the first find in 1805, the number of tablets known in Britain has risen considerably, from 12 in 1977 to 250 in 2002, following seasons of excavation at Bath and Uley in 1977–1979, and the number continues to increase, albeit more slowly. As Roger Tomlin notes (2002, 165–79), they range more widely in date than that other major source of evidence for literate expression in Roman Britain, the Vindolanda tablets; in addition, they are the product of civilian life, and illustrate the widespread belief in the potential efficacy of 'black magic'. They cast particular light on literacy among the lower strata of Romano-British Society: 'the Bath tablets do not suggest a socio-economic elite. They are prompted by quite small sums of money: 5 *denarios*, 2 *argentiolos*, 6 *argentiolos*, 6 *argenteos* 'from my purse'; Basilia in the 4th century, an age of great estates and the Hoxne treasure, spends her eloquence on a *silver* ring.'

J57 A curse from Bath 4th century AD

(a) Whether pagan or Christian, whosoever, whether man or woman, whether boy or girl, whether slave or free, has stolen from me, Annianus, son of Matuntina?, six silver coins from my purse, you, lady Goddess, are to exact [them] from him. If through some deceit he has given me ..., and do not give thus to him, but reckon? as his blood who has invoked this upon me.

(b) (On other side, 18 personal names): Postumianus (?), Pisso, Locinna, Alauna (?), Materna, Gunsula, Candidina, Euticius, Peregrinus, Latinus, Senecinus, Victor, Scutrius (?), Aessicunia, Paltucca, Calliopis, Celerianus.

[*Britannia* 13 (1982), 404–5, no 7 = Tomlin 1988, 98 = EDCS-08600464. Bath (Aquae Sulis)]

Irregular rectangle cut from a leaden alloyed sheet, found in 1979 in the votive deposit recovered from the hot spring and Roman reservoir excavated beneath the floor of the King's Bath, see Fig. 4, page 26.

Lead was the traditional material for "curse tablets", though at Bath most of them are alloys. The individual letters in each line were written left to right, but with the sequence of letters reversed from beginning to end of (a) and in each line of (b), giving privacy to what is rather a prayer demanding justice than a magical curse. Of the 18 names ten are "Roman", including two of Greek etymology, and eight are "Celtic".

The goddess addressed is Sulis Minerva: cf. **H28**, **J37–J40**. The complete collection of curses from Bath, together with a general discussion of "curse tablets", is published in Tomlin 1988. For the sacred spring see Cunliffe 1985. This is the first occurrence of the word CHRISTIANVS in the epigraphy of Roman Britain. Christianity is ignored otherwise by British curse tablets, except for the badly-damaged Eccles curse, which preserves reference to 'the house of God',' a phrase which may have Christian significance (so Hassall and Tomlin in *Britannia* 17 (1986), 428 no. 2).

J58 Loss of a silver ring ?4th century AD

Basilia gives to the temple of Mars her silver ring. If anyone is involved or knows anything about it, whether slave or free, may he be accursed in his blood and eyes and every limb, or even have all his guts eaten away, if he has stolen the ring or is involved.

[*Tab. Sulis* 97 = *Britannia* 1991, 308. 7 = EDCS-08500431. Bath (Aquae Sulis)]

The Latin of Basilia's curse 'would seem to 'a late-Roman, colloquial usage, deriving from the spoken Latin of 4th-century Britain.'

J59 The Caerleon curse Date unknown

Lady Nemesis, I give thee a cloak and a pair of boots; let him who wore them not redeem them except with his life and blood.

[*RIB* 323 add. Caerleon (Isca)]

A lead plate found in 1927 in the arena of the amphitheatre. Now in Caerleon Museum.

The writing is disjointed and barely legible, so that different interpretations are possible. The interpretation above is as amended in *RIB* 323 add. The text implies that the author has had articles of clothing stolen and that he is putting a curse on the thief. The cloak and boots are promised to the goddess if he returns them; or perhaps "handed over" to her temporarily so that she may curse the illicit wearer.

Other curses found in amphitheatres (e.g. at Carthage and Carnuntum) express ill-will towards particular performers. An altar to Nemesis was found in 1966 at the Chester amphitheatre: *JRS* 57 (1967), 203 no. 5 = *RIB* 3.3149. *Nemesis* is the goddess of justice who punishes human pride and arrogance (*hubris*); she might bring hope to worthy but less successful gladiators.

J60 Trouble at Leicester *c.* AD 150–250

I give to the god Maglus him who did wrong from the slave-quarters; I give him who theft *(sic)* the cloak from the slave-quarters, who stole the cloak of Servandus: Silvester, Ri(g)omandus, Senilis, Venustinus, Vorvena, Calaminus, Felicianus, Ruf<a>edo, Vendicia, Ingenuinus, Juventius, Alocus, Cennosus, Germanus, Senedo, Cunovendus, Regalis, Ni(g)ella, ~~Senicianus~~. I give (that the god Maglus) before the ninth day take away him who stole the cloak of Servandus.

[*Britannia* 40 (2009) 327.21 = EDCS-46400876*. Vine Street, Leicester]

A rectangle of lead 78/75 x 201 mm, cut from sheet lead c. 1mm thick, found in 2005. Neatly inscribed by a practised hand in Old Roman Cursive (c. AD 150–250 in date).

Maglus is not attested as a god, but since Celtic **maglos* ('prince') is a frequent name-element, it may be a divine title here. Those listed here are the household slaves, as is Servandus himself, presumably. The spelling of some of the Latin words shows that the writer did not pronounce *g* between vowels ('*paedagogium*' – slave-quarters – becomes '*paeda-o-ium*'); this example may indicate how far levels of literacy, even at a basic level, permeated through to the lower levels of Romano-British society.

J61 Theft of money at Leicester *c.* AD 150–250

Those who have stolen the silver coins of Sabinianus, that is Similis, Cupitus, Lochita, a god will strike down in this *septisonium*, and I ask that they lose their life before seven days.

[*Britannia* 40 (2009) 329. 22 = EDCS-46400877. Vine Street, Leicester]

A rectangle of lead 78/75 x 201 mm cut from sheet lead c. 1 mm, found in 2005.

Shallowly inscribed in Old Roman Cursive (c. AD 150–250 in date), the writing is much less neat than the example above, with letters being elongated and rather cramped. A *septisonium* (properly *septizonium* or *septizodium*) was apparently a monumental façade incorporating statues of the seven planetary deities who gave their names to the days of the week (as in modern French, Italian, Welsh etc).

J62 A curse from London — mid-late 2nd century AD

Plautius Nobilianus, Aurelius Saturninus, Domitia Attiola, and any who were absent.

[*Britannia* 34 (2003) 361.1 = EDCS-30000058. London (Londinium)]

An irregular rectangle of lead, 70 x 50mm c. 1mm thick, found in 1994, at No. 1 Poultry in the City of London, inscribed with four lines of cursive letters.

The names are probably those of the dedicatee's supposed enemies suspected wrong-doers. It is unusual for British 'curse tablets' to identify the miscreants by nomen and cognomen (i.e. as Roman citizens). *Aurel(ius)* would suggest a date after the accession of Antoninus Pius (AD 138) which fits well with the style of hand-writing which indicates a date of mid-late 2nd century.

J63 A curse from London's amphitheatre — late 2nd – early 3rd centuries AD

I give to the goddess Deana (my) headgear and band, less one-third. If anyone has done this, I give him, and through me let him be unable to live.

[Britannia 34 (2003) 362.2 = EDCS-30000062. London (Londinium)]

A lead curse tablet, c. 1mm thick, c. 85 x 105 mm, inscribed on one side in capital letters. Found at the Guildhall Yard Roman amphitheatre in the fill of a drain which occurred AD 160–250). Not folded, but nailed up, as a hole in the centre indicates.

The variant 'Deana' for 'Diana' is quite common in the imperial period.

J64 Silvianus to Nodens — Date unknown

Primary text: To the god Nodens: Silvianus has lost his ring and given half its value to Nodens. Among those who are called Senicianus do not allow health until he brings it to the temple of Nodens.

Secondary text: (This curse) comes into force again.

[*RIB* 306. Lydney Park, Gloucestershire]

A lead plate found in 1817, Now in the site museum at Lydney Park.

In the Latin of the inscription, *Devo, anilum, perdedit, demediam, nollis* and *petmittas* might more correctly have been spelt *Deo, anulum, perdidit, dimidiam, nolis* and *permittas,* Nodens was a complex Celtic god, associated with healing, hunting, the sea and lost property (see Lewis 1966, 88–92). Some time must have elapsed before Silvianus, still without his ring, felt that he had to renew his curse and added the single word REDIVIVA, *"(This curse)* comes into force again." above the original inscription.

J65 Loss of agricultural equipment — ?4th century AD

I make a note of two gaiters, an axe, a knife, a pair of gloves, whether woman or man [...] two parts to the god.

[*Britannia* 35 (2004) 337.3 = EDCS-33800075. Red Hill, Ratcliffe-on-Soar, Nottinghamshire]

An oval lead tablet, 82 x 38 mm, found in 1963 on the site of the Roman temple.

'Gaiters' and 'gloves' are both items of leather protective equipment worn by agricultural workers; the other items listed suggest woodland management. This is a good example of the value placed on everyday items of equipment by rural workers, and the ways in which they hoped that divine help might get their property back.

J66 Theft at Silchester — 4th century AD

Nimincillus. Quintinus, Junctinus (son) of Docilina, Longinus. [...*(letters hard to read, probably names)*...], him who has stolen, let the god give a nasty blow.

[*Britannia* 40 (2009) 323.16 = EDCS-55701755. Silchester (Calleva Atrebatum)]

A lead strip 60 x 103 mm, cut from sheet lead c. *1 mm. thick, found before 1901.*

The text consists of seven lines of clumsy New Roman Cursive letters fourth-century in date, inscribed line by line in reverse sequence from right to left (to maintain the secrecy of the message).

J67 A curse from Uley — *c.* AD 150–300

Honoratus to the holy god Mercury. I complain to your divine power that I have lost two wheels and four cows and very many small objects from my dwelling. I ask the *genius* of your divine power that on him who has robbed me, you do not allow the health to lie down or sit, nor to drink nor eat, whether man or woman, whether boy or girl, whether slave or free, unless he returns my possession to me and is reconciled with me. With renewed prayers I ask your divine power that you grant my petition at once and that I am justified by your majesty.

[Uley 72 = EDCS-04900617 = BM 1978,0102.148. Uley, Gloucestershire]

Lead tablet, 76 mm x 131 mm, originally folded six times. Now in British Museum.

The best preserved of the Uley curse tables, neatly written in old Roman cursive script. The collection of 140 lead tablets (86 inscribed) was found during excavation of the temple complex. They were distributed through all levels from the 2nd century onwards, with a concentration in late 4th century destruction deposits and in unstratified/ploughsoil contexts. The collection is published in Woodward and Leach, *The Uley Shrines,* London 1993 (abbreviated to 'Uley').

J68 A curse on an embezzler — 3rd century AD

[...] the man who has cheated me of the *denarii* he owed me. I give, I offer, I destine, I depute one hundred thousand *denarii* to the god Mercury, that he may bring them to the temple and treasury of the most mighty god.

[*Uley* 78 = Tomlin, 2002, page 169]

Tomlin n.44 comments that 'this is much the largest sum named in a British curse tablet, which by its handwriting cannot be later than *c.* AD 300.'

J69 Alleged harm done to livestock — 4th century AD

Docilinus asks the god Mercury that Varianus and Peregrina and Sainianus who have brought evil on my farm animal [...] I ask that you drive them to the greatest death, and do not allow them health or sleep unless they redeem from you what they have administered to me.

[*Uley* 43 = EDCS-06100391 = *Britannia* 1989, 329.3. Uley, Gloucestershire]

J70 A Latin text written in Greek letters 4th century AD

I have given the man who stole my linen and my cloak and my two silver coins, whether boy or girl, whether male slave or female, whether man or woman, whether soldier or civilian. Take away his marrow, his blood, his soul, unless he brings them back to your temple.

[*Uley* 52 = Tomlin 2002, page 175]

This text was identified as a clumsy type of 'New Roman Cursive' until it was realized that while it is *composed* in Latin, it is *written* in *Greek* letters. Tomlin comments that 'the formulas and the things stolen are more or less familiar by now, but not this presence of Greek in the British outback. It is not quantitative evidence, of course, but it gives a striking *impression* of literacy in the countryside.'

J71 A niketikon or 'victory-charm' Date unknown

Iao, Arbrasax [...], ablanathanalba, give victory and health to Tiberius Claudius Similis whom Herennia Marcellina bore.

[*Britannia* 37 (2006) 481.51 = EDCS-33800073. Billingford, Norfolk]

A rectangular tablet 51.5 x 30 mm, cut from 91% fine (almost 22 carat) gold sheet, found 'casually' in garden topsoil in 2003. Now in Norwich Castle Museum.

One side carries 10 lines of texts fluently inscribed with a very fine point; the first three are almost wholly magical signs; then come five lines of Latin text which has been written almost entirely in Greek cursive letters; the last two lines are written in Roman cursive letters, which may have been added later to 'personalize' the object. Iao and Abrasax are protective deities; *ablanathanalba* is a magical palindrome (th = θ). After being inscribed, the sheet was rolled up or folded six times into a cylindrical shape above 2.5 mm thick. It would have been kept in a container of some sort and worn as a lucky charm, probably round the neck. The client's cognomen is typical of Lower Germany, and especially Cologne, which may be where this amulet originated. It is the fourth gold amulet reported from Britain, the others being from Caernarvon (*RIB* 436), York (*RIB* 706), and Wood Eaton (*RIB* II.3, 2430.2).

J72 A spell against the plague ?late 160s AD

Abrai Barbasō Barbasōch Barbasōth.†*euliōr* (?) of divine form, send away the discordant clatter of raging plague, air-borne, †*tanuchizon*, †*nudrolees*, infiltrating pain, heavy-spiriting, flesh-wasting, melting, from the hollows of the veins. Great Iao, great Sabaoth, protect the bearer. Phoebus of the unshorn hair, archer, drive away the cloud of plague. Iao, God Abrasax, bring help. Lord Phoebus ordered mortals to refrain from †*chileōn.* Lord God, watch over Demetrios.

[*Britannia* 44 (2013) 390. 21. London (Londinium)]

A pewter strip, originally rolled up for insertion in an amulet case, found in 1989 on the site of the Roman foreshore of the Thames in Upper Thames St. in the City of London, inscribed with 30 lines of metrical Greek in 'book hand'.

The text includes magical words (italics with capital letters) and unknown words († *obelised*). It is a protective spell against plague, probably the Antonine plague of the late 160s AD. Tomlin (*Britannia* 44 (2013) 390 n. 24) points out that the letter forms employed in this document would suggest that the writer 'was bilingual (i.e. in Greek and Latin), with Latin as his first language, with the added implication that he was writing in the Latin speaking West, perhaps even in Britain.'

(e) CHRISTIANITY

J73 'Water Newton' church plate ?4th century AD

(*on outer rim*): Prostrating myself, Lord, I honour your sacred sanctuary. A ☧ ω
(*on inner rim*): Publianus.

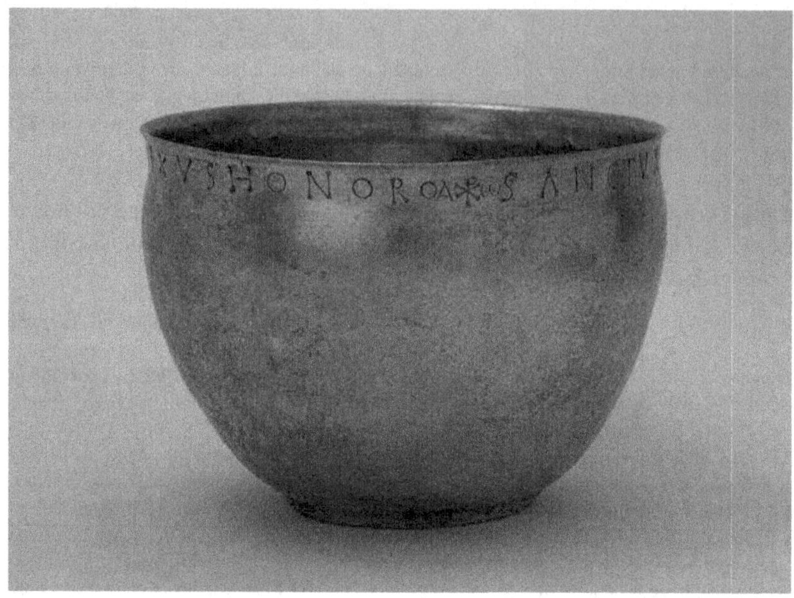

[*RIB* 2.2.2414.2 = BM 1975,1002.5. Chesterton (Durobrivae), Cambridgeshire]

Silver bowl. Found in 1975 within the Roman town. Now in the British Museum.

A Chi-Rho (first two letters of Christ in Greek) between A and Ω (the beginning and end of the Greek alphabet, therefore symbolising God) comes before SANCTVM, a second separates D from OMINE. The text forms a hexameter and runs around the outer rim of the bowl. Publianus, is most likely the name of the person prostrating himself, is inscribed on the inner rim. This cup or bowl is part of a collection of items of precious metal (often referred to as the Water Newton hoard) which appears to consist of church plate. The collection comprises one gold object (a roundel) and 27 of silver (9 vessels, 17 plaques and some fragments of silver sheet).

J74 Small silver flask with Christian symbols late 4th century AD

A ☧ ω (alpha, chi-rho symbol, omega): Eisia made this for Frymiacus' (or 'at Frymiacum').

[*RIB* 2.2.2414.20 = EDCS-48900486. Traprain Law, East Lothian]

A small silver flask 154 mm high, weight 206.95g, from the Traprain Law treasure, National Museums of Scotland.

The inscription is in capitals round the neck in double line of punched dots

J75 **Silver strainer with Christian symbols** late 4th century AD

(i) (*in the base of the bowl*): ☧ (chi-rho symbol)

(ii) (*round the upper side of the bowl*): Jesus Christ

[*RIB* 2.2.2414.21 = EDCS-48900487. Traprain Law, East Lothian]

A silver strainer with hemispherical bowl, 51mm diameter, inscribed by means of perforations in the bottom and side of the bowl and designed to be read from the outside:

J76 **A spoon bearing Christian prayers** 4th century AD

May you live in God.

[*RIB* 2.2.2420.49 = EDCS-48900350. Caistor St Edmund (Venta Icenorum), Norfolk]

Part of a silver spoon found in 1979 by a metal-detectorist in a field opposite the Roman city on the west bank of the river Tas, together with some mid fourth-century silver coins possibly associated with it. Now in private hands.

The inscription is incised on the axis of the bowl of the spoon.

J77 **Panel from a lead casket** 4th century AD

(above): ☧ (Chi-Rho symbol).

(below): Good luck to the user.

[*RIB* 2.2.2416.8 = EDCS-48900187. East Stoke (Ad Pontem), Nottinghamshire]

A panel from a lead casket, width at top 787.5 mm, at bottom 609.5 mm., height 330 mm., thickness 6.4 mm. The text is moulded in relief and bordered above and below by a cable-moulding, with a crude figure dressed in a long robe – presumably an angel – at either end.

This is one of several items in *RIB* which feature a chi-rho symbol; see *RIB* 2416.10, 12, 13, 14 (lead tanks), 2417.36, 37, 38, 39, 40, 41 (pewter vessels), and silver spoons from the Mildenhall treasure, Traprain Law, and Canterbury (*RIB* 2420. 53–62). On lead tanks, see B. Crerar, 'Contextualising Romano-British Lead Tanks: a Study in Design, Destruction and Deposition', *Britannia* 43 (2012), pp. 135–166.

J78 **Gold and Bronze rings** 4th century AD

(i) (on bezel, around figure): Venus

(on outside of ring) Senicianus, may you live in God.

[*RIB* 2.3.2422.14 = EDCS-49100229. Silchester (Calleva), Hampshire]

Gold ten-faceted ring weighing 12.02 gm with a rectangular bezel bearing a bust of Venus, found in or before 1786 during ploughing, now at The Vyne (National Trust property near Basingstoke).

'Venus' was inscribed in negative, so as to be used as a signet ring. The Christian message on a ring with Venus presumably suggests a succession of owners for this precious object. Senicianus is unlikely to have anything to do with the person of the same name mentioned in **J64**.

(ii) May you live in God.

[*RIB* 2.3.2422.15 = EDCS-49100262. Brancaster (Branodunum), Norfolk]

Gold ring, 23mm in diameter, found in ploughing in 1829. Now in Norwich Castle Museum.

This engagement ring has two busts, one male one female, crudely engraved between the lines of its inscription. If used as a signet ring, the text would appear in reverse.

(iii) (on bezel, around figure): V ☧ ꭥ
(on outside of ring): Justinus, live in God.

[*RIB* 2.3.2422.70 = EDCS-49100204. Richborough (*Rutupiae*), Kent]

A bronze ring with nine facets found in 1931 during excavations within the Saxon Shore Fort, now lost.

On the bezel, chi-rho symbol, with alpha (without cross-bar) and omega, both upside down (compare **J73**); the inscription was around the ring.

J79 A bone plaque — 4th century AD

Hail, sister, may you live in God.

[*RIB* 2.3.2441.11 = EDCS-49200284. York (Eboracum)]

Part of a bone plaque 136.5 by 9.5 by 1.5 mm with open-work letters, perhaps from a casket, found in 1901 in Sycamore Terrance, outside the north-west gate of the fortress in a sarcophagus containing the skeleton of a woman, glass drinking-vessels and some jet jewellery. Now in the Yorkshire Museum, York.

The text *vivas in Deo* is undoubtedly Christian (compare *RIB* 2420.49 (**J76**) 2422.14, 15, 70, (**J78 (i–iii)**) but its association with grave goods not often associated with Christian practice – may put the Christianity of the burial in doubt. Such mixtures of cultural practice are not unknown, however.

J80 A Christian tombstone? — 4th century AD

To the spirits of the departed: Flavius Antigonus Papias, a citizen of Greece, lived sixty years, more or less, and gave back to the Fates his soul lent for that period of time. Septimia Do[...] *(set this up)*.

[*RIB* 955. Carlisle (Luguvalium)]

Tombstone found in 1892 in the Roman cemetery on Gallows Hill, Carlisle. The lower part has been broken off. Now in Carlisle Museum.

RIB rates this as “probably Christian”. ‘More or less’ is said to be “characteristically Christian”, implying an indifference to the length of time spent in this life; a phrase similar in Latin to ‘gave back his soul’ is used on Christian tombstones elsewhere. There is as yet no certain example of a Christian tombstone from Roman Britain; this is perhaps the most promising candidate.

J81 A mysterious word-square ?2nd century AD

ROTAS
OPERA
TENET
AREPO
SATOR

Arepo the Sower holds the wheels carefully.

[*RIB* 2.4.2447.20. Cirencester (Corinium]

A fragment of red wall-plaster, on which is incised a palindromic word-square. Found in 1868 at Victoria Road, Cirencester. Now in Corinium Museum, Cirencester.

AREPO is a personal name otherwise unattested, required to make the word-square possible. Examples of this word-square are widely distributed in the Roman Empire, including Pompeii (therefore dating to before AD 79: *CIL* 4.8623 = Cooley, 2014, D100) and Dura Europos (third century AD). It can be read forwards, backwards, upwards and down wards to give the same words. The letters can be rearranged to form PATER NOSTER, "Our Father", twice over by using the central N twice, the remaining letters, two As and two Os, being understood to stand for the Greek letters Alpha and Omega, titles of Christ in *Revelation* 1.8 (compare **J73**). TENET also forms a cross. This apparent Christian connection is more difficult to sustain now that recent examples from Budapest (early second-century) and Manchester (late second-century) seem too early for a credible Christian association, though they might be the products of individual Christians rather than communities. For the Manchester example, see *Britannia* 10 (1979), 353, no. 34. There is also one, perhaps in a first-century context, at Conimbriga, Portugal. The conclusion in the *RIB* commentary on this, on which the comments above are based, is that the word-square was certainly adopted by Christians in post-Constantinian times; in earlier centuries Christians used it, but others did so also. Its origins go back to the first century and are obscure.

BIBLIOGRAPHY

Allason-Jones, L. 2005: *Women in Roman Britain*. 2nd edition. London.

Barrett, A.A. 1991: Claudius' British victory arch in Rome, *Britannia* 22, 1–19.

Birley, A.R. 1979: *The People of Roman Britain.* London. New edition 1988.

Birley, A.R. 1988: *The African Emperor: Septimius Severus*. London.

Birley, A.R. 2005: *The Roman Government of Britain.* Oxford.

Birley, E.B. 1961: *Roman Britain and the Roman Army.* Kendal.

Birley, E.B. 1966: Review and discussion of R.G. Collingwood and R.P. Wright, *The Roman Inscriptions of Britain I: Inscriptions on Stone*, *Journal of Roman Studies* 56, 226–31.

Birley, E.B. 1978: The deities of Roman Britain. In H. Temporini & W. Haase (eds), *Aufstieg und Niedergang der römischen Welt* II.18.1, 3–112.

Birley, E.B. 1983: A Roman altar from Old Kilpatrick and interim commanders of auxiliary units, *Latomus* 42, 73–83.

Bishop, M.C. and Coulston, J.C.N. 1993: *Roman Military Equipment: from the Punic Wars to the Fall of Rome*. London.

Bogaers, J.E. 1979: King Cogidubnus in Chichester: another reading of *RIB* 91, *Britannia* 10, 243–54.

Boon, G.C. 1974: *Silchester: The Roman Town of Calleva.* Newton Abbot and London.

Bowman, A.K. and Thomas, J.D. 1983: *Vindolanda: the Latin Writing Tablets.* Britannia Monograph No. 4. London.

Bowman, A.K. and Thomas, J.D. 1991: A military strength report from Vindolanda, *Journal of Roman Studies* 81, 62–73.

Bowman, A.K. and Thomas, J.D. 1994: *The Vindolanda Writing-Tablets (Tabulae Vindolandenses II).* London.

Bowman, A.K. and Thomas, J.D. 2003: *The Vindolanda Writing-Tablets (Tabulae Vindolandenses III).* London.

Bowman, A.K., Thomas, J.D. and Adams, J.N. 1990: Two letters from Vindolanda, *Britannia* 21, 33–52.

Breeze, D. J. 1997: The regiments stationed at Maryport and their commanders. In R.J. Wilson (ed.), *Roman Maryport and its Setting.* Maryport, 67–89.

Breeze, D.J. 2003: Warfare in Britain and the Building of Hadrian's Wall, *Archaeologia Aeliana* 5th series 32, 13–16.

Breeze, D.J. and Dobson, B. 1969–70: The development of the mural frontier in Britain from Hadrian to Caracalla, *Proceedings of the Society of Antiquaries of Scotland* 102, 109–21.

Breeze, D.J. and Dobson, B. 2000: *Hadrian's Wall.* 4th edition. Harmondsworth.

Burnham, B.C. and Wacher, J. 1990: *The Small Towns of Roman Britain.* London.

Casey, P.J. 1979: Magnus Maximus in Britain: a reappraisal, in P.J. Casey (ed.), *The End of Roman Britain.* British Archaeological Reports 71, London, 66–79.

Casey, P.J., Davies, J.L. and Evans, J. 1993: *Excavations at Segontium (Caernarfon) Roman Fort, 1975–1979.* CBA Research Report 90. London.

Collingwood, R.G. 1928: Inscriptions of Roman London, in RCAHM, *An Inventory of the Historical Monuments in London. Vol. III. Roman London*, Appendix II, 170–77.

Collingwood, R.G. and Richmond, I.A. 1969: *The Archaeology of Roman Britain.* London.

Collins, R. 2009: The Latest Roman Coin from Hadrian's Wall: a Small Fifth-century Purse Group, *Britannia* 39, 256–262.

Cool, H. E. M: 2014 'Which "Romans"; What "Home"? The Myth of the "End" of Roman Britain', in (ed) Haarer 2014

Cooley, A. E. 2002 (ed): Becoming Roman, Writing Latin: Literacy and Epigraphy in Roman West (JRA Supp. Series 48, Portsmouth, R1).

Cooley, A.E. 2012: *The Cambridge Manual of Latin Epigraphy.* Cambridge.

Cooley, A.E. & Cooley, M.G.L. 2014: *Pompeii and Herculaneum, a Sourcebook.* London

Creighton, J. 2009: Coins and Power in late Iron Age Britain. Cambridge

Creighton, J. 2014: 'The Supply and Movement of Denarii in Roman Britain', *Britannia* 45, 121 – 163.

Crerar,B. 2012: 'Contextualising Romano-British Lead Tanks: a Study in Design, Destruction and Deposition', *Britannia* 43 (2012), 135–166.

Crummy, P. 1997: *City of Victory: the Story of Colchester – Britain's First Roman Town.* Colchester Archaeological Trust.

Cunliffe, B. 1985: *The Temple of Sulis Minerva at Bath. Vol. 1. The Site.* Oxford University Committee for Archaeology, Monograph No. 7.

Daniels, C.M. and Harbottle, B. 1980: A new inscription of Julia Domna from Newcastle, *Archaeologia Aeliana* 5th series 8, 65–73.

Davies, R.W. 1976: *Singulares* and Roman Britain, *Britannia* 7, 134–44.

de Jersey, P. 2001: *Celtic Coinage in Britain*, Shire Publications, Princes Risborough

de la Bédoyère, G. 1998: Carausius and the marks RSR and I.N.P.C.D.A., *The Numismatic Chronicle* 158, 79–88.

Dobson, B. 1972: Legionary centurion or equestrian officer? A comparison of pay and prospects, *Ancient Society* 3, 193–200.

Dobson, B. and Mann, J.C. 1973: The Roman Army in Britain and Britons in the Roman Army, *Britannia* 4, 191–205.

Donaldson, G.H. 1988: Signalling communications and the Roman Imperial Army, *Britannia* 19, 349–56.

Donaldson, G.H. 1990: A reinterpretation of *RIB* 1912 from Birdoswald, *Britannia* 21, 207–14.

Frere, S.S. 1987: *Britannia: a History of Roman Britain.* 3rd edition. London.

Frere, S.S. and Fulford, M. 2002: The *Collegium Peregrinorum* at Silchester, *Britannia* 33, 167–75.

Gerrard, J. 2013: *The Ruin of Roman Britain: an Archaeological Perspective.* Cambridge

Grasby, R.D. and Tomlin, R.S.O. 2002: The sepulchral monument of the procurator C. Julius Classicianus, *Britannia* 33, 43–76.

Haarer, F. K. (ed.) 2014: *AD 410: The History and Archaeology of Late and Post-Roman Britain.* London

Hanson, W. and Maxwell, G. 1983: *Rome's North West Frontier: the Antonine Wall.* Edinburgh.

Harris, E. and Harris, J.R. 1965: *The Oriental cults in Roman Britain.* Leiden.

Hassall, M. 1978: Britain and the Rhine provinces: epigraphic evidence for Roman trade, in J. du Plat Taylor and H. Cleere (eds), *Roman Shipping and Trade: Britain and the Rhine Provinces.* CBA Research Report 24, 41–48.

Hassall, M. 1999: Soldier and civilian: a debate on the bank of the Severn. In H. Hurst (ed.), *The* Coloniae *of Roman Britain: New Studies and a Review.* Portsmouth, RI, 181–85.

Haverfield, F. 1918: Roman Cirencester, *Archaeologia* 19, 1917–18, 161–200.

Haynes, I.P. 1993: The romanisation of religion in the *auxilia* of the Roman imperial army from Augustus to Septimius Severus, *Britannia* 24, 141–57.

Hill, P.R. 1991: Hadrian's Wall: some aspects of its execution, *Archaeologia Aeliana* 5th series 19, 33–39.

Hobbs, R. 1996: *British Iron Age Coins in the British Museum.* British Museum Press London

Hodgson, N. 2014: 'The British Expedition of Septimius Severus', *Britannia* 45, 31 – 51.

Holman, D. 2005: 'Iron Age Coinage and Settlement in East Kent', *Britannia* 36, 1–54.

Hooley, J. and Breeze, D.J. 1968: The building of Hadrian's Wall: a reconsideration, *Archaeologia Aeliana* 4th series 46, 97–114.

Hull, M.R. 1958: *Roman Colchester.* Report of the Research Committee of the Society of Antiquaries of London. London.

Hurst, H. 1988: Gloucester (*Glevum*), in G. Webster (ed.), *Fortress into City: the consolidation of Roman Britain, First Century AD.* London, 48–73.

Jarrett, M.G. 1976: *Maryport, Cumbria: A Roman fort and its Garrison.* Kendal.

Jarrett, M.G. 1976b: An unnecessary war, *Britannia* 7, 145–51.

Jarrett, M.G. 1978: The case of the redundant official, *Britannia* 9, 289–92.

Jarrett, M.G. 1994: Non-legionary troops in Roman Britain: Part One, the Units, *Britannia* 25, 35–77.

Jarrett, M.G. and Mann, J.C. 1970: Britain from Agricola to Gallienus, *Bonner Jahrbücher* 170, 178–210.

Joliffe, N. 1941: Dea Brigantia, *Archaeological Journal* 98, 36–61.

Kennedy, D. 1977: The *ala I* and *cohors I Britannica*, *Britannia* 8, 249–55.

Keppie, L.J.F. 1979: *Roman Distance Slabs from the Antonine Wall: a brief guide.* Glasgow.

Keppie, L.J.F. 1984: *The Making of the Roman Army: From Republic to Empire.* London.

Keppie, L.J.F. 1991: *Understanding Roman Inscriptions.* London.

Keppie, L.J.F. 1995: The IXth Legion in Britain, in R. Brewer (ed.), *Roman fortresses and their legions. Essays in honour of George Boon.* Cardiff.

Keppie, L.J.F. 1998: *Roman Inscribed and Sculptured Stones in the Hunterian Museum Glasgow.* London.

Lewis, M.J.T. 1966: *Temples in Roman Britain.* Cambridge.

Lewis, N. and Reinhold, M. 1966: *Roman Civilization: Sourcebook I: The Republic; II: The Empire.* Harper and Row, New York.

Mann, J.C. 1969: *The Northern Frontier in Britain from Hadrian to Honorius: Literary and Epigraphic Sources.* Privately printed.

Mann, J.C. 1971: Spoken Latin in Britain as evidenced in inscriptions, *Britannia* 2, 218–24.

Mann, J.C. 1977: The Reculver inscription – a note, in D.E. Johnson (ed.), *The Saxon Shore.* CBA Research Report 18, London, 15.

Mann, J.C. 1991: Numinibus Aug, *Britannia* 22, 173–77.

Marsden, P. 1980: *Roman London.* London.

Marsh, G. 1979: Nineteenth and twentieth century antiquities dealers and Arretine ware from London, *Transactions of the London and Middlesex Archaeological Society* 30, 125–129.

Maxfield, V.A. 1981: *The Military Decorations of the Roman Army.* London.

Mays, M. 1992: Inscriptions on British Celtic coins, *Numismatic Chronicle*, 57–82.

Morris, F. M. 2013: 'Cunobelinus' Bronze Coinage', *Britannia* 44, 2013, 27 – 83.

Nash, D. 1987: *Coinage in the Celtic World.* London.

Painter, K. 1977: *The Water Newton Early Christian Silver.* London.

Reece, R. 1989: Lympne, in V.A. Maxfield (ed.), *The Saxon Shore: a Handbook.* Exeter Studies in History No. 25. Exeter, 152–57.

Reece, R. 2002: *The Coinage of Roman Britain.* Stroud.

Rivet, A.L.F. and Smith, C. 1979: *The Place-Names of Roman Britain.* London.

Robertson, A.S. 1980: The bridges on Severan coins of AD 208 and 209, in W.S. Hanson and L.J.F. Keppie (eds), *Roman Frontier Studies 1979*. Oxford, 131–40.

Roxan, M.M. 1990: *RIB* 2401: the Diplomata, in *RIB* II.1, 1–2.

Salway, P. 1981: *Roman Britain*. Oxford.

Sauer, E.W. 2005a: Inscriptions from Alchester: Vespasian's base of the Second Augustan Legion (?), *Britannia* 36, 101–33.

Sauer, E.W. 2005b: Forum Germanorum in north-west Italy: the home community and life of arguably the earliest known legionary veteran in Britain, *Oxford Journal of Archaeology* 24 (2), 199–211.

Southern P. 1989: The Numeri of the Roman Imperial Army, *Britannia* 20, 81–140.

Stevens, C.E. 1937: Gildas and the civitates of Britain, *English Historical Review* 52, 193–203.

Stevens, C.E. 1941: Gildas Sapiens, *English Historical Review* 56, 353–73.

Stevens, C.E. 1966: *The Building of Hadrian's Wall*. Kendal. (Updating of an article first published in *Archaeologia Aeliana* 4th series 1948, 10–49.)

Swan. V. 1992: Legio VI and its men: African legionaries in Britain, *Journal of Roman Pottery Studies* 5, 1–34.

Syme, R. 1958: *Tacitus*. Oxford.

Todd, M. 1981: *Roman Britain 55 BC–AD 400*.

Tomlin, R.S.O. 1983: Non Coritani sed Corieltauvi, *Antiquaries Journal* 63, 352–53.

Tomlin, R.S.O. 1988: The curse tablets, in B. Cunliffe (ed.), *The Temple of Sulis Minerva at Bath*. Oxford. Vol. 2, 59–277.

Tomlin, R.S.O. 1992: The twentieth legion at Wroxeter and Carlisle in the first century: the epigraphic evidence, *Britannia* 23, 141–58.

Tomlin, R.S.O. 1993a: The inscribed lead tablets: an interim report, in A. Woodward and P. Leach, *The Uley Shrines: Excavation of a ritual complex on West Hill, Uley, Gloucestershire: 1977–9*. London, 113–30.

Tomlin, R.S.O. 1993b: Roman towns and Roman inscriptions of Britain, 1939–89, in S.J. Greep (ed.), *Roman Towns: the Wheeler Inheritance. A review of 50 years' research*. CBA Research Report 93, 134–46.

Tomlin, R.S.O. 1996: A five-acre wood in Roman Kent, in J. Bird, M. Hassall and H. Sheldon (eds), *Interpreting Roman London: a Collection of Essays in Memory of Hugh Chapman*. Oxford, 209–16.

Tomlin, R.S.O. 2003: 'The girl in question': a new text from Roman London, *Britannia* 34, 41–51.

Tomlin, R.S.O. 2016: *Roman London's First Voices: Writing tablets from the Bloomberg Excavations, 2010–14*. London.

Wenham, L.P. 1939: Notes on the garrisoning of Maryport, *Transactions of the Cumberland and Westmoreland Antiquarian and Archaeological Society* 39, 19–30.

Whittick, G. Clement 1982: The Earliest Roman Lead-Mining on Mendip and in North Wales: A Reappraisal, *Britannia* 13, 113–23.

Williams, J.H.C. 2000: The Silver Coins from East Anglia Attributed to King Prasutagus of the Iceni, *Numismatic Chronicle* 160, 276–281).

Williams, J.H.C. 2002: 'Pottery stamps, coin designs, and writing in late Iron Age Britain', in A. E. Cooley, ed. *Becoming Roman, Writing Latin? Literacy and Epigraphy in the Roman West*, (JRA Supp. Series 48, Portsmouth, RI, 2002), 135–149,

Wilson, P.R. 2002: *Cataractonium: Roman Catterick and its Hinterland: Excavations and Research, 1958–1997*. London.

Wilson, P.R. 2013: Roman Britain in 2012 – Sites Explored: *Britannia* 44, p. 290

Woodward, A. and Leach, P. 1993: *The Uley Shrines. Excavation of a ritual complex on West Hill, Uley, Gloucestershire: 1977–9*. English Heritage Archaeological Report No. 17. London.

Wright, R.P. 1974: Carpow and Caracalla, *Britannia* 5, 289–92.

CONCORDANCE BETWEEN LACTOR 4, 4TH EDITION AND THIS EDITION

This edition	L.4^4
A1 (i)	
(ii)	
(ii)	
A2	1
A3 (i)	
(ii)	
A4	2
A5	3
A6	
A7	4
A8	5
A9 (i)	
(ii)	
(iii)	6
B1	7
B2	8
B3	9
B4	10
B5	11
B6	12
B7	13
B8	14
B9	15
B10	16
B11	17
B12	18
B13	19
B14	20
B15	21
B16	22
B17	23
B18	24
B19	278
B20	279
B21	25
B22	26
B23	27
B24	28
B25	
B26	
B27	
B28	280
C1	29
C2	30
C3	31
C4	32
C5	33
C6	34
C7	35
C8	36
C9	37
C10	38
C11	39
C12	40
C13	41
C14	42
C15	43
C16	44
C17	45
C18	46
C19	47
C20	48
C21	49
C22	50
C23	51
C24	52
C25	53
C26	54
C27	55
C28	56
C29	57
C30	58
C31	59
C32	
C33	60
C34	61
C35	62
C36	63
C37	64
C38	65
C39	66
C40	67
C41	68
C42	69
C43	70
C44	71
C45	72
C46	73
C47	281
D1	74
D2	75
D3	76
D4	77
D5	78
D6	79
D7	80
D8	81
D9	82
D10	83
D11	84
D12	85
D13	86
D14	87
D15	88
D16	89
D17	90
D18	91
D19	92
D20 (i)	94
D20 (ii)	95
D21	96
D22	97
D23	98
D24	99
D25	100
D26	101
D27	102
D28	103
D29	104
D30	105
D31	106
D32	107
D33	108
D34	109
D35	110
D36	111
D37	112
D38	113
D39	114
E1	115
E2 (i)	116
E2 (ii)	
E3	117
E4	118
E5	119
E6	
E7	120
E8	121
E9	122
E10	123
E11	123
E12	123
E13	124
E14	
F1	125
F2	126
F3	135

This edition	L.4[4]
F4	272
F5	
F6	127
F7	
F8	129
F9	131
F10	130
F11	286
F12	128
F13	132
F14	134
F15	133
F16	137
F17	136
F18	156
F19	
F20	151
F21	150
F22	152
F23	153
F24	154
F25	141
F26	138
F27	139
F28	140
F29	142
F30	143
F31	282
F32	144
F33	145
F34	
F35	147
F36	148
F37	149
F38	146
F39	157
F40	158
F41	159
F42	160
F43	161
F44	162
F45	163
F46	164
F47	165
F48	166
F49	167
F50	168
G1	
G2	
G3	287
G4	273
G5	274
G6	
G7	
G8	275
G9	276

This edition	L.4[4]
G10	277
G11	
G12	18
G13	176
G14	173
G15	169
G16	175
G17	170
G18	171
G19	172
G20	
G21	174
G22	177
G23	178
G24	179
G25	182
G26	183
G27	180
G28	184
G29	185
G30	186
G31	
G32	191
G33	194
G34	288
G35	195
G36	190
G37	192
G38	193
G39	187
G40	188
G41	188
G42	197
G43	198
G44	196
G45 (i)	199
G45 (ii)	200
G46	201
G47	202
H1	
H2	283
H3	
H4	207
H5	209
H6	210
H7	
H8	206
H9	211
H10 (i)	250
H10 (ii)	251
H11	205
H12	208
H13	
H14	
H15	
H16	

This edition	L.4[4]
H17	
H18	
H19	
H20	
H21	
H22	
H23	
H24	284
H25	215
H26	216
H27	217
H28	212
H29	213
H30	214
H31	
H32	
H33	
H34	
H35	289
H36	
H37	290
H38	
H39	
H40	
H41	
H42	
H43	
H44	
H45	
H46	
H47	
H48	
H49	
H50	
H51	
H52	
H53	
H54	
H55	
H56	
H57	
H58	
H59	
H60	
H61	
J1	
J2	222
J3	
J4	224
J5 (i)	218
J5 (ii)	219
J5 (iii)	
J6	220
J7	221
J8	227
J9	223

This edition	**L.4^4**
J10	225
J11	
J12	226
J13	
J14	244
J15	238
J16	
J17 (i)	240
J17 (ii)	241
J18	239
J19	242
J20	
J21	243
J22	228
J23	229
J24	230
J25	231
J26	232
J27	233
J28 (i)	234
J28 (ii)	235
J28 (iii)	236
J29	237
J30	
J31	245
J32	246
J33	
J34	247

This edition	**L.4^4**
J35	248
J36	249
J37	250
J38	251
J39	252
J40	253
J41	258
J42	259
J43 (i)	
J43 (ii)	
J44 (i)	255
J44 (ii)	256
J44 (iii)	254
J44 (iv)	
J45	
J46 (i)	26
J46 (ii)	
J47	261
J48	
J49	
J50	262
J51	263
J52	285
J53	
J54	
J55	
J56	364
J57	265

This edition	**L.4^4**
J58	
J59	266
J60	
J61	
J62	
J63	
J64	
J65	
J66	
J67	
J68	
J69	
J70	
J71	
J72	
J73	269
J74	
J75	
J76	
J77	
J78 (i)	
J78 (ii)	
J78 (iii)	
J79	
J80	270
J81	271

CONCORDANCE

A: INSCRIPTIONS

Ant. J

1961.224	D33

Bloomberg WT

6	H1 (i)
7	H16
12	H17
14	H1 (ii)
18	F7
20	G1
23	G2
29	H20
30	H41
31	H44
33	B25
37	H45
39	B27
44	H42
45	H15
48	G31
50	H46
51	H33
55	H47
62	B26
70	H19
72	H18
78	H43
79	H49

BM

1774,0715.1	J47 (ii)
1817,0308.2	J29
1817,0308.3	J22
1852,0806.3	H4
1858,0113.1	J25
1861,0218.1	B17
1862,0423.1	F21
1868,1004.1	J23
1882,0819	H31 (ii)
1883,0725.1	F48
1930,0419.1	C5
1931,0211.1	H31 (iii)
1934,1210.100	F4
1953,1002.1	H23
1975,1002.5	J73
1978,0102.148	J67
OA.248	J9
OA.252.6	J7

Britannia

1982, 404–05, no. 7	J57
1988, 496–97, no. 31	G3
1989,329, no.3	J69
1991, 308, no.7	J58
1994, 302–05, no. 34	H37
1996, 455–56, no. 48	H2
1998, 55–63, no. 16	G34
1998, 74–75, no. 44	F11
1998, 435–36, no. 7	B28
2000, 439, no. 23	F19
2000, 442, no. 39	F5
2000, 444, no. 48	H14
2000, 445, no. 49	C32, H7
2001, 392, no. 18	J48
2001, 396 ,no. 39	F34
2002, 358, no. 4	J45
2002, 359	H21
2002, 361	H22 (ii)
2003, 41–52	H35
2003, 361, no. 1	J62
2003, 362, no. 2	J63
2003, 364–65, no. 5	H24
2003, 382	F29
2004, 337, no.3	J65
2004, 344–45, no.24	C47
2004, 347, no. 27	H40
2005 476–77, no.3	B20
2005, 478, no. 4	B19
2005, 482, no. 11	F31
2005, 485, no.17	H48
2005, 486, no.20	H13
2006, 467, no.2	H36 (i)
2006, 468–9, no.3	H36 (ii)
2006, 481, no.51	J71
2007, 346, no.2	J20
2009, 256	E14
2009, 323, no. 16	J66
2009, 327, no.21	J60
2009, 329, no.22	J61
2010, 444	J53
2010, 447	J44 (iv)
2010, 448	J30
2011, 441	J54
2011, 446, no.9	H38
2011, 451	H3
2011, 459–60	G11
2011, 463–4	J33
2012, 395	J11
2012, 396	J16
2013, 381	J3
2013, 284, no. 5	J13
2013, 390, no. 21	J72
2014, 434, no 4	G20
2014, 436, no.5	J1
2014, 437, no.7	E6
2014, 443 no. 16	H32

CIL

3.2864	F6B10
5.7003	B8
1.395	B9 C16
13.3542	B1
16.69	C5

EDCS

00380552	H37
00900120*	B16
01200002	H27
01600155*	F1
04900617	J67
05000559	B19
05400255	B8
06100391	J69
07801121	J5 (ii)
08500431	J58
08600464	J57
09200330*	H59
09300321	J50
09301079	H25
09401495	H26
09800199*	D26
10600310	B1
10701776	J40
11800714	C14
11800715	D22
11800970	B28
12300273*	C5
13400109	D33
13400111	D5
13600218	B24
13600409	H31 (i)
13800058	H23
18800400	D21
20401649	H14
20500054	C19
20500225	C32, H7
23000300	C16
23900147	J48
24600984	B9
28400116	F6
28400836	B10
28500378*	H24
28500397	J43 (ii)
28500402	H22 (ii)
28500408	J45
30000058	J62
30000062	J63
33800072	H40
33800073	J71
33800075	J65
36400173	H35
37600981	H48
37600989	H13
44100155	H36
44500025	B20
44500083	J43 (i)
44500091	H36 (ii)
44600138	J52
44600269	F31
46400876*	J60
46400877	J61
46600262	J20
48900175	H50
48900187	J77
48900350	J76
48900486	J74
48900487	J75
49100204	J78 (iii)
49100229	J78 (i)
49100262	J78 (ii)
49200284	J79
49600595	H39
49602568	H34
50800214*	H57
50800391	H54
50800398	H51
50800920	H53
50801141	H52
51100300	H22 (i)
51600672	J49
55701755	J66
55701802	J33
56500302*	J54
58700044	J13
59500227*	J30
59500264	J53
59500267	J44 (iv)
64100292	H38
64100329	H3
67400303	J16
67400307	J11
69100046	H1 (i)
69100047	H16
69100052	H17
69100054	H1 (ii)
69100069	H20
69100070	H41
69100071	H44
69100073	B25
69100077	H45
69100079	B27
69100084	H42
69100085	H15
69100090	H46
69100091	H33
69100095	H47
69100102	B26
69100110	H19
69100112	H18
69100119	H49
69200370	J5 (iii)
69200366	J3

ILS

216	B16
1015	F6
1052	F1
2089	D21
2648	B9
2696	B10
2701	B8
2726	C19
2735	C16
4751	H26
7522	H27
9123	D18

JRS

1921, 102	F23
1956, 146–47	B24
1957, 229–30, no. 18	F39
1961, 192	D5
1962, 193 no.10	C3
1963, 160, no. 4	G37
1965, 222 no.7	C14
1965, 223, no. 10	D22
1965, 224, no. 11	F30
1966, 217, no. 1	J40
1967, 205, no. 16	D26
1969, 235, no. 3	J46 (i)

P. Lond.

1.215	B15

RIB

3	J55
5	F18
9	H4
11	G29
12	B18
13	G30
17	G28
19	F12
21	J4
66	G44
67	H8 (i)
69	F43
87	H8 (ii)
88	F10
91	F16
92	F17
103	F3
105	J36
108	B3
109	B4
110	H6
121	B5
132	J10
140	J26
143	J38
146	J37
149	H28
151	J35
152	F37
155	J39
156	G21
157	G22
158	G25
159	B7
161	F20
163	H5
179	F14
187	J27
191	H9
192	J34
194	H29
200	B12
201	B2
202	H11
213	J25
215	J7
218	J22
219	J29
233	F13
235	F9
247	F46
250	F21
251	H12
254	G13
255	B11
258	B22
270	F45 (i)
271	F45 (ii)
274	J9
283	C35
288	F26
291	B6
292	G12
293	F8
294	B13
306	J64
309	F44
311	F27
323	J59
327	J2
330	C1
333	D16
334	D38
358	G46
363	G45 (i)
369	G47
373	G45 (ii)
397	C3
430	D17
475	B23
476	G23
479	G24

488	G28
490	G17
492	G18
503	G26
505	G19
583	F36
587	F35
605	D39
627	D9
636	C41
637	D3
653	G16
658	G15
662	F2 (i)
663	F2 (ii)
665	C2
674	F22
678	F24 (i)
684	J8
687	F24 (ii)
707	F38
712	H30
714	F15
721	E9
722	D6
725	F47
730	D4
732	J41
733	J42
739	C13
740	D7
746	D8
757	D2
797	J6
801	C15
815	J5 (i)
816	C18
823	C17
830	J5 (ii)
887	J24
897	D37
899	F40
918	J23
933	F32
955	J80
974	C12
976	D24
978	D29
988	J17 (i)
989	J17(ii)
1008	D15 (i)
1009	D15 (ii)
1028	J46 (ii)
1030	J31
1041	G36
1047	J44 (iii)
1053	J15
1060	D30
1065	H10 (ii)
1074	J21
1085	J12
1091	D34
1092	D35
1120	J14
1124	J47 (i)
1129	J47 (ii)
1131	J51
1137	C39
1143	D19
1147	C23
1148	C24
1149	C38
1151	D13
1171	H10 (i)
1172	G33
1216	D11
1234	D10
1262	D36
1276	C26
1278	D23
1279	D25
1280	D27
1319	C6 (i)
1320	C6 (ii)
1322	C34
1329	C42
1337	D14
1340	C9
1343	G40
1356	G39
1388	G41
1389	C37
1427	C8
1463	C43
1465	D28
1534	J19
1545	J56
1550	C11
1576	J28 (iii)
1583	J18
1593	J28 (i)
1594	J28 (ii)
1602	J44 (ii)
1618	G38
1638	C7
1672	E10 (i)
1673	E10 (ii)
1695	F42

1700	F41
1706	D31
1724	G42
1736	C10
1738	D32
1778	C21
1792	C40
1795	J44 (i)
1820	C22
1843	E11
1909	D12
1912	E5
1962	F33
2022	E12
2034	C45
2059	J32
2091	G14
2110	C36
2117	G43
2122	C31
2139	C28
2142	G35
2148	C46
2191	C27
2200	C29
2204	C30
2213	G32
2243	F49
2244	F25
2250	F28
2265	F48
2288	F50
2290	E3 (i)
2291	E3 (ii)
2292	E3 (iii)
2.1.2404.1	B17
2.2.2414.2	J73
2.2.2414.20	J74
2.2.2414.21	J75
2.2.2416.8	J77
2.2.2420.49	J76
2.3.2422.14	J78 (i)
2.3.2422.15	J78 (ii)
2.3.24722.70	J78 (iii)
2.3.2434.1	B21
2.3.2441.11	J79
2.4.2443.2	F4
2.4.2443.7	H23
2.4.2443.10	G3
2.4.2443.11	H34
2.4.2443.13	H39
2.4.2446.1	H31 (i)
2.4.2446.2	H31 (ii)
2.4.2446.3	H31 (iii)
2.4.2446.4	H31 (iv)
2.4.2447.20	J81
2.5.2491.1	H51
2.5.2491.2	H52
2.5.2491.3	H53
2.5.2491.10	H55
2.5.2491.14	H56
2.5.2491.135	H60
2.5.2491.146(i)	H59
2.5.2491.146(ii)	H59
2.5.2491.147	H57
2.5.2491.148	H58
2.5.2491.150	F29
2.5.2491.159	H54
2.5.2491.209	H61
2.6.2492.24	H22 (i)
2.8.2503.127	J49
2.8.2504, 29	H37
3.03526e	F31
3.3001	J50
3.3014	H24
3.3027	D33
3.3049	J40
3.3073	B20
3.3121	B19
3.3170	J43 (i)
3.3171	J43 (ii)
3.3195	H25
3.3215	D5
3.3219	C14
3.3299	J52
3.3364	B28

Tab. Vindol.

1.154	G4
1.164	G5
1.291	G10
2.309	G6
2.310	G8
1.343	G9
2.632	G7

Tab. Sulis

30	H50
97	J58

Tomlin

1988, 98	J57
2002, 169	J68
2002, 175	J70
2003	H35

Uley

43	J69
52	J70
72	J67
78	J68

B: COINS

BM

B.95	E7
1863,0501.1	B14
1864,1128.202	E13
1919,0213.165	A7 (i)
1919,0213.179	A7 (ii)
1919,0213.323	A4
1919,0213.408	A9 (ii)
1925,1201.1	A9 (iii)
1928,0208.2	E4
1933,0414.17	E8
1935,1117.832	E2 (i)
1959,0603.1	E1
1967,0901.1	E2 (ii)
1977,0434.11	A8
1978,0108.8	A1 (iii)
1980,0634.45	A1 (i)
1988,0627.176	A5
1990,0541.1	A1 (ii)
1995,1014.32	A3 (i)
1995,1014.36	A3 (ii)
1996,1022.58	A2
2000,0301.7	A6
R.8527	A9 (i)
R.13600	C25
R.15196	D1
R.15399	D20 (i)
R.16588	D20 (ii)

Carson

3.1129	E2 (ii)

Num. Chron.

1959, 10	E1

RIC

Claudius 33	B14
Hadrian 577a	C4
Hadrian 845	C20
Antoninus Pius 719	C25
Antoninus Pius 930	C33
Commodus 437	C44 (i)
Commodus 440	C44 (ii)
Albinus 19	D1
Caracalla 108	D20 (i)
Caracalla 441	D20 (ii)
Carausius 555	E2 (i)
RIC 6 Mint of Trier 34	E4
RIC 6 Mint of Londinium 133	E7
RIC 9 Mint of Londinium 2b	E8
RIC 10.1506	E13

INDEXES

INDEX 1: NAMES OF PERSONS MENTIONED IN THE TEXTS

Listed by *nomen* (or *cognomen* if *nomen* unknown)

Members of imperial family in capitals under the name by which they are commonly known: e.g. HADRIAN not P.AELIUS HADRIANUS. The usual and ancient abbreviations of *praenomina* are used.

Roman names usually written with a J in English (e.g. Julius) are given here in the Latin form, i.e. Julius.

INDEX 2: ARMY UNITS

FLEET

NUMERI

INDEX 3: GODS AND GODDESSES

INDEX 4: LATIN TITLES

Where a title is given in **bold** it may be found in the glossary. Where a reference number is in **bold**, an explanation of the title is given in the notes to that inscription.

INDEX 5: BUILDINGS AND MONUMENTS

INDEX 6: GEOGRAPHICAL NAMES

INDEX 7: FINDSPOTS OF INSCRIPTIONS

(The numbers and letters in brackets indicate the coordinates on the map, available online at www.cambridge.org/9781009383455)

Printed in the United States
by Baker & Taylor Publisher Services